Economic Policy in Europe Since the Late Middle Ages

The Visible Hand and the Fortune of Cities

Economic Policy in Europe Since the Late Middle Ages

The Visible Hand and the Fortune of Cities

Edited by
Herman Diederiks, Paul Hohenberg
and Michael Wagenaar

Leicester University Press
Leicester, London and New York

distributed exclusively in the USA and Canada by ST. MARTIN'S PRESS

First published in Great Britain in 1992 by Leicester University Press
(a division of Pinter Publishers Limited)

Editorial offices
Fielding Johnson Building, University of Leicester,
Leicester, LE1 7RH, England

Trade and other enquiries
25 Floral Street, London, WC2E 9DS
and Room 400, 175 Fifth Avenue,
New York, NY 10010, USA

British Library Congress Cataloging in Publication Data
A CIP catalogue record for this book is available from the
British Library

ISBN 0 7185 1347 9

Library of Congress Cataloging in Publication Data
Economic Planning in Europe Since the Late Middle Ages/ edited by Herman
  Diederiks, Paul Hohenberg and Michael Wagenaar.
    p.   cm.
  ISBN 0-7185-1347-9
  1. Urban policy-Europe-History. 2. Municipal government-
Europe - History. 3. Municipal finance - Europe - History. 4. Cities
and towns - Europe - History. I. Diederiks, Herman. II. Hohenberg,
Paul M. III. Wagenaar, Michael.
HT131.V57 1992
307.76'094 - dc20   91-44056
                                                                   CIP

Typeset by Florencetype Ltd, Kewstoke, Avon
Printed and bound in Great Britain by Biddles Ltd of Guildford and Kings Lynn

Contents

Preface

On 17–19 November 1988 the Dutch branch of the International Urban History Group organised a conference on *The Visible Hand and the Fortune of Cities* at the University of Leyden, The Netherlands. Since then, the International Urban History Group has been formally organised in the *European Association of Urban Historians*. The Association has been sponsored by the European Community in Brussels. In 1991 it published its second edition of the *Register of European History Teaching, Research and Publications,* edited by Barry Haynes and Peter Clark, and published by the Centre for Urban History at the University of Leicester, United Kingdom.

At the Leyden conference, twenty written contributions were introduced and discussed. Two commentators presented their reactions. About twenty debaters added to the intellectual success of the conference. This volume is a selection of the papers presented in Leyden published in a revised form.

The organisation of the conference, of which this volume is a result, was made possible by grants from the Royal Dutch Acadamy of Sciences (KNAW) in Amsterdam, the Leyden University Foundation (LUF), the University of Leyden, the Department of Social Geography of the University of Amsterdam and the Maison des Sciences de l'Homme in Paris. Paul Hohenberg translated the French contributions into English and Leicester University Press provided a copy-editor.

Herman Diederiks
Paul Hohenberg
Michael Wagenaar

1 The visible hand and the fortune of cities: a historiographic introduction

Herman Diederiks and Paul M. Hohenberg

The theme of this volume—the visible hand—confronts us with a problem fundamental to all social history. If we define the visible hand as the set of individual actors, perhaps working together in various combinations, how is it then possible to do justice to the dual constitution of historical processes, involving both encompassing structures and the agency of subjects? We confront the simultaneity of given and produced relationships, the links among, on the one hand, the circumstances of life, production, and authority, and on the other, the experiences and modes of behaviour of those who affect and are affected by these circumstances (Medick 1987, 76–98). Lawrence Stone in particular has argued that the branch of social history that considers itself a historical social science has given too much attention to socio-economic forces at the expense of neglecting the actors (Stone 1980, 3–8). This neglect contrasts with the definite widening of the range of subjects of historical inquiry to include women, children, workers, marginal persons, etc., as implied in such terms as 'total history' or 'history from below'.

The concept of the visible hand in economic history is associated with Alfred Chandler (1977; also Carosso 1979, 233–6) who used it to refer specifically to salaried managers in the modern, multi-unit business enterprise. The system they built internalized and thus to a substantial extent replaced market mechanisms in co-ordinating the economy's activities and allocating its resources. In the present volume we apply the term to a much wider range of actors. In the specific context of the urban economy we consider the leading figures, including their relationships with the urban population as a whole and its pressure groups, with the surrounding countryside and other cities, with the king and the nobility (i.e., the territorial authorities), as well as their avowed aims and concerns in directing urban society.

This concern with élites will not imply a plea to return to an older style of political, narrative-centred history. The actors will have to be placed in the context of urban social structure and evolving systems of production: guilds, commercial capitalism, proto-industrial mode, industrial capitalism and variants of welfare societies. However, whereas most urban historical studies have explained growth and decline by anonymous forces such as the workings of the market, technological change (Sjoberg 1960), even enhanced state action, our workshop recognized that economic policy and economic fortunes are made by people: not only merchants, artisans and entrepreneurs but also those holding power at the local, regional or wider level.

The links with the sovereign and his servants must also be placed in a broader context of state formation. To be sure, states or governments can also be seen as combinations of occupational and status groups with their own interests and peculiarities. None the less, while the basic function of governments, that of organizing and controlling violence to produce protection, may be performed so as to serve the ends of those who govern, the product may also be of value to others (Lane 1976, 523). Similarly, in considering the various actors on the urban scene we need to probe to what extent certain groups have identified their particular interests with the communal interest of their town or city. That commitment influences the make-up of municipal leadership and its chances of resisting attacks on urban autonomy and liberty or privilege.

The second aspect of our theme, the fortunes of cities, also raises a number of questions. Evaluating how cities are doing is the diachronic equivalent of the concerns addressed synchronically in considering the 'importance' of cities. While one can think of many indicators, ranging from per capita income to the absence of civil strife or even the aesthetics of the built environment, in practice demographic criteria predominate, and the number of inhabitants serves more often than not as the principal if not the sole gauge, whether of prosperity, 'growth' or rank (de Vries 1984; Bairoch 1985). While the effects of economic conditions on migration and the timing of marriage offer good demographic justification for viewing population change as an indicator of urban conjuncture, cities have historically differed in their tolerance for economically surplus population: We shall return to this point.

The present volume contains a selection of the contributions discussed at a workshop at the University of Leiden in 1988. Save for the chapters by R. Morris, R. Rodger and P. Jeannin, all deal with particular towns, and their authors, apart from Ph. Guignet, focus on a single place. Within Europe the geographical spread is limited, in that only the studies of Nîmes and Naples in the eighteenth century transcend the bounds of north-west/north-central Europe. For the Early Modern period the subject cities cluster in the Low Countries and Germany, while two studies on English towns join the Dutch cities examined in the *laissez-faire* nineteenth century.

Actors and factors: the visible hand in the urban economy

Before returning to the themes that emerge from the workshop contributions, let us take up again the question of how the actors in urban economic life have fared in recent historiography. During the 1966 urban history conference at Leicester, which some see as the founding of European urban history as currently practised, the late J. Dyos spoke on this point in his 'Agenda for urban historians'. In his view, despite considerable research into the politics of major cities over relatively short periods, small cities had received scarcely any systematic study. Nor, despite considerable emphasis on working-class movements, had trade unions been given their due. Likewise, little work seemed to be in hand in 1966 on the politics of local councils or the activities of local governments (Dyos 1968, 1–46). Taking up the theme in a 1980 article in the *Urban History Yearbook*, 'The urban historian and the political will', the late A. G. Checkland recalled the 1966 conference, pointing out that it featured little discussion of the relationship between public policy and urban history (Checkland 1980, 1–11). By way of a possible answer he suggested that this neglect reflected the sense that British town development exemplifies growth through market forces. Yet could not such a study also serve as a demonstration of the ways in which public policy has had to augment and operate upon market processes in the interests of communal objectives? Checkland listed four sorts of action on the part of central and local governments:

1. providing facilities where the market has failed to do so;
2. imposing social duties on firms as well as requiring them to assume a share of the social costs they generate;
3. operating upon the morphology of towns.
4. operating upon the economic base of towns.

He also drew, in the same article, a useful distinction among three ways of viewing the city:

1. as a local economy with a structure of wealth and power;
2. as a political entity with its own initiatives;
3. as a component of the state (Checkland 1980, 8).

R.J. Morris in Chapter 13 of this volume contributes a considerable measure of answer to the issues raised by Checkland, highlighting—for nineteenth-century Britain—four primary areas of state intervention: the reconstruction of the corporations in the 1830s; the action following on the new Poor Law of 1834; the sanitary districts from the middle of the century; and the school boards after 1870.

A recent synthesis of European urbanization which shares authorship with this introductory survey continues the emphasis on market forces in explaining the evolution of urban economies and societies (Hohenberg and Lees 1985). While *The Making of Urban Europe* devotes some pages to the material construction of the baroque city and to the morphogenesis and management of industrial towns, the visible hand plays a clearly subordinate role relative to the attempt to explain urban fortunes by systemic forces generally and market mechanisms in particular. Yet if we try to understand, for example, why Bologna did so much worse than Milan during the difficult period of the late fourteenth century, the development of political power in its full sense must surely have much to do with the answer. What distinguished the capital of Piedmont was the introduction there of modern and more viable political forms (Dowd 1974, 424–52). Clermont-de-Lodève in the Languedoc provides another telling example toward the turn of the eighteenth century. The French variant of mercantilist economic policy known as Colbertism clearly inflected and weakened market forces during that period. In one specific episode, the destruction of an Anglo-Dutch convoy of 400 ships by the French fleet in 1693 gave the clothiers of Languedoc an unexpected four-year monopoly of the woollen trade to the Near East and indeed allowed them to compete with the Dutch and British for another sixty years (Thomson 1982; Foster 1985, 203–5).

To be sure, the revision of commonly accepted viewpoints does not always go in the same direction. In Chapter 4 of this volume L. Teisseyre-Sallmann stresses the point that the woes of the Nîmes silk cloth industry had less to do with Louis XIV's revocation of the Edict of Nantes in 1685 than with the organization of production, the relation to another branch of industry (hosiery) and the rivalry with the dominant centre in Lyons. Indeed, the greater or lesser emphasis on market forces may have an ideological basis. Writing of eighteenth-century Britain, P. Corfield argues that guild and corporation control and regulation functioned as adaptive forces rather than as formative agents in the differential process of urban growth (Corfield 1982, 90–3). She rejects the commonly-held view that credits the economic success of towns to freedom from regulation and the absence of municipal and guild power, and so associates old, incorporated towns and economic stagnation. Some of the variegated factors that determined the growth or lack of it of individual towns fell within the scope of policy-making; others did not. To be sure, Checkland's observations about the unique role of market forces in the British case may have referred more to the nineteenth century than to Corfield's period. Yet, however the balance between conscious actions by individuals or small groups and the workings of large-scale historical processes may shift over time and across societies, no history can afford to concentrate solely on one at the expense of the other.

Urban élites: composition and commitment

One important theme in the history of urban élites, already alluded to, treats the question of their commitment to the communal cause as opposed to their narrower individual or group self-interest. Closely related is the question of urban—'bourgeois' in the etymological sense of 'burgher'—values as opposed to the standards and ideals of a still largely agrarian and aristocratic society. The theme comes into a long-standing debate on early urban development in Britain, one that focuses on the generally poor fortunes of late medieval and Early Modern towns. The pessimistic view shared by, among others, P. Clark and P. Slack contrasts with a more positive picture painted by such scholars as A. Dyer (Benedict 1986, 169–80). Can one take at face value the complaints of townsmen about the hardships they were enduring (Bridbury 1981, 1–24, esp. 20)? The re-edifying statutes of Henry VIII (1535/6, 1540, 1541/2, 1543/4) are adduced as evidence of urban decay, yet Bridbury sees them as helping urban authorities and speculators clarify the terms of property and the ownership of houses abandoned during fourteenth-century depopulation. These statutes, he suggests, show the collaboration of the central government with urban authorities and testify to an urban upswing in the sixteenth century.

The notion of intergovernmental collaboration returns us to the theme of municipal leadership, critical to the operation of the visible hand. How willing were burghers to take on duties as sheriff and the like? Was that participation eroding as alleged by those who see the flight from civic office as a symptom, contributing cause, or both, of urban decline? Despite unmistakable problems in the fifteenth century, one may question whether English towns suffered from a lack of willing office-holders. York and Coventry found enough candidates, since the élite were intent on preserving an exclusive oligarchy (Kermode 1982, 179–98). It is easy to find *ad hoc* or *ex post* explanations: Cambridge's problems around 1474 have been attributed to the flight of artisans displaced by scholars; yet Oxford's impoverishment twenty years earlier was laid to the flight of scholars because there were no artisans (Bridbury 1981, 1–24).

Urban anthropologists have pointed to ritual and ceremony as both a symbolic thread, helping to bind the social fabric of the urban community, and an indicator of commitment. C. Phythian-Adams saw ceremony as the highest expression of the urban ideal, a living mirror (1978). Yet it may be a lagging indicator in the sense that the forms live on when the fervour has been lost. To stay with Britain for a moment, London witnessed a change in attitudes during the latter part of Elizabeth's reign, shown by growing absenteeism at livery company halls, refusals to contribute to civic enterprises, and an increase in the number who chose to pay fines rather than serve a term as sheriff, for example. Indeed, by the seventeenth century these fines loomed large in the city chamber's revenue, while a great migration to the suburbs of London took place in the 1620s and 1630s (Berlin 1986, 15–27; see also Rappaport 1989).

The question of whether urban élites were willing to serve their city is of long standing, having been raised at the time of the decline of the Roman Empire. While the answer varies, so does the interpretation we may put on it. Thus, while English flight from office may testify to urban decay (as well as aggravating it), the flight *to* urban office in the eighteenth-century Dutch Republic can be ascribed to their lucrative nature rather than to any heightened civic virtue. The reluctance of the French urban élite to devote themselves to their city does not reflect an unwillingness to hold office so much as a preference for royal appointments, which conferred immediate prestige and the promise of rising into the nobility. Y. Barel speaks of a 'feudal' bourgeoisie, referring to the alacrity with which trading fortunes were invested in lands, titles and offices (Barel 1977). B. Chevalier takes a moral stance in qualifying bourgeois investment in rural land as a cancer, a betrayal (Chevalier 1982, 129). The issue also arises for the greatest of trading republics. By the seventeenth century Venetian merchants were investing their profits in property on the mainland. P. Burke sees growing passivity as the cause, while U. Tucci refers to a new psychology, damaging to Venetian commercial acumen (Burke 1978; Tucci 1973). Yet the analysis of a specific case, the investment policy of an important seventeenth-century silk merchant, Alberto Gozzi, indicates that buying land was a symptom, not a cause of commercial decline (Rapp 1979, 269–0). In the same sense, the flight to office of Dutch urban élites in the eighteenth century can be seen as financially motivated during a time of decreasing commercial activity, when the return on government bonds looked safe and attractive (Prak, de Jong and Kooijmans 1985, 183–4).

Any evaluation of urban economic policy must begin with the question of who made it, which is why research on the composition of governing élites, including who sought and who shunned office, is so interesting. In the present volume two authors tackle this question of the make up of governing bodies for towns in the southern Low Countries (Guignet) and in Germany (Jeannin). There can be no question that wealth was a necessary, if not a sufficient, condition for holding power, and that access to the inner circle was most often closed and quasi-hereditary. Yet one must resist hasty generalizations. In Germany, some directly active burghers, whose status kept them off the council itself, could participate in intermediate bodies. Nuremberg also made provision for meritocratic advancement, something perhaps related to its uniquely long-term and comprehensive view of economic policy (von Stromer 1981, 119–9). On the other hand, the busy cities on either side of the present border between Belgium and France, where one would expect at least leading merchants to dominate urban government, elected far more lawyers and gentry than men of commerce. To be sure, one could be both a nobleman and a lawyer, while merchant families eager to be represented would make sure at least one son completed legal studies and entered a judicial profession.

City and state; state and market

However important the composition and commitment of the governing élite, caution is needed in relating the content of policy to those responsible for it. This is manifest in a recent debate concerning Early Modern Leiden. R. DuPlessis and M. Howell have argued that here, as at Lille, the élite fostered a system of small commodity production that retained anti-concentration aspects of traditional guild systems. The system did not necessarily fare well in competition with other textile centres, including nearby proto-industrial development in villages, but it contributed to social peace within the city (DuPlessis and Howell 1982, 58, 63; Duplessis 1991). In his contribution to this volume, H. Brand questions this interpretation, pointing out that the capitalists who controlled the council were not inclined to protect a system that raised wages and limited concentration.

If class interest struggled with civic mindedness for the minds and hearts of the governing élite, it is probable that in most cases the deciding vote was cast by precedent or tradition. The weight of the past certainly figured strongly in the persistence of guilds and their practices in the German lands. M. Walker, following in the footsteps of the nineteenth-century social geographer Wilhelm Heinrich Riehl, has looked at the German 'home towns' (Walker 1971). He distinguishes individualized regions from centralized ones, the latter marked by larger cities in an open landscape, the former by rolling country dotted with numerous medium-sized towns. The absolutist states and their nineteenth-century successors only gradually reduced the autonomy of towns in the individualized areas, and their guild economy reflected that durability. Indeed, despite the Cameralists' concern with these urban economies, the Empire allowed even stricter local regulation with the Imperial Trades Edict of 1731. Take as an example the journeyman's wander year, required by guild regulations but increasingly called into question toward the turn of the nineteenth century. It was feared that in seeking training in other towns, the wandering journeymen would contribute dangerously to the diffusion of both technological and revolutionary ideas. Amid considerable debate between governments and guild authorities, it took until 1853 for the obligation to be abolished (Bade 1982, 1–37). In the Habsburg lands, Maria Theresa and Joseph II's attempts to promote industry also fell foul of the urban guilds (Komlos 1986, 427–82).

As she or he contemplates the workings of urban economic policy in the pre- and proto-industrial context, the modern economist may well be ruefully reminded of industrial regulation in today's advanced mixed economies, where the regulators ceaselessly decry monopoly and yet continually fight real competition. How much did this sort of attitude have to do with a major development in the economy of Early Modern Europe, namely the loss of a quasi-monopoly of industrial production by the towns, or rural proto-industrialization? It is certainly an oversimplification to see regulatory rigidity within towns as *the* cause of the shift to rural manufactures in Early Modern Europe, and this for at least two reasons. A compelling one is that manufacturing by no means disappeared from towns, not even old, incorporated cities. The second is that rural activity benefited from good technical and economic advantages which no amount of urban economic freedom could erase, from water power to seasonally underemployed labour (Kriedte, Medick and Schlumbohm 1977; Hohenberg and Lees 1985). None the less, the long-term results of towns' unceasing attempts to preserve high wages and high profits, by maintaining the monopoly of certain activities and guaranteeing supplies of needed inputs (food, fuel and raw materials), proved exhausting as well as futile.

Even the port cities, better attuned to the rivalries inherent in long-distance trade, tried to protect their shipbuilding industries, as in the case of Danzig in the fourteenth century and Venice in the fifteenth, using subsidies and encouraging more concentrated forms of enterprise (Tucci 1987, 277–96). Yet this was enlightened policy if one compares it to the practice of excluding productive groups that appeared to threaten established positions. Ebeling in Chapter 5 of this volume shows this response—so familiar in earlier religious conflicts on the national or imperial scale, whether directed at Jews, Protestants or Muslims—at work in eighteenth-century Cologne. Bad times caused Cologne's municipal leaders to turn against

Protestant bankers and merchants in their city, thus damaging the urban economy still further.

If class interests, tradition, civic loyalty and prejudice weighted heavily in the motivation behind economic policy, ideas also had their place. The eighteenth century, in particular, saw a flowering of theory, with physiocratic ideas critical of mercantilist doctrine acting as a sort of precursor to full-scale *laissez-faire* ideology. The physiocrats' emphasis on an unfettered agrarian economy had mixed implications for the urban sector. In Germany the debate centred on the compulsory urban market—the staple—for foodstuffs such as grain and other articles: wood, tobacco, wine, flax and madder. The rulers concerned with tax revenues supported the towns who were trying to protect their food supply, while the proponents of free trade could only advance 'scientific' economic arguments. As one might expect, the grain trade was restricted to towns in 1772 (Braun 1975, 301–22). On the other hand, the élite in the Languedoc capital of Toulouse used physiocratic doctrine to promote their particular interests as great landed proprietors. Unfortunately, free trade in grain, established in 1763–4, turned out to benefit mostly the merchants of Marseilles and Bordeaux who controlled it. Toulouse instead lost revenue from reduced tolls and taxes, particularly once cheaper foreign grain began to enter France (Frêche 1974; Lacave 1976, 235–40). It was also in the name of physiocratic thinking that the municipality of Caen refused the central government's suggestion that stocks of grain be constituted to deal with potential shortages (Perrot 1975).

The most visible traces of past urban economic policy are the legacies of urban investment. Did prestigious or monumental buildings and embellishments—public and private, if that distinction is not an anachronism when applied to the baroque period—stimulate economic activity or rather strangle it with debt and taxes? P. Burke's comparison of public investment in seventeenth-century Rome, Paris and Amsterdam confirms what the eye still suggests today: in Rome prestige was the dominant consideration, in Amsterdam it was profit, while Paris falls somewhere in between (Burke 1978, 311–36). Naples offers another perspective. It was a capital until the Unification of Italy in 1860, and the city's economic activity centred on maintaining the urban residences of a large and wealthy landowning class which relied on a system of clientism and patronage, as Davis develops in Chapter 8 of this volume. Yet the most conspicuous attempts at a public building programme came during the revolutionary period and under French rule.

As a general point, one may argue that merchant cities, open to the fastmoving currents of world trade and unable to draw on a surplus from an agricultural hinterland—which they did not generally control—remained prudent both in avoiding conspicuous investment and in not allowing the population to swell too rapidly. By contrast, capitals and residence cities funnelled rural surpluses in the form of rents, taxes or tithes and other feudal dues into the city to pay for luxury consumption and grand display by the rich and a crude welfare state for the masses. Bread and circuses were provided, and the large floating population were employed in large-scale projects more often ornamental than practical. Of course, such cities suffered when rural crises disrupted the flow of payments from the countryside and threatened the luxury trades as well as construction (Hohenberg and Lees 1985, chs 4, 5). Nonetheless, their population typically remained larger than called for by economic needs. Naples is the prime example, but not the only one.

The nineteenth century: 'improvement', or coping with change

The themes, concepts and dichotomies that have served us in surveying the late medieval and Early Modern period recur in the industrial age, although in modified form: city versus state, the growth of centralized power as against urban autonomy; the visible and invisible hand, the rise and partial retreat of the hegemonic market; forces and agents, the respective roles of conscious actors and impersonal factors. As an aside, many of these questions are raised in an article by E. Bloomfield on nineteenth-century urban development in Canada (Bloomfield 1983). He identifies three areas of explicit urban policy action: railway promotion; the encouragement of new manufacturing firms; and advertising a town's good name. Incidentally, rail construction appears *not* to have influenced urban growth in nineteenth-century Germany (Lee 1988, 346–67). Early line-siting decisions favoured residence cities rather than looking to economic development needs.

While urban economic policy took on new relevance and visibility in the heyday of industrial urbanization, when problems of physical extension, social pathology, and in general the management of large, densely populated urban areas came to the fore amid widening political participation, the urban visible hand can sometimes be found where one least expects it, for example in the rural England of agricultural revolution. The provincial centres of eighteenth-century England remained modest when compared with the newer mushrooming settlements of the industrial zones. Yet they benefited from the agricultural upsurge around them. The rural élite demanded ever greater urban services and came to spend a number of weeks and months in town. The gaiety and excitement of the London social season entranced the landed aristocracy, while families of the lesser gentry and of substantial farmers joined those of increasing numbers of professional and mercantile men at assemblies, balls and other diversions in the county towns. Fireworks and fêtes were organized, there were investments for making streets passable for carriages, and county magnates were invited to participate in town politics. All this amounted to a deliberate promotional policy, as P. Clark points out (Clark 1984, 22, 23). Human actors built on favourable economic developments and the stimulating nearness of London to enhance the drawing power of their town.

As one moves forward to the later Victorian period and the English climacteric, the issue of middle-class withdrawal from urban leadership arises once more. R. Trainor recognizes that the sense of social responsibility—or the class solidarity of the wealthy—was increasingly likely to manifest itself through participation in national rather than in local politics, but on balance he advances a favourable verdict regarding the role of the Victorian bourgeoisie (Trainor 1985, 1–17). D. Fraser uses the cases of Manchester, Birmingham, Leeds and Liverpool to trace the changing structure of urban politics (Fraser 1976). A quote from the Lord Mayor of Birmingham characterizes well the 'politics of improvement' as it came to fruition in the great cities of the industrial age:

'There is no nobler sphere for those who have not the opportunity of engaging in imperial politics than to take part in municipal work to the wise conduct of which they owe welfare the health, the comfort and the lives of 400,000 people'. (Fraser 1976, 174)]

The reader will note the cautionary note, subordinating local to national ('imperial') politics. Indeed, the system of a strong mayor controlling an active political machine developed more strongly in countries such as Austria and the United States than in Great Britain, while French politicians turned the highly centralized system to advantage by combining municipal and national office once the republican form was established for good.

To the urban élites of nineteenth-century Europe it must have seemed as if every day their cities faced environmental catastrophe or a breakdown of the political order and the social fabric. Since the worst did not happen, 'improvement' is, in retrospect, the dominant theme of urban economic policy in the nineteenth century. There are good reasons for this increased municipal preoccupation. To begin with, cities all but lost any autonomous political role with the rise of the strong central state, so that they could scarcely influence, much less determine, other domains such as trade policy, regulation of professions, taxation or access to citizenship. Second, the onrushing march of technology and investment in factories and machinery, railways and canals, and the resulting concentrations of population continually threatened to overwhelm the physical and social infrastructure. Finally, and especially in the second half of the century, technology began to offer solutions as well as pose challenges (Lees and Hohenberg 1988; Tarr and Dupuy 1988). Advances in bacteriology and the harnessing of electricity stand out in terms of their urban applications.

Despite the prevailing *laissez-faire* ideology, governments made repeated attempts to control the burgeoning industrial system as well as to cushion some of the drastic human as well economic consequences. However, by the time these efforts began to take hold, local authority had become subordinated to national agencies. Of course the regulations, even when promulgated, had to be enforced, and their effects might well be other than anticipated. For example, laws against outdoor work, intended to promote factories, did not prevent London, like many large towns, from remaining the domain of the small workshop and of domestic work (Schmiechen 1975, 413–28). Far from equalizing conditions of labour, these acts contributed to its stratification and to decentralization of production, creating a dualism which to this day, allows small enterprises to survive in European cities. As for the regulation of housing, while here too the laws were made on the national level, enforcement remained local and so more subject to particular power structures and conditions (Rodger 1979, 77–91).

To return to the matter of improvements, as most services which tried to deal with the many problems—lighting, refuse, transport, water—were natural monopolies, they did not fit in comfortably with the prevailing ideology of free markets and free enterprise. The alternatives were to regulate private enterprises or to operate public ones. Both solutions were practised, and the numerous variations offer the urban historian interested in the visible hand a sort of laboratory. Here too one begins with a schematic view to the effect that almost unrestrained reliance on *laissez-faire* gradually gave way to a more collectivist view expressed in such terms as municipalization or municipal socialism. As usual, the study of specific cases forces us to modify and qualify, if not abandon, the schema and to recognize the richness of individual stories as well as the role of particular actors.

P. Kooij's study of Groningen in Chapter 9 of this volume focuses on the role of the élite, largely professional men, civil servants, and leaders of trade and industry, who promoted public utilities in which they also had a direct interest. In the much larger milieu of London, the pattern of development in the gas industry—a forerunner among capital-intensive utilities—challenges the view that ideology led the shift from private to public enterprise. Rather, changes within the industry altered the politics, inflecting public opinion and policy (Matthews 1986, 244–63). However, the equally crucial business of supplying pure water to residents and factories of British towns turned out differently (Hassan 1985, 531–47). The initial reliance on private initiatives yielded inadequate results, so that by 1907 municipal authorities controlled more than 80 per cent of British waterworks. Municipalization took hold despite the great interest of factory masters in the Yorkshire and Lancashire textile districts in tapping remote upland sources of the pure, soft water they needed.

Municipal government was active in German cities despite the centralizing efforts of a relatively autocratic Prussian and later imperial government. The social classes that governed the town were those who also promoted economic change (Krabbe 1983, 373–91). Yet the nature of the service involved influenced the path of development as well. One pattern characterized gas works. The city first contracted with a private firm, typically one that worked with British capital, technology, and technical staff. In a second phase the workings of the monopoly generated customer complaints. These led to legal proceedings by the city in a third phase, and the final outcome saw the city taking over ownership of the gas works. Electricity, on the other hand, was from the beginning generated in municipal power stations, since it was required primarily for trams, already a communal enterprise in the horse drawn stage (Krabbe 1983, 383–4).

In a newer town such as Oberhausen the central government played a greater role. While the spatial arrangement of the city centre was not successfully resolved because the political forces were too weak to offset the industrial interests, the favourable attitude of the Prussian state contributed to successful municipalization of the water supply (Reif 1982, 457–87).

The French story unfolded under the sign of strong centralism under the authoritarian liberal regime of Napoleon III. He pushed top–down modernization via encouragement of the Credit Mobilier, integration and amalgamation of railways, creation of vast public works ('Haussmannization'), and enforced modernization through exposure to international competition. Yet centralization outlived the regime. The local aspect of the story has yet to be told, according to J. Merriman (Merriman 1982, 24), although D.M. Gordon's study in the same volume of the bourgeoisie of Reims and Saint-Etienne makes a start (Gordon 1982, 117–38). He focuses on the struggle in the provinces between industrial capitalists and the more traditional mercantile manufacturers.

The present volume contains a number of chapters focusing on improvement in nineteenth and twentieth-century Dutch cities. Despite the strong and long-standing tradition of municipal autonomy, the Dutch local authorities were at least sometimes reluctant participants, intervening only after a bankruptcy in Rotterdam (van den Noort, chapter 10). On the other hand, the first World War gave a boost to government intervention in the towns of the Netherlands (e.g. Haarlem) as elsewhere (B. de Vries, chapter 11).

While local governments might lack the capacity to act or be too closely controlled by special interests, action by the central government when there was no established local authority offered no answer, as indicated by the new industrial sprawls typical of coal-mining districts. An extreme example is furnished by the case of Tsarist Odessa, which grew rapidly in the pre-emancipation period but looked like a frontier town: a desperate housing shortage, unpaved streets and no piped water system (Siegelbau 1980, 113–51; Skinner 1976). Based on the Charter of Towns issued by Catherine II in 1785, Odessa had a weak and unrepresentative local government. Delegates to the local Duma were not even paid. The central government neglected the transport network that linked the port to its hinterland, while the grain trade relied on serf labour and was largely in the hands of Greek and Italian merchants with no roots in Odessa.

In trying to compress the centuries and the hundreds of individual urban histories, we run the risk of severely overschematizing the story: state and market, individual interest and common welfare, local and national politics. Many other actors and concerns made themselves heard and felt. Two that cannot go unmentioned are the churches and the nineteenth–century social reformers. Given the political and cultural importance of the clergy in medieval European cities, it is clear that their role in regulating the urban economy—production as well as the maintenance and provisioning of the town— must have been far more central than this chapter or the Leiden workshop recognizes. Here is surely fertile ground for further research. As for the nineteenth century, organized religion had a role to play in urban politics. In the case of Britain the peak of influence has been put in the 1890s (Brown 1988, 1–14). The churches did not rely only on the persuasive power of Sunday sermons but, in Glasgow for example, gained strong representation in outwardly secular bodies such as Poor Law commissions, corporations and, after 1872, school boards. Here they could push the evangelical agenda of social reforms, such as temperance, moral control of behaviour and expression, and the promotion of religious observance. Yet these churchmen did not hesitate to tackle secular issues concerning utilities, insalubrious housing, and municipalization. They were prepared to cross party lines and even embrace collectivism to help establish the Godly commonwealth.

A flood of reformist writing on the evils of urban living and industrialism generally poured out of cities in Europe and elsewhere in the nineteenth century (Lees 1985). It is easy to forget that F. Engels' influential expose of the horrors of capitalism draws much more on the writings of urban reformers than on personal observation (Engels 1845). Historians are some-times sceptical of these reformers, questioning both the accuracy or repre-sentativeness of their descriptions and the extent of their influence. Do their voluminous writings and those of the town planners not tell us more about intellectual trends among the middle class than about changing patterns of urban life (Daunton 1983, 213)? In the middle of the century the focus of attention of urban élites, at least, changed from social concerns and broad, systemic critiques to environmental issues. Later the scope of élite activity broadened once again as civic attention moved from sewers and water to discretionary projects. One historian characterizes the development as the masking of entrepreneurial gospel as radical populism (Trainor 1985, 9).

Conclusion

The reader is best equipped to answer the question of what we have learned about the visible hand and the fortune of cities. That questions outnumber answers is neither an original nor a surprising conclusion, and if this survey has rather widened than narrowed the gap, it has not necessarily failed in its purpose. Many topics have been ignored or barely mentioned, for example the role of élites in controlling the use of urban land (chapter 12, M. Wagenaar's study of Amsterdam). The literature cited gives just a taste of the active work being done, not even a fair sample.

We may end by recalling the two senses given to the image of the visible hand. One opposes it to the market, Adam Smith's usage. Without ques-tion, the historical tension in Western history between 'free' economic activity and political or social control of the unfettered market was most often played out on an urban stage. 'Played out' is the right term, for this was melodrama, complete with suspense, conflicts, surprising reversals and dogged resistances. The other sense is that of the human actors as opposed to the abstract 'forces'or 'factors' that are as central to political and social analysis as to economic theory. The workshop took place in the context of what seemed to many a moment of transition. After more than two decades of 'new' urban history—whether influenced by Braudel, Marx, or American cliometrics—which we have traced at least in part to the impulse of Leicester, the time seemed to have come to reintroduce the actors without losing the context and the structures of thought that invite com-parison and generalization. The present volume is offered as a first step in bringing together research and encouraging more work along what we see a a fruitful line.

Bibliography

Bade, Klaus J. (1982), 'Altes Handwerk, Wanderzwang und Gute Policey, Gesellenwanderung zwischen Zunftokonomie und Gewerbereform', in *Vierteljahrschrift für Sozial- und Wirschaftsgeschichte* 69: 1–37

Bairoch, Paul (1985), *De Jéricho à Mexico: villes et économie dans l'histoire*, (English, translation, University of Chicago Press, 1988).

Barel, Yves(1977), *La ville médiévale: système social, système urbain*, Grenoble.

Benedict, Philip (1986), 'Late medieval and Early Modern urban history à L'anglaise, a review article', in *Comparative Studies in Society and History*, vol. 28, 169–180.

Berlin, Michael (1986), 'Civic ceremony in Early Modern London', *Urban History Yearbook*, 15–27

Bloomfield, E. (1983), 'Community, ethos and local initiative in urban economic growth: review of a theme in Canadian urban History', in *Urban History Yearbook*, 53–72.

Braun, Hans-Joachim (1975), 'Economic theory and policy in Germany 1750–1800', in *Journal of European Economic History*, vol. 4: 301–22.

Bridbury, A.R. (1981), 'English provincial towns in the later Middle Ages, in *Econo. Hist. Rev.* XXXIV: 1–24.

Brown, Callum, G. (1988), 'Did urbanization secularize Britain?' in *Urban History Yearbook*, 1–14.

Burke, Peter (1978), 'Investment and culture in three seventeenth century cities: Rome, Amsterdam, Paris', in *Journal of European Economic History*, vol. 7: 311–36.

Carosso, Vincent P. (1979), review of A.D. Chandler, *The Visible Hand* in *Journal of European Economic History*, vol. 8: 233–6.

Chandler, A.D. (1977), *The Visible Hand: the managerial revolution in American business*, Cambridge, Harvard University Press.

Checkland, S.G. (1980), 'The urban historian and the political will', in *Urban History Yearbook*, 1–11.

Chevalier, Bernard, (1982), *Les bonnes villes de France du XIVe au XVIe siecle*, Paris.

Clark, Peter (1984), 'Introduction', in Peter Clark (ed.) *The transformation of English Provincial Towns 1600–1800*, London.

Corfield, P.J. (1982), *The Impact of English towns, 1700–1800*, Oxford University Press.

Daunton, M.J. (1983), 'Public place and private space: the Victorian city and the working class household', in D. Fraser and A. Sutcliffe (eds) *The Pursuit of Urban History*, London.

Dennis, Richard (1984), *English Industrial Cities of the Nineteenth Century. A social geography*, Cambridge.

Diefendorf, Jeffrey M. (1980), *Businessmen and Politics in the Rhineland, 1789–1834*, Princeton University Press.

Dowd, Douglas, F. (1974), 'Power and economic development: the rise and decline of medieval Bologna', in *Journal of European Economic History*, vol. 3: 424–52.

DuPlessis, Robert S. (1991), *Lille and the Dutch Revolt: urban stability in an era of revolution*, Cambridge.

DuPlessis, Robert S. and Martha C.Howell (1982), 'Reconsidering the early modern urban economy: the cases of Leiden and Lille', in *Past and Present*, 94: 49–84.

Dyos, H.J. (1968), 'Agenda for urban historians', in H.J. Dyos (ed.) *The Study of Urban History*, London, 1–46.

Engels, Friedrich (1845, 1968), *The Condition of the Working Class in England*, reprint, Stanford.

Foster, Robert (1985), review in *Journal of European Economic History*, vol. 14: 203–5.

Fraser, Derek (1976), *Urban Politics in Victorian England: the structure of politics in Victorian cities*, Leicester University Press.

Frêche, G. (1974), *Toulouse et la région Midi–Pyrénéenne au siècle des lumières (1670–1789)*, Paris.

Gordon, David, M. (1982), 'The bourgeois of Reims and Saint-Etienne', in J.F. Merriman (ed.), *French Cities in the Nineteenth Century*.

Hassan, J.A. (1985), 'The growth and impact of the British water industry in the nineteenth century', in *Econ. Hist. Rev.*, 531–47.

Hohenberg, Paul, M. and Lynn Hollen Lees (1985), *The Making of Urban Europe, 1000–1950*, Harvard University Press.

Kermode, Jennifer I. (1982), 'Urban decline? The flight from office in late medieval York', in *Econ. Hist. Rev.*, 179–98.

Komlos, John (1986), 'Institutional change under pressure: enlightened government policy in the eighteenth century Habsburg monarchy', in *Journal of European Economic History*, vol. 15: 427–82.

Krabbe, Wolfgang R. (1983), 'Die Entfaltung der Kommunalen Leistungsverwaltung in deutschen Städten des späten 19. Jahrhunderts', in H.J. Teuteberg (ed.) *Urbanisierung im 19. und 20. Jahrhundert, historische und geografische Aspekte*, Cologne/Vienna, Städteforschung, Reihe A, vol. 16: 373–91.

Kriedte, Peter, Hans Medick and Jürgen Schlumbohm (1977), *Industrialisierung vor der Industrialisierung*, Vandenhoeck & Ruprecht.

Lacave, Michel (1976), review in *Journal of European Economic History*, vol. 5: 235–40.

Lane, Frederic C. (1976), in *Comparative Studies in Society and History*, 18: 523.

Lee, W.R. (1988), 'Economic development and the state', in *Econ. Hist. Rev.*, XLI: 346–67.

Lees, Andrew (1985), *Cities Perceived: urban society in European and American thought, 1820–1940*, Columbia University Press.

Lees, Lynn Hollen and Paul M. Hohenberg (1988), 'How cities grew in the western world: a systems approach', in Jesse H. Ausubel and Robert Herman (eds) *Cities and their vital systems: infrastructure past, present, and future*, National Academy Press, pp. 71–84.

Matthews, Derek (1986), '*Laissez-faire* and the London gas industry in the nineteenth century: another look', in *Econ. Hist. Rev.*, 244–63.

Medick, Hans (1987), ' "Missionaries in the row boat"? Ethnological ways of knowing as a challenge to social history', in: *Comparative Studies in Society and History*, 29: 76–98.

Merriman, J.M. (1982), 'Introduction: Images of the nineteenth-century French cities', in J.M. Merriman (ed.) *French cities in the nineteenth century*, London.

Perrot, Jean-Claude (1975), *Genèse d'une ville moderne, Caen au XVIIIe siècle*, Paris/La Haye.

Phythian-Adams, Charles (1978), 'Urban decay in late medieval England', in P. Adams and E.A. Wrigley (eds) *Towns in societies*, Cambridge University Press.

Prak, M., J. de Jong and L. Kooijmans (1985), 'State and status in the eighteenth century: three cities in Holland (Hoorn, Gouda and Leiden', in H. Schilling and H. Diederiks (eds) *Bürgerliche Eliten in den Niederlanden und in Nordwestdeutschland*, Städteforschung, Reihe A, vol. 23 Cologne/Vienna,: 183–94.

Rapp, Richard T. (1979), 'Real estate and rational investment in early modern Venice', in *Journal of European Economic History*, vol. 8: 269–90.

Rappaport, Steve (1989), *Worlds within Worlds: structures of life in sixteenth-century*

London, Cambridge University Press.

Reif, Heinz (1982), 'Städtebildung im Ruhrgebiet: die Emscherstadt Oberhausen, 1850–1914', in: *Vierteljahrschrift für Sozial-- und Wirtschaftsgeschichte*, 69, 457–87

Rodger, Richard (1979), 'The law and urban change, some nineteenth century Scottish evidence', in *Urban History Yearbook*, 77–91.

Schmiechen, James, A. (1975), 'State reform and the local economy: an aspect of industrialization in late Victorian and Edwardian London', in *Econ. Hist. Rev.*, vol. 28, 413–28.

Sherman, Dennis (1977), 'Governmental responses to economic modernization in mid-nineteenth century France', in *Journal of European Economic History*, vol. 6, 717–36

Siegelbau, Lewis (1980), 'The Odessa grain trade: a case study in urban growth and development in Tsarist Russia', in *Journal of European Economic History*, vol. 9 113–51

Sjoberg, Gideon (1960), *The pre-industrial city*, Free Press.

Skinner, Frederick (1976), 'Trends in planning practices: the building of Odessa 1794–1917', in *The City in Russian History*, Kentucky University Press.

Stone, L. (1980), 'The revival of narrative: reflections on a new old history', *Past and Present*, 3–8.

Stromer, Wolfgang von (1981), 'Commercial policy and economic conjuncture in Nuremberg at the close of the Middle Ages: a model of economic policy', in *Journal of European Economic History*, vol. 10, 119–29.

Tarr, Joel A. and Gabriel Dupuy (eds) (1988), *Technology and the Rise of the Networked City in Europe and America*, Temple University Press.

Thomson, J.K.J. (1982), *Clermont-de-Lodève 1633–1789: fluctuations in the prosperity of a Languedocian clothmaking town*, Cambridge University Press.

Trainor, Richard (1985), 'Urban elites in Victorian Britain', in *Urban History Yearbook*, 1–17.

Tucci, Ugo (1973), 'The psychology of the Venetian merchant', in J.R.Hale (ed.) *Renaissance Venice*, London.

Tucci, Ugo (1987), 'Venetian shipowners in the XVIth century', in *Journal of European Economic History*, vol. 16: 277–96.

Vann, James Allen (1983), review in *Comparative Studies in Society and History*, vol. 25: 725–30.

Walker, Mack (1971), *German Home Towns: community, state, and general estate 1648–1871*, Cornell University Press.

2 Urban policy or personal government: the involvement of the urban élite in the economy of Leiden at the end of the Middle Ages

Hanno Brand

Between about 1350 and 1530 the town of Leiden was the most prominent textile centre in the county of Holland. The textile industry was the leading sector in the town's economy and provided most of the population with an income. The Leideners concentrated on the production of quality cloth and depended on the wool staple of Calais for the supply of raw materials, and on the German Hansa, which handled export of the cloth, for trade. At the beginning of this century Posthumus wrote the standard work on the organization of the Leiden cloth industry (Posthumus 1908). He not only dealt with industrial organization, but also gave attention to the magistrates' economic policy. Posthumus ascertained far-reaching intervention of the town government in just about all facets of production, which he said had a capitalist nature. He was struck above all by the power of the entrepreneurs, who were supported by the town government. Up to the 1980s his findings went mostly unchallenged (Alberts 1977, 268–9). It was not until a few years ago that M.C.Howell made a critical comment (DuPlessis and Howell 1982, 49–84; Howell 1986). Without wishing to dispute that the town government intervened deeply in the town's economy, she had her doubts about the objectives of the magistrates. According to Howell, their economic policy was not aimed at preserving the power of capitalist manufacturers, but rather at the protection of the position of the small independent artisans. Leiden's economy, Howell states, was wholly geared to small commodity production.

During my research into the Leiden élites of the fifteenth century and the beginning of the sixteenth, there appeared to be little room for the small artisan in the town's political structure. As regards drapery, the magistrate worked hand in glove with the entrepreneurs. Because of this evidence of the power of the drapers, a re-evaluation of Howells' findings seemed to be in order. By examining the town's political structure and indicating in what way and with what openly revealed intentions the magistrate regulated economic life, I reveal the guiding hand of the town government and in addition shed light on the structure of Leiden's textile industry in the late Middle Ages.

Socio-economic structures

Together with northern Italy, parts of Germany, and Flanders, the county of Holland was one of the most urbanized areas of Europe in the late Middle Ages. Urbanization had so taken hold in the county that around 1500 not less than 45 per cent of the population lived within town walls, almost 10 percentage points over the 35.6 per cent which J. de Vries takes as average for the whole Netherlands. Even in Flanders this share remained at 36 per cent, despite its higher population density and the presence of large towns such as Ghent, Bruges and Ypres. Brabant and Hainault were comparable in this respect. In the other districts the agrarian component remained more sizeable (Blockmans 1983, 46–8). A high degree of urbanization does not necessarily imply that Dutch towns were large. Compared with metropolises like Florence and Ghent or with a somewhat smaller Cologne, the towns of Holland were strikingly small. The largest town in the county in the fourteenth century, the 'international' harbour Dordrecht, had around 10,000 inhabitants in 1354. In the course of the fifteenth century Dordrecht was surpassed by Leiden, which within a century expanded from a modest 5,000 to 6,000 inhabitants in 1400 to become the largest town in Holland. In 1498 the number of inhabitants reached 14,250, surpassing all towns in Holland and Zealand (Ennen 1979; Blok 1910, 68, 70–1; van Werveke 1975, 449–65; Prevenier 1975, 269–79; de Boer 1985, 88; Blockmans 1987, 238; de Vries 1984, 38, 63–4)

Leiden owed its spectacular demographical growth mainly to the cloth industry, which flourished unprecedentedly between 1350 and 1480 (van Zanden 1988, 373–5). Before 1350 industrial activities were small scale. Halfway through the fourteenth century an economic reorientation occurred, in which a large part of the international market could be secured. This favourable state of affairs lasted until about 1480. After that conditions within the city deteriorated; severe financial problems followed by an economic recession in the early sixteenth century gradually put an end to the medieval Leiden drapery (Posthumus 1908, 38–9; Brand 1991).

Because of the scarcity of sources it is almost impossible to build up a comprehensive picture of the economic situation in the city before 1350. The trade in cloth, made in Leiden or in places nearby, seems to have been dominated by the retail cloth merchants. Among them were well-off burghers who also participated in the town government (van Kan 1988, 78). In Amsterdam archeologists have found seals of Leiden cloth dating from the end of the thirteenth century and the beginning of the fourteenth, showing that retail cloth merchants were already selling their textiles there (Baart 1988, 99–101). In the first half of the fourteenth century, cloth production is also apparent from the fact that the Viscount of Leiden had the right of *ellemaat* (yardstick) as early as 1331 (Posthumus 1908, 39). This privilege meant that when retail cloth merchants wished to offer their cloth for sale in their booths in Leiden, they were first required to make a payment to the viscount. The presence in the town of fullers, weavers and dyers can be shown only indirectly. The Vollersgracht (Fullers' Canal) was first mentioned in 1316; in 1341 there was a Weverssteeg (Weavers' Alley), while four years later Leiden inhabitants paid rents on a dye works just outside the town walls (Posthumus 1908, 38). Although not much information is available, it may be safely assumed that in this early stage of the economic development of Leiden not more than limited amounts of cloth were produced. The end products were probably intended for the local and regional market.

Around the middle of the fourteenth century the Leiden textile industry must have been of some importance for employment in the town, since it already proved worthwhile to safeguard the town's competitive position in relation to the surrounding rural areas. In 1351 Leiden received a privilege from the hands of the count that prohibited all manufacture of cloth within a radius of three miles outside the town walls (Posthumus 1908, 39; Jansma 1974, 34–53). As it would later prove, this was the earliest expression of a far-reaching protectionism, which was initiated by the magistrates. Possibly this measure is linked to an important change in production methods around 1350, resulting in a considerable broadening of the commercial horizon. Production was switched to what is called the 'new drapery'. The most prosperous retail cloth merchants, who had initially concentrated on the cloth trade, became entrepreneurs called drapers. Although other types of lesser quality were also made within the city walls, the drapers focused mainly on the production of a certain type of high quality cloth (van Kan 1988, 78–80; Derville 1987, 715–24) This so-called *voorwollen* cloth was made with highly prized English wool, which was purchased by the drapers through the staple in Calais (Posthumus 1910, 20). *Voorwollen* cloth may not have been the luxury cloth or *puiken* generally acquired by the nobility and church dignitaries, but despite its somewhat lesser quality it proved to be enormously popular with the well-off bourgeoisie in many European towns, especially in the Baltic area.

The conditions for securing a sizeable portion of the international market were rather favourable at that time. The traditional Flemish textile industry, which had reached its peak in the thirteenth century, was undergoing a lengthy crisis in the fourteenth and fifteenth centuries. On the other hand the demand from the Baltic towns had increased. English wool production rose considerably in the second half of the century, and because of an anti-English cloth import policy, there was no real competition from that side until about 1500. Leiden exploited the favourable circumstances and managed to gain a large part of the market. Although knowledge of production figures is only approximate to about 1475, there is an unmistakable overall increase. During the last quarter of the fifteenth century the

Leiden drapers produced about 20,000 cloths yearly. This took up 15 per cent of the wool available in the Calais staple (Howell 1986, 51, 186).

The expansion of the textile industry resulted in increased employment in the town. Since agricultural conditions were worsening in the Rijnland countryside around Leiden, especially in the peat districts, many rural inhabitants hoped to find a new future in the new drapery. Thousands left their homes to establish themselves in Leiden. The growth of the population was, however, far from even. The recurring epidemics claimed many victims, so that up to about 1440 the urban population increased less rapidly than migration figures indicate (de Boer 1978, 144–8, 166). Although the epidemics also occurred in the second half of the fifteenth century, their intensity had lessened and an explosive population increase became possible. Many newcomers would have been soon disappointed in their high expectations of sharing in the growing prosperity. Poverty was widespread and affected a considerable part of the population. In 1438–9, when war, wheat shortages and a plague epidemic ravaged the county, the distress among Leideners increased to such a degree that the Holy Ghost Organization, responsible for the town's charity, began to run short. For weeks the masters of the Holy Ghost had to resort to collecting money from the more prosperous burghers to be able to come to the aid of the poor (Blok 1912, 12, 220, 257; G.A.L. Weeskamerarchief)

A tax lists of 1498, when a 1 per cent income tax was first levied in the town, reveals that more than a quarter of all those assessed possessed nothing. The magistrate decided to spare these paupers and to exempt them from payment. Another one-third lived just over the minimum subsistence level. Just as in most other towns with some industrial development, wealth was distributed very unequally over the populace. About 83 per cent of all wealth was in the hands of 20 per cent of the population, while the richest 6 per cent of Leideners possessed no less than 20 per cent (de Boer 1982, 8–11; de Boer 1985, 101–2, 108–9; Lis and Soly 1986, 92–4).

Compared with those in towns like Augsburg, Cologne and Antwerp, the prosperous burghers of Leiden were not very rich (Howell 1986, 63). Where it is generally assumed that the town had a capitalist structure, the gap between poor and rich was much larger than in Leiden. This observation led Howell to re-examine Posthumus' views on the structure of the Leiden textile industry. Her conclusion was that the town's industrial organization should be described as small commodity production, not, as Posthumus thought, capitalist in nature (Howell 1986, 63; Posthumus 1908, 274; Posthumus 1910, I, XVII) As will be shown below, some questions remain unanswered about Howell's argument, which makes her conclusions somewhat dubious. However, both Posthumus and Howell clearly indicate that the magistrates had a strong grip on the organization of the textile industry. According to Howell, the production system was 'a conscious product of Leiden's gerecht' (Howell 1986, 63).

Political structures

Not only wealth but also political power lay in the hands of a small part of the population. Most of the towns in the Low Countries were administrated by plutocrats: rich burghers who succeeded in appropriating political power because their high status—gained through descent, prosperity and economic power—was recognized by the town populace (van Uytven 1962, 373–409). Although power was concentrated in relatively few hands almost everywhere, in many cases parallels can be drawn between oligarchic tendencies on the one hand and economic development combined with the size of the town on the other. In large commercial or industrial centres, relatively more burghers had executive power than in smaller, economically lesser developed towns. There power was continually exercised by a small group of townspeople, who in addition managed to reserve most vacancies for their relatives (Blockmans 1987, 236–7).

Despite its modest size and as yet rather low economic development, fourteenth-century Leiden does not fit this pattern. The mobility of the Leiden administrators was only slightly less than in Ghent, while one would expect similarities with small towns like Rotterdam and Zutphen (Blockmans 1987, 240–2). Between 1340 and 1400 a political career lasted for an average of 4.6 years. Also, 77 per cent of the town administrators occupied not more than five offices in a lifetime. In the early stage of Leiden's industrial development the offices circulated at a relatively high rate within a large group (van Kan 1988, 100–2). This was probably due to the specific economic situation in Leiden and the surrounding Rijnland in the fourteenth century. The town's economic expansion offered new prospects for the less prosperous as well as the wealthy rural dwellers. This was especially so when it became clear that the profitability of farms was falling because of rising water tables and the settling of the peat moors. Both the value and fertility of the land were affected, with serious consequences for farmers and landowners.

Taking these developments into account it is hardly surprising that among the migrants to Leiden were many prosperous people (de Boer 1978, 71, 156–7, 218–23). Some of them were of knightly descent and they, in particular, had enough status to make their way in town politics without any difficulty. Between 1340 and 1420, one-third of all families whose members took seats in the town government were new inhabitants (van Kan 1988, 101). Account should be taken of the unusually high death rate in the regularly recurring plague epidemics, which might have put an early end to political careers. Still, in spite of the high degree of innovation and mobility, a certain exclusiveness can be discerned among those in power. They closed their ranks to those who did not prove capable of preserving an equal status. This consciousness was mirrored in the marriage pattern of the leading families. Of the 132 marriages traced, 112 involved political functionaries or their families. The other 20 found their partners among the rural gentry (van Kan 1988, 102).

On the political level, from the end of the fourteenth century onward, there were also signs of narrowing in the circle of town administrators.

During the last quarter of that century *vroedschappen* were established in various towns in the county of Holland. These councils of wise men—*vroed* means 'wise'—can best be seen as advisory bodies who assisted the executives, generally comprising the sheriff and the mayors and aldermen. All administrative decisions of any importance required the prior endorsement of the *vroedschap*. First mention of the Leiden *vroedschap* dates from 1386. This body consisted of those who had previously sat in the executive committee (Eibrink–Jansen 1927, 4–5; Ringeling 1936) Membership in the *vroedschap* followed immediately on resignation as a member of the executive committee. Because members of the *vroedschap* were appointed for life, and the members of the executive committee, usually referred to as *gerecht*, were selected from this circle, the Leiden town government gradually began to display oligarchic characteristics.

Especially between 1450 and 1510, a diminishing number of burghers were involved in town politics. The first signs of reduction became visible halfway through the fifteenth century. More than once the town government expressed its anxiety over the high rate of absenteeism at the meetings of the *vroedschap* and attempted to correct this shortcoming by a system of fines. This did not have much success, as it appears that the average attendance at all meetings between 1450 and 1484 was only 60 per cent. After 1484 the membership of the *vroedschap* consequently dropped, and their number, including the *gerecht*, remained fixed at fifty-six. However, the percentage of those present stayed the same so that de facto the *vroedschap* shrank to a body of about forty members (Vroedschapsresoluties 1449–58, 1465–1504, 1588–1622; de Boer 1985, 96, 99; Marsilje 1985, 60–1).

This shrinkage was partially caused by the means requirement officially in effect from 1434 for *gerecht* members. At least on paper wealth proved a necessary condition for accepting political office, because the members of the executive committee were prohibited from involvement in drapery. The requirement held only for the years of office in the *gerecht*, but because members of the family were not allowed to be involved in drapery either, it might have entailed considerable reduction in income (Posthumus 1910, 281–2).

Another factor strengthening the tendency to oligarchy was the effects of the Hoek and Kabeljauw partisan dispute. This had begun around 1350 as a struggle for power in the county between Countess Margaretha and her son William V. Strife was confined to the county as a whole at first but after both Margaretha and William V left the political stage it changed into a factional power struggle within the towns, which in times of weak princely government could expand to real party strife. In very general terms, until well into the fifteenth century the Kabeljauws championed the centralizing policies of the sovereign, especially John of Bavaria and the Burgundians, while the Hoeks were in favor of local autonomy. During the reigns of Charles the Bold and Maximilian of Austria the motivation of Hoeks and Kabeljauws is much less well defined, although the differences remain visible to about 1490 (Jansen, 1966;) This struggle, which more than once led to violence in Leiden, had far-reaching results for the constitution of the gerecht, especially in the fifteenth century (van Kan 1988, 153–60; Ladan

1988; van Gent 1987). The party or faction that could count on the support of the sovereign dominated local politics.

Between 1404 and 1420, during the reign of William VI and the unhappy years of government of his daughter Jacqueline, the Hoeks were the most powerful faction in the town. In 1420 their power came to an abrupt end when John of Bavaria sided with the Kabeljauws and managed to decide the succession struggle with Jacqueline in his favour. From that moment the Kabeljauws dominated town politics, holding on to this position until the end of the fifteenth century, apart from short intervals in the years 1445 and 1481. As a result the Kabeljauws and their relatives were overrepresented in the *gerecht* despite considerable efforts of the Burgundian rulers, who made several attempts to control the election of the aldermen and aimed for proportional representation of both factions. Around 1490 the partisan struggle was exhausted and the constitution of the *gerecht* was no longer determined by the differences between Hoeks and Kabeljauws. Nevertheless the reduction of the number of men in power continued and stabilization was reached only at the beginning of the sixteenth century.

Despite the diminution of the political élite, the town administrators never relinquished the habit of consulting the richest inhabitants of the town for difficult decisions. Many well-off burghers had no part in political decision-making. Yet when the magistrature saw itself forced to adopt far-reaching measures, it could or would not do so without endorsement from the town's wealthiest, described in the sources as the *ryckdom van der stede*. Especially at the close of the fifteenth century, when a serious crisis made itself felt but the sovereign continued to request money to pay for his wars and expanding bureaucracy, the advice of the *ryckdom* was called for more than once. When Leiden, like many other towns in the northern Netherlands, was on the link of bankruptcy, the *vroedschap* instituted several committees to reorganize the town's finances. This task was assigned to a number of members of the *vroedschap* and to other prosperous townspeople (de Boer 1985, 85–7). However, the state of the town's finances was so deplorable that the sovereign was forced to intervene. He issued a budget which regulated in detail the means that should be applied to help balance the town's income with its expenditures. When after some years the Leiden administrators did not prove able to do the job on their own, Leiden was placed under legal tutelage by a representative of the sovereign (Hamaker 1893, 181–207; Downer 1951)

When the magistrate was confronted by difficult problems concerning the textile industry, the foremost drapers were asked to attend the *vroedschap* meetings. When the economic interests of Leiden required representation in other towns, the deputation consisted not only of town administrators but also of some drapers (Posthumus 1910, 456–8, 481; Posthumus 1911, 182, 135). Because the administrative élite and other well-off burghers apparently had the same economic interests, the town administrators regularly involved economically prominent burghers in decision-making. This is hardly surprising when powerful textile manufacturers and independent artisans such as the master dyers formed part of both categories.

The political and economic élites did not overlap completely because not all rich burghers were represented in political bodies, nor were all town administrators important economically. Yet research has discovered that there were very close family ties between the two élites (Brand 1987, 49–58). Probably this resulted in an entanglement of personal, economic and public interests. As a means threshold was coupled to membership of the *gerecht* although sources do not mention an explicit level of income, it is certain that the Leiden political scene was dominated by plutocrats. Unfortunately, sources that can give an indication of the financial position of the town administrators are very scarce and difficult to interpret. It is certainly clear that the members of the *gerecht* were among the contributors to the 1438–9 collection held among the well-off citizenry. Their exact wealth, however, remains hidden. Such data have only emerged from the 1498 capital levy. Around 1500 most of the administrators were among the richest townspeople. However, some were less prosperous, since they paid even less than the town average of £Holl. 3.1. The richest paid an assessment of £Holl. 132, which confirms the earlier assumption that the economic and political élites did not overlap completely (Brand 1987, 53; de Boer 1985, 105).

Industrial organization

Although the counts of Holland often intervened in town politics and the town's finances, they were more careful in economic affairs. The dukes of Bavaria and Burgundy seem to have taken action only to confirm laws and measures of the magistrates (Posthumus 1910, 281–4). Only in a few cases, when territorial interests were at stake, did the sovereign make himself heard (Alberts 1977, 277–8). It is difficult to find a general satisfactory explanation for the extensive economic autonomy of Leiden and the other towns. The rise of the towns often resulted from local development and growth of trade and industry. Such processes were not displeasing to the monarchs because of the income they managed to extract from the expanding centres. However, their lack of administrative competence in trade and industry (and that of their council members) made it impossible to subject the towns to territorial policies, which would have undermined urban autonomy. An example of this failure is the Great Privilege for Holland and Zealand, issued in 1477. It contains just two articles on very general economic rules. The inhabitants of the county had to take into account that the new tolls could be implemented only with permission from the estates. Also, all previously issued privileges in trade and industry in towns were confirmed (Jongkees 1985, 223).

When examining the organization of the Leiden drapery, similarities with the Flemish situation are easily found. The great commercial centres in Flanders were known for their urban protectionism, which showed striking parallels with small-scale mercantilism (Munro 1977, 229–30) Such a policy, although less profound, is also easily traceable in the case of Leiden. Furthermore, Posthumus laid emphasis on the almost exclusive production of *voorwollen* cloth. Only on a very limited scale was the manufacture of top quality cloth or *puiken* allowed. The Dutch historian was influenced by Pirenne's ideas on the one-sidedness of the Flemish textile industry, which in his view was totally focused on the production of top quality cloth. This argument has been successfully challenged by Coornaert, Verhulst, Derville and Boone (Pirenne 1951, 621–43; Posthumus 1908, 254, ref.2; Coornaert 1950, 59–96; Verhulst 1972, 281–322; Derville 1987, 715–24; Boone 1988, 1–62). Recent research indicates that also in Leiden the variety in cloth manufacture may have been greater than previously assumed (Brand 1991).

The fourteenth and fifteenth-century drapers did not limit themselves to drapery. These manufacturers regulary turned up as traders or suppliers of, for example, wine and wheat or as exploiters of stone or lime kilns. Their products were regularly sold in the town (van Kan 1988, 94–7). Apparently many of them felt that concentration on drapery alone was too risky and assured themselves of extra income in various ways. However, there can be no doubt that the magistrates regarded the textile industry as the main-spring of urban prosperity.

The most important difference from the Flemish towns is probably the absence of guilds as a political factor. In Flanders the guilds had developed into powerful political pressure groups. In Holland, with the exception of Dordrecht, the established élites succeeded in preventing such develop-ments, although in the beginning the aid of the sovereign proved indispens-able. As early as 1313 Count William III forbade the formation of such guilds. In the second half of the fourteenth century the desire to found guilds was expressed sporadically in Leiden, but with the help of the drapers the town government managed to prevent the establishment of alternative power blocs. In 1393 rebellion occurred in various places in Holland and the Leiden magistrature was forced to accede to the demand to form guilds. Intervention by Albrecht of Bavaria, Count of Holland, frustrated the aspirations of the artisans. Motivated by the fact that there were Hoeks among the rebels who attempted to gain political influence in the town by means of violence, he took strong action. It was absolutely clear that the artisans wished for more independence, as they were already organized into brotherhoods which, however, were supervised by the *gerecht*. The trade organization of the weavers and the fullers, the only ones which were established in the cloth industry in the fifteenth century, had no political impact. They only supervised production and required a certain level of training. However, all activities were totally subservient to the magistrature (Posthumus 1908, 364–6).

Leiden occupied a unique position in Holland. It was the only town which proved capable of producing high quality cloth for the international market on a rather large scale. This was due to the industrial organization and the strict conditions under which production was set up. Production was led by the draper, an entrepreneur who personally purchased the raw material in Calais or charged another draper to do so. After distribution of the wool and skins between the town's drapers, their employees manufac-tured the cloth in various stages. The final product was marketed by the drapers who then pocketed the profits.

This putting-out system was wholly based on the financial power of the drapers. They were the only people with sufficient capital to purchase the raw material, to pay wages and to run some risks. Still, the part-manufacturers were not all dependent on the drapers. The master artisans in particular often ranked among the wealthier townspeople. As proprietors of workshops where processes such as weaving, dyeing and fulling took place, they required some capital to purchase the necessary materials. The dyers also showed their high degree of independence by becoming involved in drapery from time to time. Spinning, carding, combing, fulling and dyeing were done mostly by unskilled labourers, who may be reckoned among the less prosperous or even the poor.

The artisans performed their tasks in workshops near their homes. In many cases the simple work was done in the house, and both husband and wife as well as the older children were put to work. Only the masters could afford to hire helpers. As was usual in the medieval textile industry the family also formed the main production unit. Accordingly, the Leiden textile industry can best be described as a cottage industry (Posthumus 1908, 271–355).

The form of industrial organization which implied that big manufacturers controlled the means of production, and simultaneously had enormous influence on the regulation of production, is generally seen as a form of early mercantile or industrial capitalism (Lis and Soly 1986, 78–87; Derville 1987, 721–4). Following Kohachiro Takahashi, two routes can be distinguished which lead to the transformation of urban economies to capitalism. First, the producers, descendants of the circle of small independent artisans, managed to climb to the position of merchant and capitalist. Second, there is the possibility that traders began to control production directly and thus became capitalist industrial entrepreneurs. The wealthy artisans focused on the concentration of labour, i.e., they invested in central workshops where labourers were put to work for low wages in order to market the final product at the lowest possible price. They were frustrated in their aims by the entrepreneurs who involved these artisans in production through the putting-out system and thus denied them free access to the market. The entrepreneurs decentralized production and divided it into a broad spectrum of treatments. Since the various stages of production could be done by relatively simple means, and much of the work was done within the family, investments were low. This system had many advantages for the drapers and strengthened their power over the part manufacturers; it was also a result of the differentiation of tasks which resulted in little mutual solidarity among the waged labourers, so that any attempt to revolt could easily be suppressed (Takahashi 1982, 88–90, 92; Lis and Soly 1986, 78–80; Derville 1987, 721–4). Some years ago Howell and DuPlessis developed the thesis that small commodity production in medium-size towns was the most important form of industrial organization. They presented it as an alternative to the capitalism reigning supreme in the large industrial and commercial centres. In these towns the main aim was mass production and maximization of profits, which in Marxist eyes at least had to lead to repressive wage policies and the development of a workers' proletariat. Howell contrasted these capitalist elements with the characteristics of small commodity production as it would have taken place in towns such as Leiden (DuPlessis 1982, passim; Howell 1986, 27–64).

Howell gives the independent artisans a very important place in the town's economy. Their products were made in small workshops, where some waged labourers were employed besides members of the family. Corporative organizations like guilds and brotherhoods, each varying in power and independence, supervised the quality of the products, working conditions and training. Unbridled expansion and maximization of profits were not the objectives in this economic system, which focused instead on complete employment, the attainment of an acceptable standard of living, the independence of the producer and a kind of egalitarianism among the workers. Towns where small commodity production had been introduced were most often governed by rich landowners who constituted a political as well as an economic élite (Howell 1986, 38, 39). In the case of Leiden this implies that the town administrators and the drapers together attempted to safeguard the interests of the independent artisans and also wished to improve employment in the town. To reach this goal, production was regulated in detail from above, in the quality of the cloth as well as the establishment of production maxima and the implementation of a wage policy (Howell 1986, 64–9).

Town politics and economic control

Without providing much argument Derville found Howell and DuPlessis' conclusions unacceptable (Derville 1987, 85). For Leiden the arguments should be sought in the protectionistic and above all regulatory policy of the magistrates and the entrepreneurs. Sources clearly illustrate that at least until 1480 when economic conditions grew worse, they did not so much seek to safeguard the interests of the small independent artisan (Brand 1991). Rather, the drapers and town administrators attempted to force all part-manufacturers from high to low into a dependent position, so that a situation developed which resembled the capitalist transformation described by Kohachiro Takahashi. This policy, which aimed at preserving the existing balance—impeding every form of innovation and adaptation to changing circumstances, and thus contributing largely to the decline of the Leiden cloth industry in the sixteenth century—has been discussed already and requires no further illustration in this context (Posthumus 1908, 85; Howell 1986, 51–2).

The policy of the magistrature was wholly aimed at the protection of the industry. The many statutes issued during the fifteenth century were meant to strengthen the town's competitive position, ensure the quality of the cloth, preserve the existing economic relations in the town and stimulate employment for the townspeople. The contents of the statutes were not limited to the internal affairs of the town, but also included rural areas and the other competing towns. The protectionistic policy of Leiden was felt as early as halfway through the fourteenth century, which is apparent from the privilege mentioned earlier. The grip of the town on rural areas grew continually. In 1451 it was determined that no inhabitant of Leiden was allowed to contract with rural inhabitants within a radius of 200 rods outside the town walls. In 1500 this was extended to 400 rods (2,000 metres) (Posthumus 1911, 198). In order to keep employment as high as possible in Leiden and to prevent competition from towns like Gouda, The Hague, Delft and H's-Gravenzande in this particular field, statutes were repeatedly drawn up which, for example, prohibited combing, fulling and dyeing outside the town walls (Posthumus 1908, 104). At the same time control of the different phases of production was made easier. By stipulating that certain part-manufactures could take place only inside the town, rural competition was also suppressed. Only spinning was put out to rural areas, not just in the Rijnland of Holland, but even in Waterland, north of Amsterdam (Jansma 1974, 49–50; Posthumus 1908, 104–6). Yet spinning itself was also subjected to restrictions from time to time. In 1471 the magistrate prohibited the contracting out of these tasks with an eye to the unemployment in Leiden. Four years previously the urban government had used a spinning prohibition as a punishment when the publicans outside the town refused to pay the necessary liquor duties (Posthumus 1908, 106–7; Posthumus 1910, 486).

The magistrature took great pains, in close co-operation with the drapers, to prevent competition from other towns. When, in the second half of the fifteenth century, some dyers left for The Hague, it became possible for The Hague drapery to expand at the cost of the Leiden industry. The town immediately drew up a measure aimed at preventing any involvement of Leiden inhabitants with the drapery in The Hague. When a certain Aem Gerytszn. attempted to fabricate Leiden quality cloth in Overeem in Flanders, a mayor was sent to prevent such harm to the Leiden industry (Burgemeestersrekening 1486; Posthumus 1908 128, ref.4). Strict regulation also prevented the sale of looms and tools to other towns in order to forestall any competition (Posthumus 1908, 108). For that matter, in various towns people falsified cloth, often dyeing it and providing it with a Leiden quality seal for sale to Hansa merchants. In such cases the Leiden magistrature ordered the interception of bad samples, the arrest of the forgers and timely warning in the principal ports (Posthumus 1908, 129).

Many drapery statutes dealt with the quality of the cloth. The town administration prescribed very precisely the quality of the wool and dye and the type of tools. The cloth had to be of previously determined measurements, so that it could easily be recognized as a product of the Leiden drapery. Quality assurance was not only a task for the artisans and the drapers, but above all for the urban administration, which understood that the Leiden economy was helped by strict control and far-reaching regulation. To avoid harming the market, to keep prices at an acceptable level, and especially to assure the small drapers of a reasonable income, the manufacturers were tied to production quotas. Such measures were also applied to some part-manufactures to prevent the smaller artisans from being eclipsed by the larger ones (Posthumus 1908, 121; Posthumus 1910, 20, 50, 515).

Also, all skins brought into town had to be distributed and made ready for processing so that a trade surplus became impossible. In any case the drapers were not allowed to be involved in the wool trade, which could yield large profits. That the wool trade had many disadvantages for Leideners became very clear after the prohibition was repealed in 1465. Only the large drapers exploited the new possibility. Drapery at once came to rest on the shoulders of the small manufacturers, who were, however, not solvent enough to pay wages and offer trade credit. The *vroedschap* saw no other solution than the reintroduction of the prohibition (Posthumus 1908, 112–13) For the sake of taxes and of employment the town strove for stable production. Free entrepreneurship had become impossible through the intervention of the urban administration.

All this does not mean that Leideners were not involved in the cloth trade at all. Some merchants from Holland were able to break the Hansa monopoly. Especially after 1450, merchants from Holland, among whom the Amsterdamers were prominent, transported herring, dairy products and fabrics to the Wendic towns. Although an important part of the Leiden cloth was transported by Amsterdam freighters, the Leiden traders also made their mark. Between 1471 and 1474 the Wendic towns complained that Leiden traders made increasing attempts to sell the cloth themselves in the Baltic, circumventing the Hansa merchants (Spading 1973, 36, 48–52, 79–80, 159–60). It is difficult to indicate the share of the Leiden traders in the export of textiles but it probably never was of crucial importance to the Leiden economy. Leiden was to remain first and foremost an industrial town.

The cloth industry supervised by the urban government was remarkably similar to Howell's characterization of small commodity production. Entrepreneurs and master artisans were tied to production quotas; the magistrature imposed to improve employment and to protect the small manufacturers and artisans. Mass production and maximization of profits proved impossible within the system. According to Howell there were almost no signs of a repressive wage policy. Only the fullers suffered under the wage policy which the magistrature implemented with the assent of the drapers. This resulted in several strikes by the fullers and even on several occasions their departure from the town in an attempt to pressure the town government (Spading 1969, 171–5).

It could be concluded that there was a tendency to form a proletariat among the fullers. Yet Howell sees this group as a deviation from a general pattern within the Leiden textile industry. In her eyes it was not the journeymen, but the independent small artisans, the master weavers, master dyers, master fullers, dry shearers or drapers who were the dominant figures in the industrial organization. Their independence was tempered only by the fact that they received piece wages from the drapers for their part tasks. She extends this to the small manufacturers. In spite of their lack of capital for purchasing large quantities of wool and carrying out somewhat more extensive production, Howell believes that this group was crucial for the blossoming of urban industry. While the large drapers regularly subordinated their commercial interests to their political ambitions and gave up their companies for some time, their less prosperous colleagues saw to it that production continued without a pause. Howell correctly states that the small drapers were responsible for more than 50 per cent of the total production and in that way made an important contribution to the preservation of employment. For this reason the magistrature purportedly supported the artisans and small manufacturers on several fronts in an effort to guarantee production (DuPlessis 1982, 55–6; Howell 1986, 61).

Closer study of the same and other sources indicates that Howell's arguments are not tenable. First, it was not only the fullers who were the victims of a repressive wage policy. In close co-operation with the drapers the *vroedschap* also fixed the wages of the weavers, dyers and other artisans, including those of the masters. The occasion for a wage increase was usually an urgent request from the part-manufacturers, when their wages once again proved to be lagging behind inflation and price levels (Posthumus 1910, 537, 608; Posthumus 1911, 12–14, 36). The dyers also went on strike and notable artisans carried out negotiations with the *vroedschap* (Posthumus 1910, 142, 247, 349; Posthumus 1908, 347–9. Moreover, one of Howell's most important arguments is incorrect, i.e., when she wishes to demonstrate that the magistrature adapted their policy to the support of the independent artisans. To ensure their independence the administration purportedly established public dyeworks in 1477, so that production costs decreased considerably. That decision, however, had exactly the opposite effect. Because the dyers refused to accept a wage offer from the drapers, the town offered the manufacturers the possibility of processing their cloth in non-profit-making dyeworks. In this way the recalcitrant dyers were bypassed and put under heavy pressure from above (DuPlessis 1982, 56; Posthumus 1910, 60, 70). Also, Howell missed the fact that wages were kept low in another artificial way. In and around Leiden the magistrature had permitted the establishment of a substantial number of monasteries and other religious communities. Women's convents were especially numerous. For the protection of the small manufacturers and the maintenance of quality, the nuns were not allowed to drape for the market. However, the town government had no objection whatever against the contracting of nuns as part-manufacturers. They were able to work for lower wages than the artisans. To the workers' dissatisfaction—they at least once made threats against the nuns—the *vroedschap* maintained this measure, so advantageous to the drapers, throughout the fifteenth century (Jongkees 1942, 91–2, 149; Posthumus 1910, 171–2, 199).

In Howell's view the independence of the artisans was recognizable by, for example, the fact that the master weavers and master dyers themselves regulated the purchase of the raw materials. The weavers purchased the correct quality yarn on their own initiative, while the dyers were given the freedom to determine for themselves which dyes were to be used (DuPlessis 1982, 56). In the statutes Howell cites as evidence, however, this is not apparent at all. On the contrary, the draper supplied all raw materials. Even when the magistrature implemented slightly more liberal legislation in the second half of the fifteenth century, in which the artisan was allowed more freedom in this area, the draper was not denied the right to go on supplying raw material and to continue overseeing quality (Posthumus 1910, 325–6).

The arguments cited here against the existence of small commodity production as an economic system in Leiden also indicate that the policy of the magistrature was aimed at the preservation of the existing economic balance, which was to the advantage of the independent drapers. The urban government, operating in close co-operation with the entrepreneurs, realized that the textile industry would profit from the support of the small drapers. The drapery prohibition for religious communities, for example, should be seen in this light. The repressive wage policy also prevented the costs for manufacturers from escalating. By means of this strictly regulatory policy, and in the absence of politically influential guilds, the emancipation of the artisans had been prevented. The putting-out system simultaneously saw to it that they, with the exception of the most wealthy, were cut off from the market and only produced in the service of a draper. Because of the prohibition on the wool trade and the fact that the export of cloth was wholly in the hands of the Hansa, the draper should be seen as an industrial manufacturer, a figure who fits perfectly in the second option of the capitalist transformation model (Derville 1987, 274).

Conclusion

In the late Middle Ages the Leiden economy was characterized by a high degree of autonomy. The sovereign intervened only sporadically in the economic affairs of the town. Even then the intervention of the count conformed to the existing political line of the magistrature. The Leiden town government consisted mainly of wealthy burghers who were often involved in drapery themselves. At the end of the fourteenth century the administration began to take on an oligarchic form. It is striking, however, that the members of the *gerecht* and the *vroedschap* regularly called for the advice of notable entrepreneurs. Although the political responsibility was always borne by the magistrates, a climate developed in which town administrators and entrepreneurs together were able to determine economic policy.

In close co-operation with the drapers the town administrators carried out an economic policy whose main objectives were (1) the promotion of employment and general welfare; and (2) the strengthening of the existing economic balance of power. This intimate co-operation can be explained by the fact that the political and economic élites partially overlapped. The ties between two groups, apart from parallel economic interests, were strengthened even more by close family relations. As the textile industry was the basis for the town's demographic growth and increasing prosperity, it is not surprising that the drapers especially became intensely involved in town politics.

Through its dependence on English wool and the concentration on the production of a certain type of cloth, the town's economy was highly sensitive to shifts in supply and demand. Town administrators and drapers attempted to compensate as much as possible for the vulnerability of the drapery by controlling all stages of production and holding down wages with a repressive wage policy. At the same time a far-reaching protectionism attempted to guarantee employment in the town. The Leiden economy was wholly directed by a town government which, by preserving the existing balance, also safeguarded the interests of all independent drapers. These entrepreneurs were industrial capitalists who frustrated the emancipation of the artisans by way of the putting-out system and a repressive wage policy. The artisans' way to the market was cut off and they were robbed of any possibility of organizing in politically influential guilds.

Bibliography

Alberts, W.Jappe, H.P.H. Jansen m.m.v. J.F. Niermeyer (1977), *Welvaart in wording. Sociaal-economische geschiedenis van Nederland van de vroegste tijden tot het einde van de middeleeuwen*, The Hague: 2.

Baart, J.M. (1988), 'De materiële stadscultuur', in E.H.P. Cordfunke e.a. (ed.) *De Hollandse stad in de dertiende eeuw*, Zutphen; 83–112.

Blockmans, W.P. (1983), 'Verwicklungen und neue Orienterungen in der Sozialgeschichte der Niederlände in Spätmittelalter', in W. Ehbrecht and H.Schilling, *Niederlände und Westdeutschland. Studien zur Regional-und Stadtgeschichte im Mittelalter und in der Neuzeit*, Keulen, Wenen; 41–60.

Blockmans, W.P. (1987), 'Mobiliteit in stadsbesturen 1400–1500', in D.E.H. de Boer and J.W. Marsilje, *De Nederlanden in de late middeleeuwen*, Utrecht: 236–60, of which 238.

Blok, P.J. (1910), *Geschiedenis eener Hollandsche stad I. Eene Hollandsche stad in de middeleeuwen*, The Hague.

Blok, P.J. (1912), *Geschiedenis eener Hollandsche stad II. Eene Hollandsche stad onder de Bourgondische en Oostenrijkse heerschappij*, The Hague.

Boer, D.E.H. de (1978), *Graaf en grafiek. Sociale en economische ontwikkelingen in het middeleeuwse 'Noordholland' tussen ca. 1345 en ca. 1415*, Leiden.

Boer, D.E.H. de (1982), ' "Te vongelinc geleyt", sociale en economische problemen in Leiden aan het einde van de 15de eeuw', in *Leidse facetten, tien studies over Leidse geschiedenis*, Leiden.

Boer, D.E.H. de (1985), 'Die politische Elite Leidens am Ende des Mittelalter, eine Zwischenbilanz', in H. Schilling and H. Diederiks, *Eliten in den Niederlanden. und in Nordwest Deutschland*, Keulen, Wenen: 85–105.

Boone, M. (1988), 'Nieuwe teksten over de Gentse draperie: wolaanvoer, produktiewijze en controlepraktijken (ca. 1456–1468)', in *Bulletin de la commission royale d'histoire CLIV*: 1–62.

Brand, A.J. 1987, 'In politieke kringen, de familie Paedze van Sonnevelt en de verdeling van de macht in Leiden aan het einde van de middeleeuwen', in *Leidschrift*; 40–65.

Brand, A.J. (1991), 'Crisis, beleid en differentiatie in de laatmiddeleeuwse Leidse lakennijverheid', in J. Moes and B.M.A. de Vries (eds) *Stof uit het Leidse verleden. Sociale- en economische facetten uit de geschiedenis van de Leiudse textielnijverheid*.

Coornaert, E. (1950), 'Draperies rurales, draperies urbaines. L'évolution de l'industrie flamande au moyen âge et au XVIième siècle' in *Belgisch tijdschrift voor filologie en geschiedenis*, 59–96.

Derville, A. (1987), 'L'héritage des draps médièvales', in *Revue du Nord*, 69 no. 275: 715–24.

Downer, W. (1951), De financiële toestand van de stad Leiden (unpublished lecture, available only at the Gemeente Archief, Leiden).

DuPlessis, R.S. and M.C. Howell 1982, 'Reconsidering the early modern urban economy; the cases of Leiden and Lille', in *Past and Present*, 94: 49–84.

Eibrink-Jansen, E.A.M. (1927), *De opkomst van de vroedschap in enkele Hollandsche steden*, Leiden.

Ennen, E. (1979), *Die europäische Stadt des Mittelalters*, Göttingen, 3.

GAL, Secretarie Archief I inv. 381–4, vroedschapsresoluties 1449–1458, 1465–1504, 1588–1522.

GAL, SA. I inv. 560 Burgemeesterekening 1486 fo. 113.

GAL, Weeskamerarchief inv. no. A1, III B1 RA.

Gent, M.J. van (1987), 'Hoeken en Kabeljauwen 1477–1481; een nieuw overzicht', in *Leids Jaarboekje*, 35–62.

Hamaker, H.G. (1893–5), 'De stad Leiden in staat van faillissement', in *Verslagen en mededelingen Oud-Vaderlandsch*, recht 3 181–207.

Howell, M.C. (1986), *Women, production and patriarchy in late medieval cities* Chicago and London.

Jansen, H.P.H. 1966, *Hoekse en Kabeljauwse twisten*, Bussum.

Jansma, T.S. (1974), 'Het economisch overwicht van de laatmiddeleeuwse stad t.a.v. haar agrarisch ommeland, in het bijzonder toegelicht met de verhouding tussen Leiden en Rijnland', in *Tekst en Uitleg*, The Hague, 34–53.

Jonkees, A.G. (1942), *Staat en Kerk in Holland en Zeeland onder de Bourgondische hertogen 1425–1477*, Groningen, Batavia.

Jongkees, A.G. (1985), 'Het groot privilege van Holland en Zeeland (14 maart 1477)', in W.P. Blockmans (ed.) *1477. Het algemene en de gewestelijke privileges van Maria van Bourgondië voor de Nederlanden*, Kortrijk, Heule, 145–234.

Kan, F.J.W. van (1988), *Sleutels tot de macht. De ontwikkeling van het Leidse patriciaat tot 1420*, Leiden.

Ladan, R. and A.H. Netiv, 'Leiden 1445. Hoeken in verzet', in *Leids Jaarboekje*, 24–49.

Lis, C. and H. Soly (1986), *Armoede en kapitalisme in pre-industrieel kapitalisme* (Poverty and Capitalism in Preindustrial Europe), Antwerp, Weesp.

Marsilje, J.W. (1985), *Het financiële beleid van Leiden in de laat-Beierse en Bourgondische tijd ca. 1390–1477*, Hilversum.

Munro, J.H. (1977), 'Industrial protection in medieval Flanders: urban or national', in H.A. Miskimin, D. Herlihy and A.C. Udovitch, *The Medieval City*, New Haven and London, 229–30.

Pirenne, H. (1905, 1951), 'Une crise industrielle au XVIième siècle. La draperie urbaine et la nouvelle draperie en Flandre', in *Bulletin de l'académie royale de Belgique. Classe des lettres* (1905), reprinted in H. Pirenne, *Histoire économique de l'Occident médiéval*, Bruges, 621–43.

Posthumus, N.W. (1908), *De geschiedenis van de Leidsche lakenindustrie I. (veertiende tot zestiende eeuw)*, The Hague.

Posthumus, N.W. (1910), *Bronnen tot de geschiedenis van de Leidsche textielnijverheid I (1333–1481)*, The Hague.

Posthumus, N.W. (1911), *Bronnen tot de geschiedenis van de Leidsche textielnijverheid II (1481–1573)*, The Hague.

Prevenier, W. (1975), 'Bevolkingscijfers en professionele structuren der bevolking van Gent en Brugge in de 14de eeuw', in *Album Charles Verlinden*: 269–79.

Ringeling, J. (1936), Het ontstaan van de Leidse vroedschappen (unpublished dissertation, Amsterdam, available in the Gemeente Archief, Leiden).

Spading, K. (1969), 'Streitkämpfe des Vorproletariats in der Holländische Tuchstadt Leiden im 15. Jahrhundert', in *Wissenschaftliches Zeitschrift der Ernst-Moritz Arndt Universität Greifswald* 18: 171–5.

Spading, K. (1973), *Holland und die Hanse im 15. Jahrhundert*, Weimar.

Takahashi, Kohachiro (1982), 'A contribution to the discussion' in R. Hilton and others. The Transition from Feudalism to Capitalism, London, 3.

Uytven, R. van (1962), 'Plutocratie in de oude democratieën der Nederlanden', in *Handelingen der Koninklijke Zuidnederlandse Maatschappij voor taal-en letterkunde en geschiedenis*, 16: 373–409.

Verhulst, A. (1970), 'De inlandse wol in de textielnijverheid van de Nederlanden van de 12de tot de 17de eeuw; produktie, handel en verwerking', in *Bijdragen en mededelingen voor de geschiedenis der Nederlanden*, 85/1: 6–18.

Verhulst, A.E. (1972), 'La laine indigène dans les anciens Pays-Bas entre le XIIième et le XVIIième siècle. Mise en oeuvre industrielle, production et commerce', in *Revue historique*, CCXLVII: 281–322.

Vries, J. de (1984), *European urbanization 1500–1800*, London.

Werveke, H. van (1975), 'Het bevolkingscijfer van de stad Gent in de 14de eeuw. Een laatste woord?', in *Album Charles Verlinden*, Ghent.

Zanden, J.L. van, 'Op zoek naar de "missing-link" ', in *Tijdschrift voor sociale geschiedenis*, 14/4: 359–86.

3 Holders of power and economic activity in German merchant towns in the sixteenth and seventeenth centuries

Pierre Jeannin

It is certainly hazardous to speak generally about German cities, even with the proviso of limiting oneself to merchant towns, when the most thorough and scholarly works, in intent as well as in fact, generally treat no more than the history of a single place. The ground rules of our present discussion aggravate the problem, since they invite us to reflect on the influence various holders of power may have had on the vitality of the urban economy. The diversity of Germany and the nature of the period in question (the sixteenth and seventeenth centuries) offer plentiful divergences and indeed often contradictory developments. Without in any way seeking to cover the full range of examples, and while retaining the conviction that monographic research remains crucial, I suggest that a provisional synthesis can help sort out the diversity and divergences. Two themes will guide this exercise. First, what position did those who exercised urban power occupy with respect to economic activity? The idea here is to identify one or several relevant élites. Second, how did economic interests contend in the political arena? This should help provide a context for the analysis of particular economic policies.[1]

Economic activity and urban power

In German towns of the Early Modern period, public affairs were directed by an oligarchy: power was exercised by a minority whose composition depended on a variety of criteria which always included wealth. Putting it this way, though banal, avoids having to speak of economic and political power in the same hands as if it made sense even theoretically to see them as held separately. The two categories were not then perceived separately; rather one envisaged a natural and fitting order in which each occupied his proper rank. The order of rank differed little from one city to another. While we shall consider some interurban differences, generally minor, let us first highlight distinctive German traits that conditioned, objectively and subjectively, the existence and reproduction of urban élites.

The first of these traits is the real importance of urban autonomy, despite the setbacks imputable to the rise of territorial states driven by the modern monarchic ideal. The long-term trend forced the cities into closer dependence on the royal courts, though these poles of centralization by no means controlled the bulk of German social and political space at the end of the seventeenth century. Only after that time did a bureaucratic infrastructure give substance to state control; the eighteenth century, as a consequence, shows a generalized contrast between dynamic residence cities and stagnant imperial cities. In our period the most populous and active German cities were still free. Think for example of the relative weight in 1700 of a territorial capital such as Munich compared with the great imperial cities nearby, Augsburg and Nuremberg, however much these might have already lost of their sixteenth-century glory. It should be added that urban autonomy, though direct for imperial cities, did not require that status.

To unify their territorial state, princes naturally sought to extend or affirm their authority toward the cities under their suzerainty. This pressure began in the fifteenth century and could lead to armed confrontations, such as the action of the dukes of Mecklenburg against Rostock in 1487 concerning the placement of the episcopal see. Even in the sixteenth century, however, these actions managed little more than to nibble at the autonomy of the smaller towns. Often the lord in question was weak himself, as in the case of the Abbott of Corvey facing his town of Höxter. The Thirty Years War hurt the precarious autonomy of these tiny units. Size and complexity of functions distinguished true cities, and they generally weathered the trials of war, however severe, with no irreversible loss of economic and demographic potential. Even where princely authority had been long restored, municipal resistance continued to thwart the express objective of centralisation. Long after the bishop had regained power in Münster, the attachment to civic liberties protected good Protestants there; some non–Catholics still held municipal office early in the seventeenth century. Wherever outside pressure led to decisive change, as in Braunschweig in 1671, dissensions within the town proved a factor. None the less, for a long time it was hard to distinguish in either form or content the internal struggles of towns that would succumb to outside force from what was happening in imperial cities whose autonomy remained intact.

The visible signs of autonomy included such things as physical separation, i.e. the lack—noted also in many territorial cities—of a royal fortress or residence, or else a rather isolated royal enclave; the absence of a functionary transmitting royal orders; judicial and fiscal administration not subject to royal command. The qualifications one can and eventually must bring to this picture cannot change its underlying message concerning the socio–political structure of towns. If one bears in mind the high position state officers occupied in French towns, the absence of any group of agents representing a higher power strongly characterizes the German case. The exclusion of the nobility provides another characteristic trait, so long as we do not oversimplify matters here. In Upper Germany, for example, certain patrician families had long had noble status, and others acquired it over the period. However, the rule linking citizenship and ownership of urban land remained quite general. In Hamburg no noble could own a house. A point that applies to Protestant towns is the small number of clergy, in contrast to the Catholic norm that gave the clergy very great social weight in a city. The juridical definition of the city as a community of burghers corresponded well to the general perception. In a functional sense, the wider and more diverse the links to the outside world, the more 'urban' the city. Yet, most clearly in Germany, the city formed a separate universe, reserving to itself the task of awarding leadership roles.

The concept of political élites takes on particular meaning in this context. In each town only a few families provided or could provide the members of the Council, where power concentrated. Enjoying senatorial prestige, this body functioned on the urban scale as a true government, which simultaneously legislated, administered directly and adjudicated on appeal, with only the law—whose guardian it was—to answer to. Only appeals to law could lead, in some cases, to division of powers in this or that domain, as for example in recruiting Council members, but such modifications implied no basic change in the system. Whatever variety of agencies and procedures a comparative study of municipal institutions may turn up, it is quite legitimate to speak of a single system or a common base.

Some cities were ruled by a single council. In Lübeck it normally included eighteen members, four of them burgomasters. This simple model, common in small towns, did not function everywhere in the same way. While in Hamburg and Lübeck a senator retained the position for life, retiring but rarely owing to advanced age or following a bankruptcy, other councils were renewed periodically or even annually. Yet these renewals, which might take the form of alternating between holding office and reserve status, did not prevent the same men from becoming fixtures, possibly with a year of 'rest' in between. A multi-stage system was the rule in southern Germany. The Nuremberg variant gave power to a Little Council composed of patricians only; the Great Council played a largely ceremonial role, even though its *Genannte* came from families representing the cream of the bourgeoisie. Matters became more complicated when the urban entity included several incompletely blended communities; Braunschweig had five councils, one per *Weichbild* (precinct), so that the Plenary Council consisted of over one hundred members and effective government had to be exercised by an Inner Council of twenty-five.

As in the matter of term length, the varied electoral systems yielded a similar result. Pure co-optation was expressly forbidden (in Hamburg the changing rules were intended to limit nepotism), but the outgoing Council might designate an electoral college to name the members of the new body. How far actual practice diverged from what was possible in theory is illustrated by the example of Cologne. The regime that was established late in the fourteenth century divided the burghers into twenty-two groups (*Gaffel*), which elected thirty-six members of the Council who then chose another thirteen members. By the sixteenth century the burgomasters elected from among these forty-nine councillors invariably came by turns from the same ten or so families. This result is not the paradox it seems, since the *Gaffel*, like the southern German *Zunft*, though comprising members of one or more trades, was much more a clan than a guild in the craft sense; the merchants and other notables who figured in the membership alongside artisans in fact exerted a dominant influence.

During the struggles of the seventeenth century, opponents of council arbitrariness tried to enforce rules against conflicts of interest. It was already the case that a son could not sit alongside his father. Extending the prohibition to the son-in-law was a small step forward but hardly a blow to the power of familial ties. Constitutional details aside, access to municipal honours was governed by social distinctions more or less reflected in juridical statutes. A first line of cleavage concerned the *degree of participation of artisans*. Their access to the exercise of power varied inversely with the size of the city: in small towns masters, at least from certain trades, held a number of Council seats. A homogeneous social structure went along with this situation. The local merchants and the most prosperous artisans were not divided by great disparities of wealth or status; indeed, the grandest among them would have cut a modest figure in a wealthy city such as Augsburg or Cologne. We have already seen how Cologne's artisans failed in fact to exercise their theoretical role. Frankfurt had a different solution; while the Council included artisans, they sat on a third bench, were chosen by the occupants of the first two benches, and had no real part to play. Overall, artisans counted for little or nothing in the ruling bodies of the larger towns. Northern cities openly confirmed this exclusion from senatorial functions by statute.

In some cases there were no further barriers. In Hamburg and Lübeck any citizen save a manual worker was fully eligible in principle, so long as he was 'honourable' in a vague sense to which we return below. Elsewhere the closed patriciate was constitutionally recognized, as in Nuremberg with its famous *Tanzstatut* of 1521. This ordonnance specified the list of forty-two families, henceforth practically unchanging, who were permitted to dance at the town hall and, by the same token, to hold seats on the Council. In Frankfurt, access to the two front benches similarly defined the political élite: until 1611, a closed club, the Limpurger, enjoyed a near monopoly, which it shared after that date with a second patrician society, the Frauensteiner. The contrast is clear with the north, where the senatorial élite allowed new men to emerge. Of the merchants who joined the Hamburg Council in the seventeenth century, a quarter had acquired citizenship after immigrating. Lübeck shows the same sort of renewal, despite the presence there of patrician elements with the same pretensions and aspirations—right down to the titles of nobility—as their counterparts in Upper Germany. Six or seven families retained an almost uninterrupted membership in the Council for two to three centuries, every one with twelve to fifteen senators and several burgomasters, and all were members of the *Zirkelgesellschaft*.

In moving from a biographical to a statistical view, we must beware of oversimplification. Having tallied the number of 'new men' and the sons and grandsons of senators, what can we conclude from the rate of renewal and its variation over time or from one city to another. Meaningful and significant coefficients can be obtained only if one controls for complicating factors: non-periodic vacancies, related to the longevity of senators; and biological extinction or possible loss of interest within senatorial lineages. The small numbers to be analysed can also foster an illusion of precision. Yet certain structural traits emerge quite clearly. The families making up the class of senators exercised greater control than even the frequency of certain patronymics suggests, owing to kinship ties sustained by endoga-mous alliances. The truly new men who rose to Council honours almost invariably clustered to these established lineages, whether the matrimonial alliance came before or after they joined the Council. Those among the new men who belonged to an élite family in their city of origin form a special category. Heinrich Wedemhof, supposedly the wealthiest man in Lübeck (joined the Council in 1588, died in 1589), was the son, nephew, and cousin of councillors in Münster.

Those who, where no statute forbade it, rose to senatorial rank were merchants, and it must be noted that even long-standing members of councils could maintain their business activity. The case of Hamburg mentioned earlier may seem the farthest removed from that of Nuremberg. Yet in this port city, where merchants could aspire to political careers, more and more jurists occupied Council seats. The strengthening of relations of cities with the outside world required increasing legal capabilities, and this accounts for a growing professionalization of senatorial functions which could result in a majority of lawyers. Hamburg had to call a halt to this evolution, specifying in the *reces* of 1663 that the Council would have twelve merchants and twelve lawyers, with at least one merchant among the four burgomasters. In a different context, Frankfurt's lawyers competed with patricians rather than merchants. Of course, many lawyers came from merchant families. In Hamburg the two types belonged to the same milieu, with its roots in commerce. When a patriciate closed its ranks, social distinctions grew sharper to the extent (largely unknown) that these families refused to accept outsiders as marriage partners. The patricians were largely *rentiers*, more or less feudal landowners in the area controlled by the city or beyond. However, in the world of trade these patricians disdained, wealth also included real estate, though difficult it is for us to assess its amount and allocation. The allocation for Hamburg seems to have been small, perhaps because the city controlled so little territory, but matters were different in Cologne. In Erfurt, the wealth tax revealed that in 1569, 57 per cent of the wealth consisted of real estate. Those who argue against strong typological contrasts can point to a rather wide range of portfolio choices among the leading holders of wealth.

Whether access to municipal honours was slightly open or totally closed, only the rich could partake of power or hold offices that were honorific in principle. To be sure, even before senators began to receive official compen-sation (no later than the seventeenth century), public service was not without tangible rewards, which were customary if not legal. Yet paid or not, no one could claim honour without wealth. Once this is granted the question remains as to which variant of the system was the more plutocratic. In many larger cities fiscal practices were such that we are unable to gauge the distribution of wealth. In Nuremberg, Hamburg or Lübeck, the burgher paid tax on his wealth without having to declare either the basis or his liability, simply by swearing he had paid what he owed. Council members were sometimes exempted from tax; this was not the case in Höxter, however, where seventeen Councillors were among the twenty-four who paid the highest tax in 1516. Among larger cities where such precision might be possible is Augsburg, but unfortunately F. Hartung limited himself to statistics. What is left, subject to the vagaries of preservation, are individual inventories. They allow the tentative conclusion that even those patrician families that remained firmly in political control might well be far less wealthy than certain merchants, and not merely the magnates among these like Johannes Ochs of Frankfurt. In Hamburg the growth of commercial wealth was so intense that the oligarchy was more plutocratic than elsewhere. Yet the distinction holds true: government only by the wealthy did not imply government by the wealthiest.

Among the élite in the most active centres were merchants who settled there but, typically for religious reasons, did not apply for citizenship. Integrated with a contract, as in Hamburg, or in some other way, these residents and their families might well be wealthier than the richest of the citizens, with whom they also contracted alliances. Such a ranking in terms of wealth emerges clearly from the list of large accounts in the Bank of Hamburg around 1620, or from the turnover in maritime trade in the 1640s. The powerful wave of immigration to Frankfurt at the same time thrust the Dutch into the lead among traders there. A thorough search might well turn up analogous traits in Nuremberg also. Cologne did not lack wealthy foreigners undergoing progressive assimilation; as elsewhere, one discovers that they functioned as part of the multinational networks. Non-burghers who were overrepresented among the richest group of merchants remained (by choice?) generally outside the political sphere. So, however, did many rich merchants, given the disproportion between the number who could qualify and the limited number of places with real access to power. Let us go back and sum up the case of Hamburg: a dozen or so senatorial seats and as many *Oberalten* (twelve before 1685, fifteen after that date). Although these elders, who headed the parish councils, had no true political authority, the position could be a stepping-stone on the way to a seat on the Council. A maximum total of thirty places, then, with vacancies at the mercy of Providence (*Oberalte* were named for life). Compare this to the number of merchants rich enough to aspire to office. How many? Martin Reismann plausibly estimates their number at several hundred.

A problem of information disparity arises here. Historians either know or can fairly easily find out the names and even the origins of political actors. Sometimes even their wealth can be estimated, whereas such is not the case for the leading figures in economic life, who cannot usually be counted, much less classified by wealth or status. Given fiscal registers detailed enough to include occupations, nominative analysis could do something to dispel the sociological fog. Yet it is agreed that merchant fortunes waxed and waned faster than others, while the desired classification rarely reveals clearcut thresholds that would designate an undisputed élite. One thesis would seem to hold for those towns whose trade went beyond the narrowly regional: many affluent and established merchants were socio-economically hard to distinguish from the senatorial class in the same town. Some of them may have chosen not to join the council, while others surely remained outside for lack of places.

A shorthand summary, which need not even exclude those regimes where a governing élite quite rejected any infiltration, would focus on informal understandings (*connivences*). Holders of municipal power formed a narrow circle embedded in the wider circle of those who dominated economic life. The sharp boundary which divided the two, on which political history has focused closely, relegated much of the economic élite to the heterogeneous civic conglomerate of citizens that made up the *Bürgerschaft*. Yet the ground common to the two élites, all the harder to explore because its limits were elastic, in fact defines the locus of meaningful exercise of power in the direction of what may be loosely called an economic policy.

Political clashes and economic interests

The groups exercising political dominance have been presented in a static framework, leaving out change over two centuries both within cities and around them. To take one example, a victorious Charles V imposed constitutional changes on many southern German cities. Furthermore, most towns experienced repeated troubles, sometimes in the form of lengthy refusals to implement council orders, sometimes genuine sedition that led to the ousting and even the death of some council members. Although these movements resulted only in occasional elimination of unpopular leaders, they should be seen as more than accidental. Their clustering, for example, in the initial phase of Reformation provides adequate evidence of a wider crisis. However, the very fact that dramatic conflicts can be traced back to a complex set of tensions, generally combining religious fervour and economic interests along with rivalries or feuds among organized groups and clans, gave each case an individual history affecting circumstances and timing. Thus the *Fettmilch* riots of 1613–14 in Frankfurt stand out in a relatively calm period.

Conflicts of this type remained in each city's collective memory. Yet even when the protesters were successful for a time, the episodes did not represent any major discontinuity in the system of power nor, especially, did they substantially alter the ruling élite. In raising the issue of urban conflicts, omitted from this chapter until now, I must add a word of caution. Historians have tended to take at face value the legal and political issues raised by the antagonists. In doing so they have exaggerated the civic homogeneity of the citizenry (*Bürgerschaft*) and failed to bring out the practical significance for the exercise of power of social cleavages between men of wealth and the rest. This becomes clear when one looks at the

conservative nature of the final resolutions; they clearly involved accommodation within the élite groups I sketched out earlier. None the less it is
instructive to examine the dysfunctions revealed in urban tensions and the
conflicts to which they could lead, since these affect our theme, the role of
power in economic life.

Economic grievances, more or less clearly spelled out, were prominent
whenever a part of the population rose against the council. Complaints
about the price of grain put the blame on greedy merchants, including
council members, who exported it. Never mind that such imputations were
simplistic; after all, the council in their patriarchal capacity were responsible
for the subsistence of the population if not for their welfare. Complaints
against tax increases were more frequent and general; when added to an
outcry against waste of public monies—as in the 1520s—they took on an
explosive character. Politically, the issue involved financial control or audit
independent of the council. Early in the sixteenth century there were
accusations that council members were embezzling municipal funds or
diverting revenues or lands for their own use. A weak economy contributed
to aggravating the political climate; yet the oldest revolts were about gross
abuses of power rather than disagreements over the conduct of economic
policy.

After the great wave of troubles during the Reformation the struggles
assumed a more sophisticated tone, both in terms of the issues and because
highly learned jurists took a greater role. Protestant cities undertook a
thorough organizational springcleaning. Church property passed to the
parishes or to welfare and educational establishments, while the new administrative bodies, though often headed by a Council member, included
honourable (ie. prosperous) burghers. In Hamburg the *Oberalten*, mentioned earlier, made up the peak of a pyramid-shaped structure of 'burgher
colleges' which took shape between 1527 and 1529. Elsewhere the form
might differ while the function—mediating between the magistrates and the
populace—was analogous. A similar idea lay behind the *Kämmereibürger*, a
Hamburg body outside the Senate that controlled all receipts and expenditures after 1563. Lübeck followed the same route, though more slowly and
timidly: certain revenues instituted early in the seventeenth century were
entrusted to joint management. Not that any city even by the end of the
century could be said to have a completely centralized and open fiscal
system. However, progress in that direction was everywhere coupled with
practices involving co-operation in administrative tasks resulting from the
city's need for funds. Participatory management also extended to bodies
that carried out economic policy.

The reality of conflict underlay such working compromises, since it
hindered the council from taxing the population arbitrarily without consent
at least from the *melior pars*. The fact that some of these worthies participated in the protests brings out a further point of contact between the issue
of political struggles and that of economic policy. Since some of those who
incited subversive movements were of high social rank, we can reasonably
interpret certain struggles as no more than the 'outs' against the 'ins'. Some
examples involved a single senatorial family, with one member leading the

anti-council movement to protest against the nomination of his relative. Another and more significant type of case, evidenced at Lübeck in 1598–9, involved strong opposition led by members of the merchants' group. Since these merchants dominated the 'burgher colleges' in that city, what we have is simply a push by the new money—some of whom took the place in the Senate for which they were fully qualified—with a set of demands involving specific actions in favour of trade. We must avoid interpreting this incident as showing generalized antagonism between mercantile interests and the senatorial structure of power.

We have suggested a dual perspective in order to provide a framework for detailed analysis of public actions with respect to work, to provisioning, and to trade. Whether one wishes to consider goals, methods of implementation, or positive and negative effects, such analysis needs to steer clear of an anachronistic vision of the concept of economic policy.

Note

1. Detailed references are inappropriate in a synthesis too short to allow inclusion of new material. The following few references represent only an arbitrary sampling from an enormous literature, yet they incorporate most of the information and some of the ideas I drew on for this chapter.

Bibliography

Blendinger, F. (1973) *Die wirtschaftliche Führungsschichten in Augsburg 1430–1740*, Limburg.

Helbig, H. (1973) *Führungskräfte in der Wirtschaft im Mittelalter und in der Neuzeit 1300–1800*, Limburg.

Hsia, R.Po-chia (1984) *Society and religion in Münster 1535–1618*, Yale Historical Publications, Miscellany 131.

Jochmann, W. and H.D. Loose (eds) (1982) *Hamburg—Geschichte der Stadt und iher Bewohner*, Volume 1, Hamburg.

Kellenbenz, H. (ed.) (1975) *Zwei Jahrtausende Kölner Wirtschaft*, Volume 1, Cologne.

Mauersperg, H. (1960) *Wirtschaft-und Sozialgeschichte zentraleuropäischer Städte in neuerer Zeit. Dargestellt auf den Beispielen von Basel, Frankfurt am Main, Hamburg, Hannover und München*, Göttingen.

Pfeiffer, G. (ed.) (1971) *Nürnbergs—Geschichte einer europäischen Stadt*, Munich.

Reissmann, M. (1975) *Die hamburgische Kaufmannschaft des 17. Jahrhunderts in sozialgeschichtlicher Sicht*, Hamburg.

Ruthing, H. (1986) *Höxter um 1500. Analyse einer Stadtgesellschaft*, Paderborn.

Schildhauer, J. (1959) *Soziale, politische und religiöse Auseinandersetzungen in den Hansestädten Stralsund, Rostock und Wismar im ersten Drittel des 16. Jahrhunderts*, Weimar.

Soliday, G.L. (1974) *A Community in Conflict. Frankfurt society in the seventeenth and early eighteenth centuries*, Hanover, New Hampshire.

Spiess, W. (1966) *Geschichte der Stadt Braunschweig im Nachmittelalter, vom Ausgang des Mittelalters bis zum Ende der Stadtfreiheit 1491–1671*, 2 vols. Braunschweig.

4 Urban economy and industrial development in the Early Modern period: Nîmes in the seventeenth and eighteenth centuries

Line Teisseyre-Sallmann

The seventeenth and eighteenth centuries were a period of growth in Nîmes urban economy. From the reign of Henry IV the city specialized within the secondary sector, and the growth of manufacturing, centred on textiles, led to true industrial development in the eighteenth century. Progress, however, was neither uniform nor linear. Until the second half of the seventeenth century, woollens led the recovery from the disasters and wars of the fifteenth and sixteenth centuries. A complete transformation during the 1660s and 1670s saw silk and hosiery take the place of woollens. The change in raw materials and the rise of a wholly new industry signified a profound change in the urban economy.

The evolution that concerns us placed the forces promoting development squarely in a rich and tangled web of power relationships, political as well as economic, which played themselves out on the local as well as on the national scale. We can sense the issues and stakes affecting this urban economy by considering the chronology—the story begins as Louis XIV is beginning his reign; the urban tradition regarding occupations—the city's prosperity rested on the absence of restrictions; the conditions and nature of industrial development—decline of woollens, revitalization of silk, and launching of hosiery; and the social and religious state of the city—two-thirds of those employed in textiles, whether as workers or supervisors, were Protestant.

The struggles for influence crystallized around two opposing principles: that of liberty in its various meanings—freedom of enterprise and occupation, freedom to trade and manufacture, municipal and religious liberties; and that of regulation (*dirigisme*). In the various struggles these principles conditioned the positions of the protagonists: drapers and silk masters who favoured total economic freedom; hosiers who also wanted free entry into the trade but formed a corporate body (*jurande*) with control over a region;

the municipal authorities backed by the long-established privileges the city enjoyed; the silk men of Lyons trying to preserve their monopoly; the small Cévennes towns resenting control by Nîmes; the representatives of royal power committed to the strictest economic control and to religious absolutism; and Catholics and Protestants whose mutual hostility was economic as much as it was spiritual. It must be said that some of these players did not hesitate to draw cynically on both principles as suited their interests.

In the late sixteenth and again in the early eighteenth century, the nature and character of Nîmes industrial development brought about confrontation between social and political forces as well as between economic élites whose interests were not merely divergent but opposed and even irreconcilable. Their influences and interactions, their alliances, conflicts and compromises conditioned Nîmes economic fortunes in the Early Modern period. My present aim is to analyse the power relationships which in turn furthered development or retarded or even arrested it. After examining the development and characteristics of the two principal industries, I shall look at the role of the various parties in their establishment and finally at the factors conditioning industrial growth.

Silk and hosiery: two industrial trajectories

The paths and fortunes of the two industries differed: a complex and troubled course for silk, steady and constant progress for hosiery. Silk first grew in the middle of the seventeenth century. From 1640 to 1680 new apprentices quadrupled in number. Among the Huguenot population the number involved with silk tripled in a generation. The scope of the industry changed as well, from mere ribbon-weaving to trade and manufacture of fabrics. By 1673 the Protestant side of the trade was well set up, with thirty-six merchants and twenty-five manufacturers. Socially and symbolically, this growth manifested itself in the presence of silk men among the city's economic élite. When the Duke of Noailles, Lieutenant-General of the Province entered Nîmes in 1682, the silk trades led the procession: 'In the first row, the company of principal merchant burghers, another company of silk merchants, taffeta and ribbon masters, and silk workers'.[1]

After this period of general growth, the end of the century saw a more differentiated picture within the silk cluster. The 1691 listing of occupations indicates stagnation in clothmaking in contrast to the other activities. While spinning and dyeing showed growth, the commercial activities and ribbon-weaving held their own.[2] Yet after the end-of-century trough, the production of silk fabrics grew throughout the eighteenth century, the 1730s and 1760s delimiting three discernible phases within the trend. Using employment as an indicator, one notes slow recovery during the first three decades followed by acceleration, beginning in 1731 for masters and in 1736 for apprentices. The peak was reached in the 1760s and the number of apprentices fell slightly after 1770, although the lack of data for masters and journeymen makes it impossible to generalize this loss to the labour force as a whole.[3]

It is likely that knitting-frames (*métiers*) were introduced in Nîmes at the end of the 1670s. The weaving of stockings was taken up enthusiastically and continued to flourish for over a century. Data on supervisory personnel and the amount of equipment show slow but steady growth from the end of the seventeenth century into the 1770s. Starting from nothing, the production of stockings was well established by 1692, twenty years on, and growth accelerated at the turn of the century (the labour force grew by 357.8 per cent and the number of frames by 153.7 per cent from 1692 to 1705). Growth continued for another three-quarters of a century, at a slower pace to be sure, as both supervisory personnel and the amount of equipment doubled over the eighteenth century.[4]

Trying to understand the forces that produced these two patterns of change leads us to examine the characteristics of these two industries, so different from each other with respect to conjuncture, technology and structure as they sought to establish themselves in Nîmes and within the larger economic context. Their circumstances in the crucial years of the later seventeenth century were in no way comparable. The manufacture of silk cloth had been carried out in Nîmes for over a century but it was now to be brought out of a somnolent state to confront the Lyons and Avignon manufacturers in the national and international market. On the other hand, the aim of the nascent hosiery industry was to gain a foothold on the Nîmes scene as a separate trade alongside the established woollen and silk branches, at a time when the last two faced difficulties.

The most flagrant contrast between the two industries, and one which conditioned all their differences, resulted from the product itself: on the one hand a rich stuff used for festive or ornamental dress, on the other an article of clothing, no doubt necessary but hardly on a par with the grandeur of brocades and satins. Both the period of production and the cost of the raw material made the silk trade highly capital-intensive compared with the hosiery business, since the knitting of a pair of stockings took a few hours and used a most ordinary kind of thread.[5] Hosiery began with wool and only gradually shifted to the use of silk, the changeover coming in the 1730s and wool disappearing in the 1760s. As the workshops became standardized and the products more diversified, the wool–silk distinction was replaced by one that ranged from fine silk through ordinary silk to floss silk (silk–cotton mixture).[6]

Hosiery represented a conception of work quite foreign to the silk trade, success being dependent on the quality of the frame rather than on know-how and the ability of a highly skilled labour force. The prowess of the machine replaced the competence and experience of the worker. The production of a silk cloth was a long and complex process, entailing thirteen distinct operations, a team with at least nine skilled people and sixteen quite specific and different types of instruments.[7] Beyond the raw material, it took a twofold—physical and human—investment in capital to mount a silk workshop, since one had to produce the means of production and train the labour force. Not everyone could manufacture silk cloth, whereas anyone could knit stockings.

A solid stocking required a single operation whose trouble-free course depended only on the frame. However complex it may have seemed, working the machine was almost childishly simple. 'The work is well within the means of women who do it as well as men, and one sees many young people of fifteen who can make up to five pairs of men's silk hose in a week.'[8] Setting up a hosiery workshop required chiefly the building and buying of looms. 'The stocking-frame is an iron machine made up of three thousand five hundred pieces' and its manufacture was the job of iron workers.

It is thought that a skilful locksmith needs four or five months to make one, and even then he requires the services of two journeymen to forge the larger pieces, a plater, a needlemaker, a foundryman for the copper pieces that control the iron ones, a fitter to adjust and assemble the pieces, and finally a carpenter for the frame. This leads one to conclude that the most skilled clockmaker, even with suitable help, cannot produce so many as three looms a year.[9]

Once the new hosiery industry took conscience of itself, it would still have to face the question of the scope and limits of its activity.

Despite their differences the two industries had similar structures. At the beginning of the eighteenth century each had two types of entrepreneurs: the merchant manufacturer who organized production and sale on behalf of master artisans or manufacturers working to order, and the independent merchant manufacturer or master manufacturer. This system, where traditional artisans coexisted with enterprises of a capitalist type, changed rapidly during the eighteenth century. By the middle of the century the intermediate category of men who both traded and produced had disappeared, leaving a clear separation between the worlds of capital and labour.

The break in hosiery came around 1740. Whereas in 1736 there were 98 merchants, 54 master manufacturers, and 669 master artisans, by 1746 the 175 merchants—'taxed according to their means'—were listed separately (for the first time since 1706), ahead of the master artisans who were assessed on the frames they owned, if any, or on the labour force they employed. In the silk trade, a decree by the Parlement of Toulouse in 1761 legalized the separation, ordering the establishment of two communities: 'a body of merchants organizing the production of silk fabrics' and 'a body of master artisans making silk fabrics for others'. There were then 40 merchants and 529 manufacturers.[10]

Freedom of enterprise

The two industries received no direct help either from the central or the regional authorities. Through the seventeenth and eighteenth centuries no subsidy was given, no (royal) manufacture created. They grew only through individual initiative and private capital. Freedom of enterprise was a recognized privilege of the city, which indeed based its policy of economic recovery on an influx of capital and labour attracted by the ease with which outsiders could establish themselves within the city. The silk and hosiery industries were drawn in opposite directions by self-interest, and their position on the principle of free enterprise—hosiery in favour, silk against— proved a determining factor in their subsequent history. Whereas the hosiers were hindered from pursuing their struggle, the silk trade received backing in its quest for a monopoly.

The rise of silk production in Nîmes between 1640 and 1680 is related to the issue of freedom of enterprise. Some historians have attributed it to Colbert's protectionism, notably the exclusion of Avignon-made products which supposedly led to ruin in that city and the emigration of its skilled workers. While Nîmes profited from Avignon's troubles, the growth of silk there was already a decade old and part of a larger transformation of the textile trades. In fact, Avignon and the Comtat Venaissin suffered little from French protectionism, since it was loosely enforced. Brief squabbles between King and Pope did block trade from 1667 to 1770, but it picked up thereafter, as shown by the fact that the admission of masters in Avignon recovered to new heights in the 1770s after a clear-cut but short-lived drop.[11]

The momentum of Nîmes silk trade was broken sharply in 1682. The crisis has long been attributed to the revocation of the Edict of Nantes in 1685. However grave the effects of that action may have been, no religious policy can bear the burden of causation for a major economic phenomenon. In fact, the drama of renewed religious absolutism has hidden the effects of equally absolute economic regulation. This is not to deny the impact of the royal action. Two months before the revocation, a plea to the King signed by some thirty merchants ended a recital of the industry's woes by asking for religious liberty, including the right of all to practise the silk trade, pointing out that almost all Nîmes merchants belonged to the 'itself-proclaimed' (*prétendue*) reformed religion.[12] Even the flight of vital human capital, supposedly a critical factor in the decline of silk, needs to be re-examined. Emigration was limited and selective, severely affecting only silk and involving mostly workers, whose motivation was as much tied to employment opportunities as to religious convictions.[13]

The change in religious policy helped precipitate a latent conflict, based on social and economic rivalries, in which regulation proved a decisive weapon. Breaking with the city's libertarian tradition in order to free themselves of Protestant domination, the Catholic manufacturers asked the Council to establish a guild. Their request received a quick and favourable response. The rules promulgated in 1682 subjected the silk trade to the authority of four sworn guardian masters (*maîtres gardes jurés*) who were to be 'men of probity professing the Catholic, Apostolic, and Roman Religion', sworn in before the Lieutenant-General and authorized to inspect workshops regularly. While the religious restrictions hurt, the technical articles (sixty-four articles compared with four regarding religion) were just as nefarious for an industry that had counted on free entry and unregulated production to catch on in the most highly regulated of industrial sectors. The generalized concern that followed finished the task by driving away investors, whether Catholic or Protestant, commoner or aristocrat.

By contrast, the *dirigiste* legislation worked in favour of the hosiery trade.

Here is why. The whole city had initially taken up this new activity, and everyone either wove hose or organized others to do so.[14] The wool and silk merchants were determined to capture this source of profit by controlling the distribution of the product. A royal declaration of July 1672 established the title of master in hosiery for the whole kingdom, promoting the trade as a separate and distinct sector. This divided the city, with the hosiers pushing for an independent profession, and the economic élite and city fathers—for once on the same side—arguing for freedom. From 1690 to 1712 the two sides sought the favour of the intendant and the Council, who thrice decided in favour of freedom. Yet in the end the hosiery trade, without establishing either a formal guild or rank of master, achieved the same end. The merchant manufacturers controlled entry and imposed all the usual rules, from payment of dues to fixing the terms of apprentices and journeymen.[15]

The struggle involved more than the city of Nîmes. From 1700 the juridical framework established the authority of the city's capitalists over the whole region. While knitting had spread widely in town and country, the act of 1700 authorized stockings to be woven in only eighteen towns nation-wide, in Lower Languedoc only Nîmes and Uzès (the latter unable to compete with its dynamic rival). Merchants and manufacturers of the region had to come to Nîmes to join the governing body, pay dues, and register their workers, and the rebellious were soon put back into line. While an edict of 1754 deregulated the trade, Nîmes was by then too well established to be successfully challenged.[16]

While the hosiers used the regulatory apparatus when it suited them, they could sound like the most enlightened liberals when it was to their advantage. They confronted the locksmiths in a long conflict over the building of frames, lasting from the beginnings of the trade to the establishment of a separate profession of frame builder in 1767. The locksmiths claimed jurisdiction over an activity that used their skills. Fearful of losing control, the hosiers hired away the skilled labour they needed for the complex task of building and repairing the knitting-frames. The regulators favoured the hosiers in 1698 (Baville's order), a position reversed in 1701. After a number of lawsuits, the rival parties had to bow to market forces and sink their differences. When the export of frames became legal in 1754, the hosiers changed sides once more and backed the frame builders who were trying to establish their independence from the locksmiths. This appeal to liberty should not deceive anyone; the supposedly independent profession of frame-builder was in fact closely controlled by the hosiery trade.

Freedom of production

Both the silk and the hosiery industries had built their initial success on the principle of freely exercised production. They shared a modern concept of market supply and demand, dependent on the cultivation of clients; adapting to customer needs and resources; diversification, on lower quality goods; and on competitive pricing. From the seventeenth century this policy faced a challenge from *dirigiste* government. Although in theory analogous for the two industries, both of which incorporated national norms into their statutes, regulation worked quite differently in practice: in favour of hosiery and against silk fabrics.[17]

Hosiery was subject to the rules governing the Paris branch, which specialized in luxury products for a restricted clientele, the Court, and did not seek to control production in the nation as a whole. Nîmes export earnings made the authorities lenient, despite highly critical reports from the inspectors. By contrast, after 1682 the silk trade was subject to the full panoply of regulation and suffered in consequence. Not until 1751 was the stranglehold of regulation eased, after which production expanded from just five or six types of cloth to more than 120. The problem was that the rules imposed in 1682 were intended for luxury fabrics, for which Nîmes had neither the human nor the financial wherewithal. Lyons, the silk capital, enjoyed the prestige, the strength and the legal backing (a monopoly granted by François I) to brush aside any techniques not in keeping with its traditions. Finicky enforcement of accepted production practice was the Lyons style, and this made it impossible for Nîmes to establish a niche that would afford its production any secure scope.[18]

Once the Council had restored freedom to the Nîmes trade, in 1750 the latter showed how adaptable and vigorous it could be.

Far from fearing the inconstancy of the consumer, as producers must who always do one thing, we excite this inconstancy by repeatedly offering some slight novelty, whether in the design, the fringe, the composition of the stuff, the warp count, etc. The consumer's taste is like a raging torrent; it must be satisfied, since no regulation of the trade can stop it. No fabric is good or worth making but that which sells, and none sells at a profit save that which pleases.[19]

While Lyons and Tours remained pre-eminent in the high quality, long-lived silk fabrics suitable for upholstery and decoration, Nîmes took advantage of the desire for novelty and lightness in fashion to capture a wider clientele attracted by lower prices.[20]

None the less, Nîmes failed to achieve complete independence, losing to Lyons the struggle for control over trade in silk thread. As early as 1540 the customs at Lyons exercised a monopoly on imports — typically from Italy or Spain — which supplied the entire French market. Not only did this detour lead to additional costs and delays for the Nîmes manufacturers, but the extra handling could cause damage to the delicate fibres. After 1603 new taxes were added to the royal levy on silk; these were then made permanent and reaffirmed in 1687. Although their protests had fallen on deaf ears around 1700, the merchants of Nîmes resumed the struggle after 1748 under the new conditions prevailing in the middle of the eighteenth century. While the Bureau of Commerce was in principle on their side, its advisory was quite timid: although the Lyons taxes would still be paid, they could be levied anywhere in the kingdom. Moreover, while the state sustained the principle of Lyons' monopoly, it attempted to appease the men of Nîmes a policy of support for the development of silk cultivation in the area.

An ordinance in 1752 offered subsidies for the planting of mulberry trees and these, in effect until 1759, gave a decisive push to that activity in the Cévennes. Despite their control over Cévennes sericulture, the merchants of Nîmes remained dependent on the Lyons trade, since locally-grown silk could not compete with the Italian product.[21]

Nîmes became the industrial metropolis of Lower Languedoc in the eighteenth century. While the *dirigiste* policies, and the way they were applied, by turns helped and hampered the urban economy as pressures from divers interest groups caused the agents of royal power to advance, retreat, reverse or hesitate, the liberal push after mid-century proved mostly positive. However impressive its growth, the city none the less proved unable to extend the reach of its activity into commerce and finance and so achieve major importance in the regional economy. Whether because the élites were too poor or too timid, whether their production was limited by technological choices or by structural conditions, the city stood well behind Lyons and Montpellier. The latter remained the administrative and financial capital of the region. Despite support from both intendants and inspectors of manufactures, the city failed in its repeated efforts after 1726 to acquire a consular court. The key was that Nîmes lacked banking facilities so that merchants had to go regularly to Montpellier in any case. As the intendant put it succinctly: 'Nîmes is less a commercial than a manufacturing town.'[22] However profitable in the short term, the city's high degree of specialization acted as a barrier to transformation and further development.

Notes

1. AD (Departmental Archive) Gard, 1F 115. *Demographic notes of Dr. Albert Puech*, fol. 70 gives the number of apprentices: 1641–50 = 60; 1651–60 = 110; 1661–70 = 246. Also, AD Gard 1Mi 75 R3–4, *Livre long de l'imposition protestante*, for 1647, 65 silk workers (55 ribbon weavers, 6 winders, 2 dyers, 2 merchants); for 1673, 169 total (36 merchants, 25 factors, 94 ribbon weavers, 12 winders, 2 dyers). The overall role of silk in the urban economy cannot be gauged for lack of global sources. See A. Puech, *Les Nîmois dans la deuxième moitié du XVIIe siècle: la vie de nos ancêtres d'après leurs livres de raison*, Nîmes, 1888.
2. AD Hérault C 2774, *Etat des corps de métiers de la ville de Nîmes*, 1691 shows for taffeta, 19 masters; for silk winding, 42 masters and 9 apprentices; for dyeing, 11 masters and 4 apprentices; also 34 silk merchants and 100 master ribbon weavers.
3. AC (Communal Archives) Nîmes IVE 190–5. The registers for 1703 to 1789 show annual averages for taking in of masters: 1703–30, 14.1; 1731–60, 30.1;

1761–70, 46.2; for placing apprentices: 1703–35, 9.1; 1736–60, 25.7; 1761–70, 85.1; for registering journeymen: 1761–75, 86.7.

4. AN Paris G7 1685, 89, *Statistique des manufactures du royaume par généralités*, 1692 shows 109 masters and 350 frames. AC Nîmes IVE 24–8, Registre *des visites générales, 1717–1761* and IVE 76–83, *Registre de répartition de la taxe, 1705–1781* show the following:

1705	merchants:	42	manufacturers:	457	frames:	888
1717		15		489		975
1727		78		658		1241
1736		98		723		1497
1746		175		762		1536
1759/60		133		852		1770
1772		144		913		1800.

5. For silk, see R. Gascon, *Grand commerce et vie urbaine au XVIe siècle. Lyon et ses marchands*. Volume 1, Paris and The Hague, 1971, pp. 55–65.
6. See AC Nîmes sources in n. 4.
7. L. Teisseyre-Sallmann, 'Les gains de productivité dans l'industrie de la soie sous l'Ancien Régime', *Actes du Ve colloque sur le patrimoine industriel* (Alès, 1983). Paris, CILAC, 1984, pp. 25–50.
8. J.-C. Vincens Baumes, *Topographie de la ville de Nîmes et de sa banlieue*, Nîmes 1802, p. 503.
9. AD Hérault, C 2646, letter from an intendant to the chief clerk for finances, 1761.
10. AC Nîmes, IVE 76–83, *Registres de répartition de la taxe dans le corps des marchands-fabricants de bas, 1705–1781*; IVE 189, *Arrêt du parlement de Toulouse, 1761*; IVE 200, *Répartition des taxes sur les marchands et fabricants en étoffes de soie.*
11. H. Monin, *Essai sur l'histoire administrative du Languedoc pendant l'intendance de Bâville, 1685–1719*, Paris, 1884, pp. 347–64. L. Dutil, 'l'industrie de la soie à Nîmes jusqu'en 1789', *Revue d'histoire moderne et contemporaine*, X, 1908, pp. 318–43. R. Moulinas, 'Industrie, conjoncture et fiscalité. La fabrique de soieries d'Avignon et les privilèges de regnicoles des habitants de cette ville à la fin du XVIIe siècle et au début du XVIIIe', *Annales de la faculté des lettres et sciences humaines d'Aix*, V. 42, 1967, pp. 69–118.
12. H. Monin, op. cit., p. 349.
13. AD Hérault, C 2199, *Requête des marchands de soie de Nîmes, 8 août 1685.*
14. M. Sonnenscher, 'The hosiery industry of Nîmes and the Lower Languedoc in the eighteenth century,' *Textile History*, vol. 10, 1979, pp. 142–60.
15. L. Dutil, 'La fabrique des bas à Nîmes au XVIIIe siècle', *Annales du Midi*, 1905, pp. 218–51.
16. AC Nîmes, IVE 16, 'Arrêt . . . pour les maîtres ouvriers faiseurs de bas . . . de soie . . .', 30 March 1700; IVE 78, *Répartition de la taxe sur les fabricants de bas*, 1727.
17. AN Paris, F12 659A, pièce 45 *Observations du sieur Holker fils sur les manufactures de la province de Languedoc*, 1774.
18. AD Hérault, C 2648, *Mémoire des syndics des marchands faisant fabriquer les étoffes de soie de Nîmes à l'intendant*, 1777.
19. AN Paris, F12 653, file 3, *Lettre de l'inspecteur des manufactures de Nîmes Imbert de Saint-Paul au contrôleur général*, 15 June 1776.
20. Municipal Library of Carcassonne, ms. 82, Ballainvilliers, *Mémoire sur le commerce du Languedoc*, 1789, ff. 103–4.

21. G. Charlety, 'Le régime douanier de Lyon', *Revue d'histoire de Lyon*, 1902–3; Bâville, *Mémoires pour servir à l'histoire du Languedoc*, Amsterdam, 1734; AN Paris, F12 1436, pièces 9, 10, 12, 13, 1748–9.
22. AD Hérault, C 2755, *Juridiction consulaire de Nîmes*, 1726–86.

5 Structural crisis of the economy and political leadership: the example of Cologne in the eighteenth century

Dietrich Ebeling

It has been noted since the very beginning of modern urban historiography that the roots of urban development in the Middle Ages and the Early Modern period are to be found in the particular economic function of towns and cities. Mass commercial production of high quality goods was not compatible with an agrarian society characterized by feudal structures. The market for a limited regional area first grew out of this functional differentiation. Later, in the large centres of production, a special distribution sector for commercial products developed. Although it is not possible to detect any clear product specialization in the trade sector, this necessary complement to craft production geared to distant markets must be viewed quite separately in analytical terms from the long–distance trading function which some towns took on solely as a result of their favourable geographical location.

This separation between the spheres of agricultural and craft production formed the basis for the first phase of urbanization since classical antiquity. However, it is particularly important that we do not lose sight of this fact when dealing with the urban history of the Early Modern period, because this basic function was in part fading and being replaced with or over–shadowed by other functions. Moreover, at least a second urbanization phase under way was determined, according to de Vries, by particular functions in the world market on the one hand, and by the growing role of the Early Modern state on the other (de Vries 1984).

The 1986 Berne Economic History Congress devoted an entire section to the decline of individual towns and cities or whole categories of towns, a decline which, as Gutmann noted, always implied a functional loss, too. Moreover, in his latest book on the development of craft and industry in Early Modern Europe Gutmann argues that the loss of this basic function of the medieval city and its monopoly of craft production played a decisive role in stimulating commercial development between 1500 and 1800 (Gutmann 1986, 28; Gutmann 1988). Without doubt a major cause of the decline of many older commercial towns was the spread of mass production rural industries, which began in a few regions in the sixteenth century and reached a peak in the late eighteenth and early nineteenth centuries, attaining a more significant share of overall commercial production *vis-à-vis* the towns.[1]

This proto-industrialization was able to establish itself in those areas where the rigid constraints of the feudal system had been eased or completely removed. It was here that the decisive advantage held by the autonomous towns in the Middle Ages was lost. Apart from the structural obstacles, the higher wage levels in the towns represented a great disadvantage in work-intensive Early Modern commercial production. Even in the most developed form of rural industry the producers were able to obtain part of their vital needs via non-commercial activity. Whereas the urban worker was forced to purchase the food he required in the market-place, where price levels were inevitably higher than in rural areas because of transport and shipment costs, the completely landless workers in rural industry make use of a small garden or received payments in kind for work performed in the farming sector and were thus able to obtain at least part of their food requirements in this way.

In contrast, the specialization and the high degree of division of labour in towns proved to be a disadvantage for at least some sectors of craft production, which was the main reason why these towns lost their economic function. The response to this situation can, according to Gutmann, be classified into two categories. The conservative answer was the usually hopeless attempt to retain the monopoly by the use of force. On the other hand, the more successful towns were those which managed, at least temporarily, to maintain the attractiveness of their labour markets by dis mantling protective social mechanisms, to gain a competitive advantage by specializing in high quality processes involving the widespread introduction of mechanization, or simply to take on completely different, non-commercial, functions (Gutmann 1986, 42–4).

Apart from the political activities in the towns which, to this end, were directed at the external environment, a long conflict within the towns themselves finally decided the course the town was to take. Using the example of the city of Cologne I shall demonstrate the problem of a loss of function, and against this background, examine the political conflicts.

Cologne had already clearly passed the peak of its development in the sixteenth century, both in absolute terms and in comparison with the other large European cities. The number of inhabitants declined and stabilized at about 40,000 until well into the nineteenth century. This constant population level conceals, however, the far-reaching structural crisis, particularly in the export-oriented trades. From its renaissance in the Middle Ages Cologne was primarily a craft centre and trading city; its rise to become the largest city in north-western Europe occurred in that first period of urbanization. At that time the city produced nearly the entire range of goods produced in the Middle Ages for the supralocal and supraregional markets.

The trades which processed wool, cotton, cloth and silk attained predominance in Cologne in line with the significance of textile manufacturing. With the exception of the dominance attained by the woollen cloth manufacturing trade during the fourteenth and fifteenth centuries, there was no specialization in any single leading product, as was the case in Lyons with the manufacture of silk. With very few exceptions all the different trades were organized in craft guilds. From the seventeenth century onwards the only exceptions to this rule were in those cases where a new trade began manufacturing a previously unknown product and did not encroach upon the activities of any of the established craft guilds.[2]

The structure of the once progressive putting-out system became a handicap in the manufacture of woollen cloth. In order to exclude dependence upon merchant capital from outside the craft guilds, it had been decided that only members of the craft guild concerned could become putting-out capitalists. This gave rise to a monopoly which proved hostile to innovation, and which made the majority of wool weavers dependent upon a few craft guild members, finally bringing about the ruin of the entire trade. Whereas at the end of the fourteenth century about 6,000 people were dependent upon wool processing, at the end of the eighteenth century there were only two dozen self-employed master craftsmen in woollen cloth manufacture.[3]

In Aachen under similar conditions the merchant capitalists had left the town and established modern wool processing in the immediate vicinity, with elements of both putting-out and manufacturing structures, which in a short time enabled them to conquer an important part of the international market. In those areas where exploitation of wage differentials were prevented by those affected, the economically liberal territorial state used military force to enforce the owners interests if the need arose.[4]

Cologne's silk production suffered a similar fate to that of the wool industry. In the fifteenth century silk production was still numbered amongst the great export trades. Here too a lack of flexibility with regard to changes in fashion and resistance to technical innovations were decisive. While the old silk trade died, the manufacture of silk ribbon, which had been brought to Cologne as late as the sixteenth century by Protestant immigrants, managed initially to keep pace with developments.

Although the silk ribbon weavers were formally organized in a craft guild, the putting-out system run by merchant capitalists dominated from the outset. A monopoly like that of the woollen cloth manufacturing trade was unable to establish itself. During the conflict surrounding the introduction of the mechanical weaving loom, which spread throughout the entire Reich in the second half of the seventeenth century, the putting-out capitalists were able largely to prevail. Nevertheless, Cologne was, only of modest significance as a manufacturing centre in the eighteenth century.

The merchant capitalists in this sector were mostly Protestants who faced increasing restrictions upon their economic activities in Catholic Cologne. Politically speaking, they had no rights and they suffered discrimination when practising their faith. When, at the beginning of the eighteenth century, a large group of Protestants including some of the most important silk merchants left the city, they did so because of the obstacles placed in their path and the disadvantages they suffered in the trade as a result. Christoph Andreae established a highly successful silk manufacturing business on the other bank of the Rhine at Mülheim, under the protection of the Palatinate government, which directly took work away from Cologne's silk ribbon weavers. Silk manufacturing in Cologne faced further competition in the surrounding area also from the Krefeld-based company owned by van der Leyen, who put out material to rural producers and organised the complex final production process in a factory in a similar way to the production of woollen cloth in Monschau.

In the last third of the eighteenth century Cologne's silk ribbon manufacturers exploited the infrastructure in the vicinity of the city to put pressure on the ribbon weavers who had to put up with wage cuts and the truck system. Their attempt to use the craft guild as an instrument to defend their interests failed. The merchant capitalist Herstatt, who later became a banker, countered this move by arguing that he had concluded contracts with the individual artisans and not with the craft guild.[5]

As the eighteenth century drew to a close there were only 274 self-employed mastercraftsmen in Cologne's textile industry. Only about one in five employed a journeyman. It is impossible to ascertain how many unskilled workers were required. It is certain that some of the 864 day labourers, who alone were responsible for 10.6 per cent of households, were employed in the textile trade. Many of the 480 single women who ran one-person households stated that they worked as knitters, weavers or spinners. It is not possible to quantify the numbers of married women and children who, as in other places, formed the large pool of temporary workers.

The predominance of the small artisan shops is not the only indication that the remaining textile craftsmen did not have very favourable prospects in the trade. When in 1798 taxes were collected, it was established that nearly 80 per cent of textile craftsmen were below the taxation threshold compared with 64.2 per cent of all craftsmen and 23.0 per cent of merchants and entrepreneurs. Three-quarters of the textile craft workers did not own a house and most of them had to be content with the worst possible accommodation (Ebeling 1987).

However, during the eighteenth century some branches with potential did emerge outside the sectors organized by craft guilds and did indeed offer the prospect of new prosperity. Tobacco above all should be mentioned here because of its positive effect upon employment. In 1736 Heinrich Joseph DuMont, who originated from the Liège area, set up his business, followed in 1764 by Franz Foveaux and in 1779 by Johan Breuer. Despite the downturn in the tobacco processing branch it still employed between 1,200 and 2,000 people. The low level of qualifications required in this profession is illustrated by the fact that in the 1797 address book and the 1799 census only forty-one household heads described themselves as tobacco spinners. As in the case of temporary workers in the textile trades a large number of people in tobacco processing were classified as day labourers or the like or were women and children.

The census carried out in 1799 by the French revealed that day labourers and single working women accounted for 2,012 (24.6 per cent) of the 8,174 households in Cologne. Apart from paupers unfit for work, these people represented the lowest rung on the social ladder. They were nearly all exempt from income tax collection in 1798. Their accommodation, which only one in ten owned, was among the worst the city had to offer. Moreover, one-third of them had to share their accommodation with one or more other households.

The social gap between the remaining group of textile craftsmen and the very lowest social class was smaller than the gap separating them from the group of guild craftsmen who largely supplied the local market. The food trade in particular had divided up the city market between guild members, partly internal craft guild restrictions and by administrative restrictions on the number of businesses in such a way that most craftsmen enjoyed an adequate or a comfortable existence. Two-thirds paid tax on a middling income and 10 per cent even paid taxes on a higher income. Half of these people owned their houses and a quarter even had two or more houses. Judging by the value of their homes most of them lived in good to very good accommodation. While one in four self-employed textile craftsmen had to share his accommodation with at least one other household, this applied to only 7.5 per cent of bakers and butchers.

Everywhere there was a rush to join those vocations and to participate in those activities which drew upon the local market. At the same time resistance to excessive entry mounted in the trades organized in craft guilds. The instruments ranged from increased entry and examination fees, extended training periods and compulsory, varied experience for journeymen, to a complete closure of the craft guild to new entrants. Only the sons of master-craftsmen remained exempt from such measures. Declining standards in the export trades as well as the less demanding activities in the non-guild branches led to a decline in the qualification of employees. According to cautious estimates the proportion of unqualified employees rose during the eighteenth century from about 10 per cent to about 20 per cent. When a series of manufacturing plants were set up in Cologne during the French period, the entrepreneurs found that there were not enough qualified workers in the city (Wankell 1949, 14–24).

Since its beginnings in the Middle Ages Cologne's economy had been based on the dualism of export trade and local commerce. However, the decline of the export trade was also accompanied by a fall in active trading. The type of merchant connected with a particular trade had disappeared with one or two exceptions. The continuing significance of the trading sector was based on the very favourable location of the city straddling the transportation routes. In contrast to the trading centres in Upper Germany, Cologne did not lose its importance as trade shifted from the Levant to the Atlantic. Rather, commerce profited from the increased efforts of the Dutch since the end of the Thirty Years War. The Dutch were set on opening up the Rhineland area for new products from overseas. However, in this context Cologne's merchants were allowed to take on functions relating to transportation or to sell on commission.

Transit trade had gained such an overwhelming importance in the eighteenth century that Mathieu Schwann wrote in his history of the Cologne Chamber of Commerce: 'Cologne's businessmen were only making money out of business deals conducted by others' (Schwann 1906, 55). Cologne secured a monopoly of trade on the Rhine between Dordrecht and Mainz by means of the staple (the right to register and handle goods in transit) (Kuske 1939; Feldenkirchen 1975, 21–6). Only a few dozen families were able to live lavishly from the commission and transport business. As a rule, however, one also ran one's own trading operation on the side. Indeed, in general it tended to be the exception if someone devoted himself entirely to one trading sector.

Wine remained through the centuries one of the most profitable trading products. The high level of capital outlay limited the number of wholesalers to a few families. Some of them had wine warehouses in the city which could hold up to 7,500 hectolitres. At the end of the century such a quantity of wine had a value of 600,000 francs. These families belonged to the inner circle of the economic and political establishment (Ebeling 1987, 65 ff.).

The other classical export products of the Rhineland, which mainly entered the European trade via the Netherlands, also in part went through the books of Cologne's merchants. However, where one of these sectors had been completely restructured and had taken on much larger dimensions, for example the emergence of the trade in long-cut timber at the end of the seventeenth century, Cologne's merchants hardly made an appearance (Ebeling 1988).

One gains the impression that in the eighteenth century a type of merchant dominated in Cologne who was satisfied with the security of the commission and transportation business and with carrying on his father's business and did not seek to maximize his personal profit.

Another type of merchant also operated in the city, people who since the sixteenth century had been making a great effort and taking great risks to break down the craft guild system, or in the case of the tobacco processing industry, to operate in niches on the market free of interference by the craft guilds. These were immigrants who, due to their confession or lack of social status, had no chance of entering the ranks of the business leaders. They were the only people who took new initiatives to the extent that the fossilized economic structures allowed. Mostly they imported ideas for new production processes from their home countries. The Protestants amongst them were subjected to increased discrimination at the beginning of the eighteenth century. Although Protestants were granted equal status in formal terms by the French authorities, Protestant merchants remained excluded from integration by the business establishment despite their considerable economic successes. In contrast there were, however, close ties with early Protestant entrepreneurs in the Rhineland.

Catholic immigrants from Italy and northern France did not have to overcome these obstacles, and the most successful amongst them were able to enter political bodies and established families. Nevertheless, they initially had to seek their success in the business world outside the classic trading sectors, as did the Protestants. The Farinas made their way up the ladder with the production of eau de Cologne, which had until that time been unknown in the city. The tobacco manufacturing families Faveaux, DuMont and Breuer exploited another new opportunity, introducing new production and processing techniques from France.

These immigrants were not motivated by their minority religious position alone but by the fact they were forced to begin anew under unfavourable conditions. They compensated for their lack of capital with experience and ideas brought with them from their economically more advanced countries of origin. In the case of the Protestants, additional motivation may have been derived from the fact that after attaining economic success they remained excluded from socio-political integration as well as from participation in the classic trades. They were forced to explore new avenues and were not distracted from their economic objectives by political and social obligations. However, the sharp religious divide should not close our eyes to the social integration which existed outside the political and family sphere. In the leading lodge of Freemasons an enlightened élite gathered towards the end of the eighteenth century, comprising members ranging from the Cologne aristocracy to local Protestant merchants.

Despite their business activities these merchants cannot be compared with the great early entrepreneurs of the Rhineland such as the Scheiblers and the von der Leyens. They did not devote themselves clearly enough to one particular company. This situation did not change fundamentally after the lifting of craft guild barriers. In Cologne the general trading sector continued to offer better prospects for attaining profits (Ebeling 1985).

The survey of incomes and living conditions shows just how lucrative the wholesale trade was in the eighteenth century for the people operating it. In 1798, 691 merchants contributed a total of only 43.1 per cent of overall taxation while accounting for only 8.5 per cent of households. One should, however, note that small traders are included in this figure. In 1810 the newly founded Chamber of Commerce put the figure of important wholesale merchants at eighty-nine, stating that they had on average 467,000 francs in capital. They distinguished themselves from the masses by virtue of their very lavish lifestyle, including grand houses with a large number of servants. While according to a list compiled in 1798 the average value of houses in Cologne was 1,269 livres, only a few wholesalers lived in houses with a value of less than 5,000 livres. The house of a wine wholesaler called Bettendorf was valued at 15,000 livres and was in no way inferior to the houses of the aristocratic and the old patrician families. While servants were only employed in one in five households in the city, the wholesalers had on average 2.3 servants. Some, like the banker Abraham Schaafhausen, even had five servants (Ebeling 1987, 105–38).

In view of the great opportunities for profit-making in the wholesale trade it is not very surprising that under the changed conditions of the French occupation nearly all the efforts of the merchants were directed towards maintaining their trading privileges (Schwann 1906, 79–208). Apart from a few dozen rich merchants, the top of the social ladder in Cologne was occupied by those families that enjoyed income from capital and rents from sinecures and public offices. In 1798, of the ninety-seven people who paid the most income tax, sixty-one were merchants, fourteen were *rentiers*, six priests, three hotel proprietors, two brokers four with academic positions, and seven members of other professions.

Undoubtedly, the process of modernization of Cologne's commercial economy was hindered by the continuingly favourable and, above all, low risk opportunities to make profits in the wholesale trade. Whereas in the eighteenth century there were still obstacles caused by the remains of the guild constitution, once they had been completely abolished in the wake of a fully liberal economic policy very little merchant capital flowed into the production sphere.

The political system in the city favoured those who persevered. In the phase of expansion in the Middle Ages Cologne had won free status within the Reich, and it managed to maintain political autonomy until the French occupation in 1794.[6] Thus it was primarily the power structures within the city which were responsible for the reactions to the economic decline. In accordance with the growing significance of the export trade and craft production in the fourteenth century, these power structures had shifted in favour of those segments of the population most active in the economy. Twenty-two *Gaffeln* acted as electoral bodies for the official positions in the city's government, and they were drawn largely from the craft guilds and to a lesser extent from the corporations of merchants and the patricians associations. For this reason, earlier urban historiography tended to classify Cologne as one of the craft guild democracies. In fact this system largely reflected the relative importance of the several economic forces in the late Middle Ages while at the same time leaving sufficient scope for upward mobility. Biographical studies show that the export trades were not represented by craftsmen producers but by the merchant capitalists. There can therefore be no question of the existence of a craft guild democracy (Herborn 1977).

In the period of decline in the seventeenth and eighteenth centuries the occupants of jobs in the municipal administration were drawn mainly from the members of the *rentier* patricians, from the active merchants, from wealthy guild craftsmen in local trades and, to an increasing extent, from professional jurists. Long tenure of employment, the coupling of various offices held, and the amassing of new positions were an expression of the formation and existence of a political class which was no longer so heavily committed to particular interests (Nicolini 1979).

For this reason its stance in the conflicts being carried out between the conservative and innovative forces was therefore seldom unequivocal. Decision-making took years and even decades. This can be illustrated by the following example: at the end of the sixteenth century some Italians and Dutch who had immigrated to Cologne attempted to introduce a new dyeing technique for silk which was customary in Upper Italy and Antwerp (Witzel 1907, 432–48). The Cologne silk weavers guild raised objections on the grounds of quality, although the market had long since accepted the new products. The political leadership, which mainly comprised people with merchant expertise, realized that a go-it-alone policy of banning the weighting of silk would inevitably not be in Cologne's economic interests.

To comply with the wishes of the silk guild the city's representatives raised the matter at the convention of municipal authorities in Speyer (1592) and Ulm (1593) but no uniform action against silk grieving resulted. The import of weighted silk from upper Italy could not be controlled anyway. The Cologne Council did in fact take the initiative in invoking a ban on the new technique by the Reichstag in Regensburg in 1594, and shortly before it had acted in favour of the silk guild within its own walls. At the end of 1593 large quantities of silk were confiscated. Furthermore, the dyeing vats belonging to the silk dyers involved were destroyed. The silk guild was able to assert itself throughout the economy and many merchants left the city.

Four years later such action was repeated and many of the merchants, who had subsequently returned to the city, were hit once again. However, this time some of the merchants who had violated the ban on silk weighting turned out to be members of the silk guild who were no longer able to resist market forces. The processing of raw silk in Cologne was damaged irreparably. The silk guild was on the verge of being dissolved.

The quarrel about the new dyeing technique pushed the conflict over technical innovations in silk spinning and weaving into the background. As far as both merchants and the silk guild master craftsmen were concerned, the import of raw silk and dyeing was the more profitable side of the silk business. Indeed, until 1724 the von der Leyens of Krefeld had their silk dyed in Cologne before they finally established their own dyeing plant (Koch 1907, 86). The abortive attempt to force rival commercial towns in the Reich to adhere to Cologne's own conservative line was not repeated on other occasions.

While it is possible to see clearly the differing economic interests behind policy in the preceeding case, it is not possible without further analysis to attribute directly political action taken in many other conflicts to the specific economic interests of certain groups and forces. The motives for political action in many individual cases and in fundamental decisions in favour of a 'conservative' or 'progressive' policy were concealed by the dispute surrounding the admission of the Protestant faith and the scope its members should be given. The treatment of Protestant immigrants always concealed the restriction or expansion of their latitude for economic activity. Since the arrival of the first wave of immigrants in the 1560s the Protestants had always been excluded from the craftsmen's guilds, the retail trade and nearly all other forms of business activity in the restricted local market. This led to a tough selection process, which, in the final analysis, allowed only Protestant merchants with enough capital to set up a business in Cologne (Schwering 1908, 9).

When the city's economy went into decline, even their right to work as wholesalers was challenged. At first, the lucrative trade in wine was taken away from them. Then at the beginning of the eighteenth century they lost the commission and transport business, which was, apart from the wine trade, not only the most lucrative business but also provided a basis for most trading activities and the putting-out business. Cologne's economy was deprived of huge amounts of capital with the exodus of the most important Protestant merchants from the city (Schwering 1907). There can be no doubt that the interests of the local merchants were behind these claims to a monopoly and here the rather vague term 'local merchants' is not chosen at random. This circle was by no means restricted to a few large wholesalers. The usual process of integrating large wholesale and retail trading practised by Cologne's Protestants also hit those people in Cologne who earned their living mainly in the retail trade (Schwering 1910, 6).

The anti-Protestant sentiment, which flared up again in the mid-eighteenth century and was shared by a broad section of the population, came at a time when the Council bodies had just increased again the scope for the Protestants' business activities and thus cannot be interpreted in any other way. Many people earned all or part of their income from working as small shopkeepers and tradesmen, jobs which depended upon consumer spending in the city and its outlying areas, a source of income which was not inexhaustible. The apparent or real threat posed by this sector revealed the deep distrust nurtured by the lower middle classes in Cologne against the Protestants, which basically served as a symbol of changes in old structures and distribution mechanisms posing a threat to their existence. Even if, apart from their activities in the retail trade, the repeated and partially successful attempts by the Protestants to break down craft guild structures in the textile trade did constitute real inroads into established positions, their impact was slight and the reactions of the lower middle classes reflected more their fear that more was to come.

The strong Cologne clergy skilfully exploited this mood for its sharply anti-Protestant stance. At the end of the eighteenth century people travelling through the city made the surprising discovery that in the centre of the Rhineland, which tended to have a liberal and enlightened climate, a prevailing anti-Protestant sentiment was close to provoking a pogrom (Bayer 1912).

There was a group in the political establishment, by no means small in number, which advocated a liberal attitude *vis-à-vis* the religious minority without at the same time pursuing any particular economic interests of its own. This group believed that the economic activities of the Protestants would tend to benefit the city as a whole. This faction was opposed primarily by an opposition movement developing outside the constitutional organs and drawing mainly on lower middle-class support. It was no coincidence that it was backed most strongly by the guild of textile crafts-men (Müller 1982, 126; Weingärtner 1913; Becker-Jakli 1983, 55–92). In institutional terms this movement—like the Council bodies—had its power base in those craft guilds whose members mainly felt that their interests were no longer being represented by the ruling class. The anti-Protestant stance adopted by this group did not arise from a claim to a confessional monopoly—which was the case as far as the clergy were concerned—but was attributed to a conservative outlook and a desire to restore past privileges.

In spite of the fact that this movement soon achieved an institutional character at the polls, and consequently influenced the city's constitution, the Council was very tentative in dealing with this challenge. By blocking off the safety valve which the lower middle classes had created to vent their dissatisfaction, the Council would merely have increased the explosive force arising from growing social deprivation caused by economic decline. The organization became ensnared in the legal machinery of Reich jurisdiction, which it had itself declared, and finally ran out of steam. However, it achieved complete success, at least symbolically, in the decisive question of the treatment of Protestants. The city's oligarchy shied away from confrontation for the sake of internal peace. It thus lost the chance to push forward the changes which had already taken place in the areas surrounding the city.

The view shared by many people in the political establishment that it was necessary to usher in fundamental changes, did not have the support of the majority. Furthermore, one should not confuse enlightened sentiments with a purposeful approach dictated by unequivocal economic interests. As long as commerce promised lucrative profits capital remained committed. The pressure exercised by relatively insignificant business circles was too weak and its political weight too insignificant to have a far-reaching effect.

This was confirmed during the French occupation when political power was no longer in either the hands of the city's oligarchy or those of the organized lower middle classes. The economic views of the French administration, expressed in the complete abolition of the craft guild system and the promotion of commercial enterprises, did little to change existing structures.

Even after the abolition of *Stapelrecht* and later, when a customs frontier was established along the Rhine, all the efforts of the economic élite were directed towards supporting trade. Although as a result of the establishment of the customs post many enterprises located on the eastern bank of the Rhine moved to Cologne, relocation was short-lived and ceased when the Napoleonic system collapsed. In the nineteenth century, Cologne only gradually regained the impetus it had had during the early phase of industrialization in the Rhineland.

Notes

1. For an account of the proto-industrialisation concept, see above all Mendels 1981; Kriedte, Medick and Schlumbohm 1977; an overview of the debate on this concept is provided in Clarkson 1985, and finally Mager 1988.
2. For an account of the structure and development of the Cologne economy in the late Middle Ages and Early Modern period, see above all the state of research of representative papers by Irsigler, Kellenbenz, Gramulla and Pohl amongst others in Kellenbenz (ed.) 1975.
3. For an account of the wool-processing trades, see in particular Arentz 1935 and Oberbach 1929; the employment figures for the fourteenth century are taken from Kuske 1948, 101; the figures for the eighteenth century are from Ebeling 1987, 36f.
4. For an account of the case of Aachen and the genesis of cloth production in Burtscheid and Monschau, see summary by Kisch 1981, 258–316.
5. Koch 1907 gives an account of the Cologne silk trade; details of the influence of Dutch immigrants in Witzel 1907; for an account of the founding of the Andreae manufacturing plant, see Thimme 1914; for an account of the Krefeld silk trade

from a comparative angle, see Kisch 1981, 66–161 and Kriedte 1983; Riedl 1952 provides a direct comparison between the silk trade in Krefeld and Cologne; an account of the role played by the putting-out capitalist Herstatt in Arentz 1935, 105.

6. For an account of the dominance of the trade even in the first decades of the nineteenth century, see Ayçoberry 1981 as well as Kellenbenz (ed.) 1975, vol. 2; for an overview of Cologne's political constitution in the eighteenth century, see Kellenbenz (ed.) 1975, vol. 2; 14–22.

Bibliography

Arentz, L. (1935), *Die Zersetzung des Zunftgedankens, Kölnischer Geschichtsverein*, Cologne.

Ayçoberry, P. (1981), *Cologne entre Napoléon et Bismarck, Aubier-Montaigne*, Paris.

Bayer, J. (ed.) (1912), *Köln um die Wende des 18. und 19. Jahrhunderts (1770–1830)*, Cologne, Bachem.

Becker-Jakli, B. (1983), *Die Protestanten in Köln*, Cologne, Rheinland-Verlag.

Clarkson, L.A. (1985), *Proto-Industrialization: The first phase of industrialization?*, London, Macmillan.

Ebeling, D. (1987), *Bürgertum and Poebel*, Cologne/Vienna, Böhlau.

Ebeling, D. (1988), 'Rohstofferschließung im europäischen Handelssystem der Frühen Neuzeit am Beispiel des rheinisch-niederländischen Holzhandels im 17./18. Jahrhundert', *Rheinische Vierteljahrsblätter* 52: 150–70.

Ebeling, D. (1985), 'Die wirtschaftlichen Führungsschichten Köln im Spektrum der rheinischen Frühindustrialisierung des 18. Jahrhunderts', in Heinz Schilling and Herman Diederiks (eds) *Bürgerliche Eliten in den Niederlanden und in Nordwestdeutschland*, Cologne/Vienna, Böhlau, 401–20.

Feldenkirchen, W.P. (1975), 'Der Handel der Stadt Köln im 18. Jahrhundert', PhD thesis, Bonn.

Gutmann, M.P. (1988), General Report to the section 'The Dynamics of urban decline in the late Middle Ages and Early Modern times: economic response and social effects' of the 9th International Economic History Congress Berne 1986, in *Debates and Controversies*, Zurich, Verlag der Fachvereine.

Gutmann, M.P. (1988), *Towards the Modern Economy. Early industry in Europe 1500–1800*, Philadelphia, Temple University Press.

Herborn, W. (1977), *Die politische Führungsschicht der Stadt Köln im Spätmittelalter*, Röhrscheid, Bonn.

Kellenbenz, H. (ed.) (1975), *Zwei Jahrtausende Kölner Wirtschaft*, 2 vols, Cologne, Greven.

Kisch, H. (1981), *Die hausindustriellen Textilgewerbe am Niederrhein vor der industriellen Revolution*, Göttingen, Vandenhoeck & Ruprecht.

Koch, H. (1907), *Geschichte des Seidengewerbes in Köln vom 13. bis zum 18. Jahrhundert*, Leipzig, Dunker & Humblot.

Kriedte, P. (1983), 'Protoindustrialisierung und grosses Kapital. Das Seidengewerbe in Krefeld und seinem Umland bis zum Ende des Ancien Regime', *Archiv für Sozialgeschichte*, 23: 219–66.

Kriedte, P., H. Medick, and J. Schlumbohm (1977), *Industrialisierung vor der Industrialisierung. Gewerbliche Warenproduktion auf dem Land in der Formationsperiode des Kapitalismus*, Göttingen, Vandenhoeck & Ruprecht.

Kuske, B. (1948), *Die Wirtschaft der Stadt Köln in älterer Zeit*, Cologne, Bachem.

Kuske, B. (1939), 'Der Kölner Stapel und seine Zusammenhänge als wirtschaftspolitisches Beispiel', *Jahrbuch des Kölnischen Geschichtsvereins*, 21: 1–46.

Mager, W. (1988), 'Protoindustrialisierung und Protoindustrie: vom Nutzen and Nachteil zweier Konzepte', *Geschichte und Gesellschaft*, 14: 275–303.

Mendels, F.F. (1981), *Industrialization and Population Pressure in Eighteenth Century Flanders*, New York, Arno Press.

Müller, K. (1982), 'Studien zum Übergang vom Ancien Regime zur Revolution im Rheinland. Bürgerkämpfe und Patriotenbewegung in Aachen und Köln', *Rheinische Vierteljahrsblätter*, 46: 102–60.

Nicolini, I. (1979), *Die politische Führungsschicht in der Stadt Köln gegen Ende der reichsstädtischen Zeit*, Cologne/Vienna, Böhlau.

Oberbach, E. (1929), 'Das Kölner Textilgewerbe von der Wende des Mittelalters bis zum 19. Jahrhundert', PhD, Cologne.

Riedl, Th. (1952), 'Die Ursachen für den Niedergang des Kölner Seidengewerbes und für den Aufstieg der Krefelder Seidengewerbe im 17. und 18. Jahrhundert', PhD thesis, Cologne.

Schwann, M. (1906), *Geschichte der Kölner Handelskammer*, Volume 1, Cologne, Neubler.

Schwering, L. (1907), 'Die Auswanderung protestantischer Kaufleute aus Köln nach Mülheim a.Rh. im Jahre 1714', *West-deutsche Zeitschrift für Geschichte und Kunst*, 26: 194–250.

Schwering, L. (1908), 'Die religiöse und wirtschaftliche Entwicklung des Protestantismus in Köln während des 17. Jahrhunderts', *Annalen des Historischen Vereins für den Niederrhein*, 85: 1–42.

Schwering, L. (1910), 'Zur äusseren Lage des Protestantismus in Köln während des 18. Jahrhunderts', *Annalen des Historischen Vereins für den Niederrhein*, 89: 1–29.

Thimme, H. (1914), *Geschichte der Firma Christoph Andreae in Mülheim a.Rh. 1714–1914*, Cologne.

de Vries, J. (1984), *European Urbanization 1500–1800*, London, Methuen.

Wankell, M. (1949), 'Beiträge zur Wirtschaftsgeschichte der freien Reichsstadt Köln im 18. Jahrhundert unter besonderer Berücksichtigung der Industrialisierung', PhD thesis Cologne.

Weingärtner, G. (1913), 'Zur Geschichte der Kölner Zunfunruhen am Ende des 18. Jahrhunderts', PhD thesis Münster.

Witzel, G. (1910), 'Gewerbegeschichtliche Studien zur niederländischen Einwanderung in Deutschland im 16. Jahrhundert', *Westdeutsche Zeitschrift für Geschichte und Kunst*, 29: 117–82, 419–51.

6 Capital policies of the Hohenzollerns in Berlin (1650–1800)

Helga Schulz

Capital policies are pursued by extremely centralized states or those striving to such an end. The absolutist monarchs in baroque Europe, moreover, commensurately appointed and extended their capitals. Indeed, they pressed ahead with construction, cultural institutions and economic life whilst consciously neglecting the other cities in the country in order, on the one hand, to consolidate state power through centralization while on the other hand, ensuring an impressive framework for the ostentatious public appearances of royalty. Paris, Vienna, Madrid, Berlin, Stockholm and Copenhagen were all decisively influenced and developed during the seventeenth and eighteenth centuries through such capital policies. Tsar Peter the Great even went as far as to have St Petersburg completely rebuilt on the mouth of the Newa. In fact, apart from Russia at that time, capital policies were no more energetically pursued in any other European state than in Brandenburg-Prussia where every possible effort was undertaken to boost the status of an insignificant region in the plains away from trade routes and cultural centres to become, or more precisely, to attain the level of (Mittenzwei 1987) the smallest European major power. Indeed, the overall development of Berlin became a distinct state policy concern of the visible hand.

The impressive ascent of Berlin from being just one of many rather indistinguishable German residencies to emerge finally as a European metropolis was, for a long time, considered solely the achievement of the Hohenzollerns. Above all, two regents have remained to the present time as city promoters: the Brandenburg Prince Elector Frederick William (1640–88) and his great-grandson, the Prussian King Frederick II (1740–86), both of whom during their lives and today once again called 'the Great' by some people, originally on account of their military successes, currently however because of their political shrewdness.

Looking objectively at Figure 6.1, essential misgivings arise through such a close interconnection between monarchic stature and urban heyday. Berlin experienced her greatest population explosion during the era of the pomp-loving first King Frederick I (1688–1713), equally the most profound geographical expansion of all, which continued under the 'Soldier King' Frederick William I (1713–1740). Trade blossomed above all towards the end of the reign of Frederick II and then until the 1790s under his insignificant successors. Such disproportions, moreover, corroborate that even such a conscious and deliberate capital policy as pursued by the Hohenzollerns does not attain its goal by direct means, simply subordinated to the cause–effect mechanism but solely within the framework of manifold regional and even European limitations.

The three principal pillars of Hohenzollern capital policies were trade promotion, the procurement of colonists and urbanization. However, as can easily be determined, these props were interconnected for the trade sector required labour and these workers in turn needed accommodation. Moreover, the three pillars were not always of identical height and consistency and, thus Berlin's social welfare edifice was occasionally undermined.

Trade policies represent the latest, specifically Prussian element of capital policies. Until the death of the first king in 1713 Berlin had been a capital like many others, only smaller and less significant. Commerce and trade both thrived through the luxury consumption of the court. Private traders also did extremely well. Merchants imported, above all, French and Dutch products — cocoa, tea, silk, perfumes, etc. — and waxed rich as court suppliers. The services, mainly haute cuisine and transport expanded more rapidly still than the crafts. A society of nobles emerged around the court with the wealthy and extravagant residents of other German states and foreign powers playing the tune. However, apart from the noble palaces and stunning festivities there developed ever greater poverty in the suburbs, particularly amongst newcomers, thwarted fortune-hunters, dropouts and vagabonds. All this has also been shown to hold true for the common socio-economic structural features of absolutist capitals (Hohenberg 1985, 137–71; Schieder 1983).

This state of affairs was fundamentally changed by the 'Soldier King' Frederick William I. His accession to the throne shocked the capital's citizens and, it is said, prompted thousands of Berliners to flee the city. The King reduced court outgoings to an absolute minimum, dismissing artists and leading officials and even 'flattening out' the Dutch pleasure-grounds which were subsequently used for drilling. He also installed a garrison of over 20,000 men in the city which, as the Saxon envoy sarcastically remarked, far more resembled a military camp than a residency (Kathe 1976).

In fact, this 'Soldier King' is also the initiator of a further decisive change in the capital. The army cost money and needed uniforms, so the ruler solved the problem through the compulsory promotion of a viable woollen sector in Berlin which also exported its products. The initiative for the capital's economy was taken by the visible hand. The richest Court and military suppliers of the deceased king were forced to set up a warehouse, which shortly afterwards became state-owned, for the woollen trade. Now Brandenburg wool could be sold only to Saxony on pain of death, and consequently, the Saxon textile sector faced serious raw material problems and many weavers were compelled to emigrate to Brandenburg-Prussia.

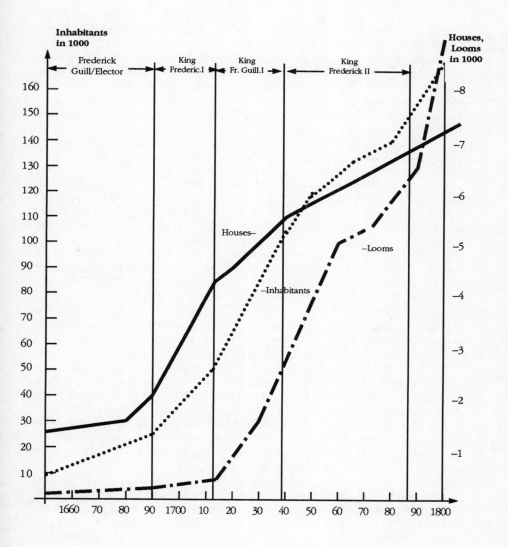

Figure 6.1 Growth of Berlin 1650–1800

Beggarwomen and hawkers secured the enactment of a royal edict on wool spinning and knitting. By means of idleness the King sought to kill two birds with one stone: poverty and luxury. He forbade the wearing of colourful cotton dresses and men were not allowed to wear foreign cloths. Thereby, by administrative means, a civilian market was created for Berlin woollens alongside their military outlets. Berlin's guesthouses were desolate as the reign of Frederick William I drew to a close. The sedan chair bearers had disappeared from the city along with their clients but more than 3,000 looms were thundering. Moreover, the newly emerged textile entrepreneurs and merchants were doing at least as good business through their military supplies as their predecessors had conducted with the Court during the period of the first king (Hinrichs 1933).

Frederick II pursued similar policies but with marked modifications. Resorting to Lyons' institutions and weavers he established a silk sector in Berlin, employing in due course thousands of hands. Even then, however, it was not possible to meet fully the needs of the Brandenburg-Prussian rococo society for silk. Luxury was again permitted. and thus there emerged the Berlin porcelain manufactory, initially as a private foundation and subsequently state-owned. A wide range of crafts and manufactories were once again available for the better-off citizens. However the army, especially the Berlin garrison, remained the most important customer for manufactures. Military suppliers and regimental commanders alike dealt on a large scale with woollen, leather and metal goods manufacturers. Indeed, the intertwining of state, army and economic interests, which was characteristic for Prussia, exerted a particular influence in the capital. Indeed, this amalgamation affected, even deformed, the political attitude of the trading and guilds bourgeoisie (Mittenzwei 1979).

The manifold measures undertaken by the powerful king to boost crafts in the capital have often been praised, whilst financial assistance granted to manufacturers and entrepreneurs has been investigated in detail and fully documented. On the other hand, Berlin's economic viability suffered severe blows through the long wars, the European financial débâcle following the Seven Years War and as a consequence of the restrictive Customs and Excise tax imposed by the Prussian state. The impressive development of Berlin as one of the foremost German trade centres ensued not only through but frequently also in opposition to absolutist state policies.

One example is cotton processing. Initially suppressed as an undesirable competitor with the woollen sector, later accepted but never promoted, the cotton trade specifically precipitated an upsurge towards the end of the eighteenth century, paving the way for technical and technological innovations which heralded the industrial revolution in Prussia as well. Herbert Kisch once strikingly contrasted the ineffectiveness of the state pampered and administered Berlin trade sector with the free capitalist spirit of the Rhenish entrepreneurs, whereby he surely perceived the Berlin conditions in a distorted and exaggerated manner. However, his conclusions contain more than merely a grain of truth (Kisch 1981, 152–61). Yet the trade policies of the Hohenzollerns, concentrating as they did on manufactories and finance in the capital, caused Berlin to develop in a way which soon proved advantageous compared with other capitals and residencies. Indeed, the Prussian metropolis with its distinct economic structure had always constituted a far more expedient point of departure for the industrial revolution than Vienna or Paris, let alone even smaller German residencies such as Dresden and Munich.

The population influx endured for an entire century from the last ruling years of Elector Frederick William to the death of Frederick II and was constantly a principal concern of state policies. Depopulation of the central and eastern regions made it necessary to take seriously the cameralistic principle that people constitute the greatest wealth of the state. This attitude changed only towards the end of the eighteenth century. Partly under the influence of the ideas of Malthus, more so through the French Revolution, King Frederick William III (1797–1840) perceived the need to restrict the population growth in the capital. Moreover, meanwhile fear of disturbances in Prussia had become greater than concern for taxpayers, soldiers and workers.

Initially the capital had not been a focal point of immigration policies, probably because it had been spared the ravages of direct military action in the seventeenth century. As he enacted his famous Potsdam edict in 1685, offering the persecuted Huguenots refuge in Brandenburg, the Elector was not thinking of Berlin. In fact, the edict cited Magdeburg, Halle and Frankfurt-on-Oder besides smaller towns such as Stendal, Werben and Rathenow. None the less, almost half the refugees coming to Brandenburg settled in the capital. Where else might they have hoped to be so fortunate and utilize their craft skills? The residency gained considerably in attractiveness after Berlin became the capital of the kingdom in 1701. The number of immigrants rose markedly, producing an annual growth rate of 4 per cent (Wilke 1987).

It was only under King Frederick William I that settlers, especially workers for the woollen sector, were directly encouraged to opt for Berlin. In a manner comparable to the infamous soldier recruiters, Prussian officials went to the Protestant trading regions of Saxony, Thuringia, Hessia and southern Germany to stimulate settlement in the capital of factory owners and workers. They were promised support and assistance in house-building and rent payments, equally in obtaining equipment and materials. Moreover, these commitments were generally met and honoured from public funds. In addition, the capital was exempted from compulsory publicity and military recruitment (canton system), a most advantageous privilege in Prussia (Hinze 1963). This settler policy became more selective under Frederick II for the King preferred only skilled specialists or wealthy immigrants.

Most newcomers at that time came spontaneously without royal backing to the capital on the Spree, attracted by its ever brighter radiancy, the lessons of past events and hopeful for their own good fortune. Similarly, as regards immigration, economic factors clearly exerted a more profound influence than state policies. Such economic influences included, first and foremost, the expanding market of both the capital and the residency. However, legend has it that in the settler arena everything meritorious is

attributable to the monarch, and legends are more compelling than historical dates and facts. In a certain respect these legends are also more befitting,
for in actual fact, royal settler policies interacting with trade strategies
constituted a catalyst for the rise of capital. This was, moreover, necessary
to attract a nucleus of experts and wealthy, enterprising entrepreneurs to
Berlin to bridge the gap between the Brandenburg residency and the west
and central European trading centres.

Hohenzollern capital policies were also able to minimize the social contrasts in Berlin compared with other European capitals (Figure 6.2). It
seems that the number of available workplaces in the trading sector
increased more or less in line with the population growth. The number of
poor people rose only as a result of unemployment in crisis periods.
Moreover, as in Dresden, Vienna, Paris and St Petersburg, the households
of the nobility were extremely modest in size and standards. Nor did they
attract beggars. The city's economy hinged on extensive guild trading,
equally on small and medium-sized manufacturing outlets unconditionally
loyal to the monarchy, perceiving their fate to be intrinsically linked with
the development of the state.

Most state funds certainly did not accrue to colonization and trade but
were used to expand and beautify Berlin. The new towns of
Friedrichswerder and Dorotheenstadt had been founded under Elector
Frederick William, however construction operations were restricted to the
castle precincts and a limited area nearby and in the new towns for government officials and court craftsmen. The new towns, including Friedrich-
stadt, were established in line with the population expansion under the first
king. His successor promoted this activity using both public funds and
draconian measures (even blackmailing rich Civil Servants and others disin-
terested in building projects). By 1740 Berlin already had the basic structure
it was to retain for the rest of the century. Generally speaking, modest
houses were built, regularly spaced like tin soldiers alongside wide roads,
envisaged for the anticipated influx of colonists with soldiers' rooms on the
upper floor for the powerful garrison. The churches were not costly whilst
the portals featured no pretentious triumphal arches. The squares remained
empty and virtually predestined for military parades. The provident King
undertook building operations with an eye on the future, and for many
years the Berliners bemoaned that the new houses were attracting thieves
but not tenants. Around 1740 an equilibrium had been reached between
available housing and demand.

Frederick II, the King's successor, clearly entertained quite different
town-planning ambitions. Residing permanently in Potsdam, it was he
who bestowed upon the spartan trading and garrison town residential urban
splendour and a metropolitan exterior. The Friedrichsforum with the opera,
library and Catholic cathedral are all his work along with the boulevard
Unter den Linden. Adjacent to centrally positioned squares and thorough-
fares the king, out of his own pocket, had modest residential blocks raised
by one or more storeys and adorned with Italian-style facades (Gut 1986;
Goralczyk 1986).

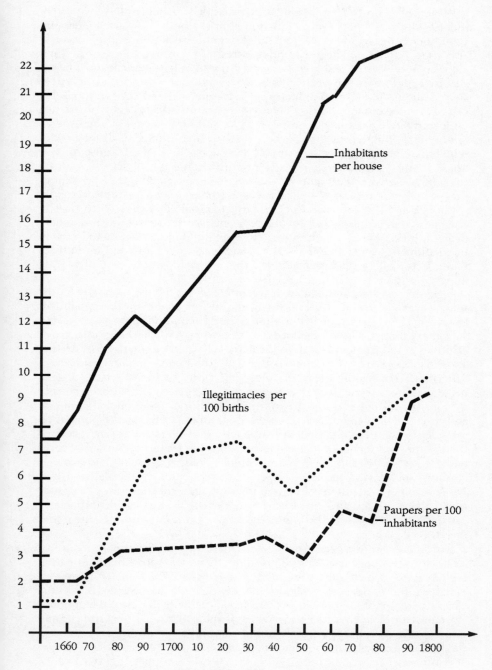

Figure 6.2 Signs of modernization in Berlin 1650–1800

Meanwhile, however, housing construction was completely neglected. Indeed, although the city's population almost doubled between 1740 and 1800, increasing from 90,000 to 172,000, there was no longer any systematic civic building. The unrelenting stream of immigrants had at their disposal only a small building workers' settlement in the north and a rather shabby conglomeration of dwellings in the suburbs. Accommodation density (as shown in Figure 6.2) increased between 1734 and 1800 from twelve to twenty persons per house. This was still substantially less than Vienna with thirty-five persons per house in 1790, although Viennese houses were undoubtedly bigger. As a result there was a veritable housing shortage with whole families living and working in one room. Weavers, because of their noisy looms, encountered the greatest difficulties of all in the housing market. Moreover, with rents accounting for between 20 and 25 per cent of the annual earnings of a skilled worker, this outlay was most certainly greater than anywhere else in Germany. A royal edict in 1765 to protect tenants, which superseded the basic principle 'purchase thwarts rents', brought little respite. The transformation in building policies is reflected in population and trading policies. The state withdrew more and more from these sectors of capital policies, leaving the field wide open to private initiative and entrepreneurial speculation (Skoda 1975).

Ever greater state influence is perceptible in the police hierarchy in the widest sense of the word. Following the fusion of the Berlin constituent towns in 1709, the municipal authority had become nothing more than a subsidiary body of the absolutist state. Moreover, the king intervened arbitrarily, and frequently also to the detriment of urban matters, in staffing and finances. Under Frederick II the Chief of Police became the leading official directly responsible to the King. In fact, his sphere of activity shifted more and more to the latter field although, originally, he had been equally responsible for supervising the municipal authority, trade policy and law and order in the capital (Schrader 1963; Straubel 1984). As the population grew along with the numbers of manufactory workers and journeymen, so too did the sources of conflict in Berlin. Since the 1770s a secret police force had been established in the city along French lines. A dense network of area commissions existed meanwhile to control stringently all citizens' activities. Draconian punishment was imposed to ensure general compulsory registration. When strikes and disturbances occurred (as happened particularly often in the 1790s under the influence of the French Revolution), the police director called in the army.

Social policies were meanwhile intermeshed with security operations. Thus, the price of cereals figured prominently in the reports on the situation in the capital, which were submitted to the king by the Chief of Police.

Indeed, the avoidance of starvation in the capital soon became an essential element in upholding public order. In 1719 the King had the military storehouses opened in order to provide the hungry population with cheaper grain—a measure much admired abroad and repeated during crises, but in the final analysis proving inadequate to ward off the general price increases and mitigate needs in the big city (Naudé, 1901). A copper engraving of the coronation of Frederick II in 1740 shows homage being paid to the background of public bread distribution during this cold year with its bad harvest.

Supply policies for the capital were effected by setting up state-run poorhouses. Moreover, during the expansion of the city in the first half of the eighteenth century, the Great Frederick Hospital was established as an orphanage and poorhouse, the Charité as civic hospital and maternity ward for unmarried mothers and the invalids' house. All these facilities helped, by comparison, to keep the illegitimacy rate in Berlin low (Figure 6.2) and virtually ruled out infanticide. A foundling hospital, which the 'Soldier King' Frederick William I had ordered to be constructed for population policy considerations shortly before his death, was not built. His successor utilized the means for a big poorhouse, significantly the sole public building set up in Berlin during the Seven Years War. This social aspect of capital policies was embodied poignantly by the principle of 'the carrot or the stick' which Bismarck was later to formulate as guideline for handling the workers' movement. On the one hand Berlin's pauper institutions assumed responsibility for public assistance which could no longer be handled properly by the dismembered communal family and guild associations in the increasingly anonymous capital functioning in accordance with capitalist economic basic principles. On the other hand, such institutions, especially, the poorhouse, served to discourage begging and other antisocial and illegal activities (Sachße 1980; Krüger 1958) The public assistance functions of these institutions diminished, relatively speaking, during the eighteenth century with their restricted capacity revealing to a growing extent a disproportion between numbers of inhabitants and needy persons.

By and large, however, Hohenzollern capital policies throughout the eighteenth century ensured a relatively steady development of Berlin, which, in turn, curbed social conflicts and prevented the emergence of a political opposition.

Bibliography

Goralczyk, Peter (1986), 'Wunschvorstellung und Realität in der städtebaulichen Entwicklung Berlins im 18. Jahrhundert' in Karl-Heinz Klingenburg (ed.) *Studien zur Berliner Kunstgeschichte*, Leipzig.

Gut, Albert (1986), *Das Berliner Wohnhaus des 17. und 18. Jahrhunderts*, Berlin.

Hinrichs, Carl (1933), *Die Wollindustrie in Preußen unter Friedrich Wilhelm I*, Acta Borussica. Denkmäler der Preußischen Akademie der Wissenschaften, Berlin.

Hinze, Kurt (1963), *Die Arbeiterfrage zu Beginn des modernen Kapitalismus in Brandenburg-Preußen 1685–1806*, 2nd edn, Berlin.

Hohenberg, Paul M. and Lynn Hollen Lees (1985), *The Making of Urban Europe 1000–1950*, Harvard University Press.

Kathe, Heinz (1976), *Der 'Soldatenkönig' Friedrich Wilhelm I. Eine Biographie*, Berlin.

Kisch, Herbert (1981), *Die hausindustriellen Textilgewerbe am Niederrhein vor der industriellen Revolution. Von der ursprünglichen Kapitalistischen Akkumulation*, Göttingen.

Krüger, Horst (1958), *Zur Geschichte der Manufakturen und der Manufakturarbeiter in Preußen. Die mittleren Provinzen in der zweiten Hälfte des 18. Jahrhunderts*, Berlin.

Mittenzwei, Ingrid (1979), *Preußen nach dem Siebenjährigen Krieg*.

Auseinandersetzungen zwischen Bürgertum und Staat um die Wirtschaftspolitik, Berlin.

Mittenzwei, Ingrid and Erika Herzfeld (1987), *Brandenburg-Preußen 1648–1789. Das Zeitalter des Absolutismus in Text und Bild*, Berlin.

Naudé, Walter (1901), *Die Getreidehandelspolitik und Kriegsmagazinverwaltung Brandenburg-Preußens bis 1740*. Berlin.

Sachße, Christoph and Florian Tennstedt (1980), *Geschichte der Armenfürsorge in Deutschland vom Spätmittelalter bis zum Ersten Weltkrieg*, Stuttgart.

Schieder, Theodor and Gerhard Brunn (eds.) (1983), *Hauptstädte in europäischen Nationalstaaten*, Vienna.

Schrader, Kurt (1963), 'Die Verwaltung Berlins von der Residenzstadt des Kurfürsten Friedrich Wilhelm bis zur Reichshauptstadt', unpubl. diss., Humboldt University Berlin.

Skoda, Rudolf (1975), 'Wohnhäuser und Wohnverhältnisse der Stadtarmut (*ca.* 1750–1850). Erläutert anhand von Beispielen aus Quedlinburg; Halle, Hamburg und Berlin', in *Jahrbuch für Volkskunde und Kulturgeschichte*, 17.

Straubel, Rolf (1984), Der Berliner Polizeidirektor und das Textil gewerbe der brandenburgisch-preußschen Residenz. Ein Beitrag zum Verhältnis von Lokalbehörde und wirtschaftsentwicklung (1740–1789), unpubl. diss., Akademie der Wissenschaften der DDR.

Wilke, Jürgen (1987), 'Die französische Kolonie in Berlin', in Helga Schultz, *Berlin 1650–1800. sozialgeschichte einer Residenz. Mit einem Beitrag von Jürgen Wilke*, Berlin.

7 Municipal oligarchies and bourgeois merchants as separate social groups: comparisons on either side of the Franco–Belgian border in the eighteenth century

Philippe Guignet

The Leiden colloquium sought to stimulate discussion and debate on the respective roles of urban economic élites, municipal authorities and the state in the development of cities. The scientific organizers concentrated on the interactions among these three major loci of decision-making. It is scarcely feasible to delve into the problem as a whole in a short chapter particularly in view of the rich urban heritage of the region with which I am concerned: northern France and southern Belgium.[1] Rather than risk a superficial analysis for want of space, I shall simply try to remove certain stereotypes which cling to the conventional view, focusing on the social composition of the boards of aldermen (*échevinages*) in six major towns on either side of the Franco–Belgian border: Lille, Valenciennes and Douai on the French side; Tournai, Ath and Mons on the Belgo-Austrian side.

If a single myth pervades the historiography of the region, it is surely the view, however qualified, that municipal governments were extensions of the leading merchants and more generally of the business bourgeoisie. One example is from a major if older, historian of the French Low Countries: M. Braure argues that the merchants of Lille, a commercial aristocracy, controlled the Council as they did the Chamber of Commerce, and thus ruled the city.[2] Other historians may put it more cautiously but do not disagree. P. Goubert, speaking of the expansionist matrimonial strategies of business families, even doubts the value of studying social composition, even though it is abundantly clear that many aldermen had nothing to do with either trade or manufactures.[3] Some historians, such as J. Sentou who works on the Revolution, go farther and argue that 'one cannot conflate a class with its representatives, who may not belong to it', thus calling into question this entire approach to policy analysis.[4] There is some truth in the argument, in that those who hold power may not in the long run serve the interests of their group of origin. However, it is paradoxical to deny that the daily occupation and the source of income of those who wield authority condition both their perception of and their vision for the city they govern.

Without ignoring the arguments often raised against social analysis of holders of political power, I remain unconvinced, the more so as patient genealogical reconstitution yields quite a different picture from the one suggested by Goubert. Moreover, the value of knowing where the leaders came from is all the greater in that these cities maintained their autonomy *vis-à-vis* the central state much more successfully than was the case elsewhere in France. Absolutism did nibble at the fiscal and military authority of the 'great magistrates' but failed to capture all of it. In the Austrian Low Countries the urban governing bodies did much better still in preserving the ancient liberties and privileges. With their power, prestige and moral authority, the aldermanic patriciate remained at the heart of the urban system of power.

For each city under study we shall note the social composition of families newly represented on municipal councils between 1750 and 1789, considering occupation as well as status (noble or commoner), both of which varied between towns.

On the French side of the border: a minority position for business families.

The thirty-seven families joining the Lille Council during the second half of the eighteenth century fall into three groups: merchants, noblemen (often garrisoned in the capital of Flanders), and men of law. Merchants represented almost 40 per cent of the newcomers; generally natives of Lille, by the time they joined the Council at an average age of 42 they had gained substantial business experience. While they typically married into other merchant families, they formed part of the élite, each being a sometime member of the Consular Chamber or the son of a Consular judge.[5] Thus accession to the Council was the last step in a long-term progress involving an entire extended trading family.

A quarter of the newcomers were fully-fledged aristocrats in military service at Lille. Some of these squires were foreign born, for instance the Jacobite O'doyer. They became magistrates shortly after marrying into the local nobility.

Men of law and holders of judicial offices were fewest in number. Usually native Lillois, they made the grade earlier than others (33 years old, on average), and to do so needed to overcome a legal barrier, specific to Lille, which barred lawyers from serving in the municipal government, which explains why they were relatively few.

The tripartite analysis of new magistrates may fail to bring out fully the role of the nobility. First, only 45 per cent of the families represented on the Council during the second half of the century are mentioned in the list of newcomers; second, the holder of a law diploma could be a nobleman. Occupations and social status were not fully congruent.

If one compares the proportion of nobles among new aldermen in two periods, 1700–19 and 1770–89, one is struck by how greatly that role increased: the number of men bearing the title of squire or knight increased from 41 per cent to 64 per cent of the total.[6] In the last class, that of 1785, nobles took fully eleven of thirteen posts. To be sure, these were not aristocrats of long standing: Louis Jean-Baptiste Huvino de Bourghelles's family had been noble since 1697, that of Charles François Joseph Libert de Beaumont since 1700, while Ignace Albert Joseph Cardon de Broncquart was a nobleman since 1721 and Jacques François Denis du Péage only since 1769.[7] Yet all were true noblemen, psychologically detached from the bourgeoisie for decades. In other words, while nobles remained a numerical minority among new magistrates, it is clear that as the most established bourgeois families acquired noble status, urban government was becoming steadily more noble. Note also that we are dealing with Lille, where merchants and men of business enjoyed positive status. How about elsewhere?

Matters were quite different in Valenciennes, where fully one-third of the new aldermen were nobles in the classes between 1702 and 1718, and just under 30 per cent between 1772 and 1789. While the decline is small, it confirms the point that the nobility was and remained a distinct minority. The social make-up of the newly chosen families is quite clear: of the twenty-six families involved from 1750 to 1789 twelve were graduates in law and were in practice, many as lawyers or notaries, five were local merchants, and as many were noblemen, often retired officers (no information is available about two families).

In contrast to Lille, men of law dominated recruitment of magistrates in Valenciennes, while men of business occupied a secondary place. To be sure, Paul-Joseph Nicodème, a leading merchant and writer on trade served for eleven years as a magistrate between 1764 and 1779 before being elected to the Constituante, but this eminent man, who read the Philosophes and corresponded with Fontenelle, is the exception.[8] Not until November 1789 did merchants flock to the ranks of new magistrates.[9] There is no evidence that the screening of candidates by the governor or the intendant discouraged merchants.[10] What then, can account for their relative absence? Documents cannot tell us whether merchants were put off by the pressure of business, by a perception that the Council was hostile to them, or by a sense that government was properly the business of men of law.

Given the composition of Douai's population, it is not surprising that representatives of commerce had such a small share in its government: only two out of thirty-nine families admitted to the magistrature in the last four decades of the *ancien régime*.[11] By contrast, 28 per cent of the newcomers were at least squires, i.e., aristocracy though this substantial share cannot hide the major role taken by men of law. Of the thirty-nine families, nineteen (49 per cent) were represented by a lawyer, sixteen commoners and three aristocrats.[12] The remainder of the aldermen were professionals, really urban administrators close to the legal milieu. It is here rather than in the *Parlement* itself that the electors found suitable new recruits from time to time.

These findings are all the more noteworthy in that if one goes back to the late sixteenth century, the Municipal Council of Douai was firmly in the hands of the bourgeoisie—*rentiers* and merchants—with few aristocrats.[13] Early in the seventeenth century, and pushed along by the establishment there of a *Parlement*, the decline of merchant participation in the Council began. From 1716 electors were exclusively chosen from non–business groups: magistrature, university, government and religious chapters. There was a clear attempt to deprive commoners of modest means of the vote, since they could be unreliable. In a 1708 memoir to the intendant they were accused of plotting to elect a young tanner, son of a blacksmith, in prefer- ence to a long-established gentleman, and of preferring a nobody to a canon of the church. The 1716 measures did what they were supposed to do; the new electors from the university, the judiciary and the church felt no cultural or social affinity with the 'active' bourgeoisie and were not inclined to elect grain merchants and other businessmen.[14]

In summary, in none of the French cities did men of commerce take the major share of seats on councils, not even in Lille where they fared best. Most magistrates were chosen from among men of law and aristocrats. How did matters stand on the other side of the border?

Tournai, Ath and Mons: clear supremacy of legal and noble families

Tournai offers no scope for analysis of recruits to the magistrature, since there were only eleven newcomers between 1750 and 1789. Moreover, the sample is disturbed by a special event: when the *bailliage* of Tournai- Tournaisis was abolished, several councillors immediately joined the newly created Provincial Council of Tournai, while three men who lost positions there were compensated with posts in the city's magistrature. To make up for these facts, it is best to look in detail at the lists of potential candidates on the five occasions between 1752 and 1789 when the City Council was renewed.

Information on the lists coupled with other data make it possible to classify virtually all the families involved.[15] Merchants and manufacturers comprised 11.4 per cent; together with commoners holding law degrees (18.6 per cent) they remained firmly in the minority compared with the profession of squires and knights (62.9 per cent of seats). This latter share stabilized throughout the period, with a minimum of seven aristocrats in 1789 compared with nine (out of fourteen) in 1752, ten in 1759, and again nine in 1764 and 1774.

Tournai's Council was in the main a body of aristocrats and never more so than in the second half of the eighteenth century. In seeking a point of comparison a century earlier, one is faced with the absence of lists of recommendations, but for the 1680s one can at least determine who could claim the title of squire or knight. For all nine renewals in the decade, five to eight out of fourteen members were aristocrats gaining fifty-two out of the 126 (41.3 per cent) places filled. Already a dominant position but not yet one of hegemony. With reduced turnover in the eighteenth century competition was heightened, and so was the share taken by the nobility. Not only did they tend to hold the high offices (provost and mayor), but they did so at the expense of men of law as well as men of business. To be sure, many squires took care to acquire a legal education and a diploma. Despite the lack of much documentary evidence, it is clear that men of business were frustrated in their desire to gain status by holding municipal office. Denis-Joseph Vandale, in a petition to the minister plenipotentiary, Count Koenigsegg-Erps, noted that 'There are no longer any merchants in the Tournai magistrature. There always were in the past and the good of business requires that there be at least two.' This confirms the trend toward exclusion of all save the aristocracy from the Tournai Council.

Compared with Tournai, Ath was a small, though not inglorious town. We lack recommendation lists, and there are other deficiencies in the data, as so often is the case on the Belgian side of the border. The archival records of the Council of State and the Austrian Privy Council yield official lists for elections in 1721, 1724, 1751, 1752 and 1771. Together with detailed genealogical analyses, including research in parish registers, the data make it possible to classify all but 8.6 per cent of the families involved. Holders of law degrees accounted for 37.1 per cent of newcomers on the five lists, merchants 22.9 per cent, and holders of medical degrees 14.3 per cent. By contrast, those who could claim the title of squire held fewer than one seat in ten (8.6 per cent), although they might count as natural allies an equal number of men who administered the estates of the aristocracy.

Of course, this small sample can yield only orders of magnitude. Yet commoners clearly gained a majority of new seats, and even men of business were not so peripheral as elsewhere. Throughout the century the names of major linen trading families appear on the lists—Depestre, Taintenier, Delwarde and Ducorron—showing that in Ath a merchant family could expect to crown its success by having a member rising to aldermanic office. None the less, the mechanism for recruiting office holders depended vitally on men of law, even though here, as elsewhere in small cities, physicians also played a part. Note that many of these lawyers came from families enriched by the linen trade. Take the case of the Taintenier: in the first half of the eighteenth century they were a solid family of bourgeois merchants, and they remained active in business, as shown by a petition to the Estates of Hainaut by the Taintenier brothers in 1768 concerning their linen printing factory. Yet Philippe-Joseph, Bachelor of Law, practised before the sovereign Council of Hainaut, while the economist François-Joseph seems to have had more on his mind than the putting-out and finishing of linens.

As regards the aristocracy, it seems that belonging to the council of so small a city as Ath simply did not confer the sort of prestige and social recognition that a similar post would yield in Tournai or Mons. This point should not be overstated, to be sure; the Council at Ath included members from wealthy and titled families, and rather more as the century wore on.

Nicolas Joseph Pollart de Warnifosse held an important position from 1776 to 1785 and became burgmaster in 1782; Robert Charles Marie Charlez de Vrequem held a seat from 1786 to 1789. While one cannot conclude with certainty that the attitude of the aristocracy grew more positive in this regard, it may be noted that the position of burgmaster was held by aristocracy from 1776 onward, a change from the past.

Let us look briefly at the seven families who joined the ranks between 1775 and 1789. The parish registers of Saint-Julien and Saint-Martin in Ath tell us little about Joseph de Courtray's social position, or about André-Joseph Ghislain (save that he appears to be related to the Taintenier family through his mother), or about Jean-Baptiste Limbourg. However, we do learn that when Jean-Baptiste Limbourg's daughter Marie-Catherine married Charles Lebrun in April 1778, the witnesses were none other than Toussaint Delecluse and his brother Nicholas François Joseph, Lord of Relaix. This detail makes it possible to place Limbourg in the sphere of influence of a family group that included the Delecluses. Three other lineages of which we can learn something had been fairly recently ennobled. Joseph-Ernest Hoffay Esquire was from Brussels. When he married in 1784, Nicholas François Joseph Delecluse, then a lawyer licensed before the Hainaut Council, served as witness. Shortly after moving to the city, Baron Spandl, from an old Bohemian family titled since 1576, married in 1774 and rose to the Council in 1776. As for Nicholas Joseph Pollart de Warnifosse, his elevation hardly shook the foundations of the municipal oligarchy. His older brother was lord (*châtelain*) of the manor for Ath and the family had been granted letters of nobility on 7 September 1695 for services rendered during the French blockade of Mons.

Thus only one truly new man rose to the Council from 1775 to 1789: Jean-Baptiste Jaubert. This Frenchman from Barcelonnette (diocese of Embrun in the Upper Alps) was an apprentice in a Lyons trading house when he was sent to the Austrian Low Countries to buy 'various products of those regions'.[16] Attracted by the civilized and busy life he found there, he decided to settle in the 'Belgian provinces', and in October 1775 married the daughter of a Tournai merchant. Domiciled in Ath as a trader in linens and Lyons silks, he became a citizen and soon acquired a strong reputation in the town. No wonder we find this 'self-made man', bright and quick to seize opportunities, participating in a comprehensive welfare scheme devised by François-Joseph Taintenier. Yet if the *Journal des troubles des Pays-Bas* is to be believed, he did not neglect his own affairs while working in public business, using loans from the house of Depestre to good effect. Clearly, this outsider with his energy, subtlety and willingness to take risks was an exceptional figure in a city whose élites tended to resist innovation.

The members of the Mons magistrature enjoyed far greater prestige than their colleagues in Ath. Was their social background different? Unfortunately the nomination lists are of little help; in the latter part of the century they do not even give the nominee's Christian name, let alone other data. From time to time it is specified that so-and-so exercises the honourable profession of lawyer, but one must look elsewhere for the information needed to specify the social background. I have used genealogical research as well as the numerous letters of recommendation that flowed into the offices of the Dukes of Arenberg. For the groups chosen in 1783, 1788 and 1789 I was able to use the excellent set of nominative files compiled by Marie Arnould for her Master's thesis.[17]

A total of forty new families were involved from 1750 to 1789 in the staffing of the Mons Council. It may seem strange that not one of the new men had even the slightest business connection. Yet our biographical research only corroborates Fonson's *Petit tableau de la ville de Mons* in which he states quite plainly: 'In the Magistrature, shopkeepers and merchants are not admitted.' He cites a merchant who confess that he reluctantly sacrificed everything to make sure his eldest son was admitted to the bar.[18] The true originality of Mons in terms of recruiting aldermen emerges if one notes that only three of the newcomers were not lawyers. In this capital of Belgian Hainaut, lawyers before the Sovereign Council of the province and law graduates held an unequalled share of Council seats. That was considered appropriate. As Antoine-François de Behault de Warelles wrote to the Duke of Arenberg: 'The public wants to be sure that the Magistrature is entrusted insofar as possible to men qualified for judicial functions.' Moreover, matters were no different in the province as a whole. The increase in the role of lawyers in the Sovereign Council was a clear trend in the second half of the eighteenth century. The *Calendrier du˙Hainaut*, in its annual list of practising lawyers, shows the striking increase in their numbers: about 130 in 1765–70; 200 in 1781; and no fewer than 340 in 1788!

Marie Arnould's study of the renewals of 1783, 1788 and 1789 confirms our findings, with fully 92 per cent of those involved being men of law. Only slightly less clearcut is the dominance of the aristocracy, since they comprised 56 per cent of the Council and Magistrature in those three years. While the data lack a full count in the first two decades of the century, scattered information suggests that the aristocracy held fewer than a quarter of the seats, thus showing their increasing strength.[19]

The Revolution and municipal authorities: the commercial bourgeoisie's hour strikes

The transformations brought about by the Revolution clearly proceeded differently on each side of the border. On the Belgian side municipal power was affected only by the 'missionaries in boots' who came from France, once after the battle of Jemappes and again—to stay—after the Battle of Fleurus.

France: the great shift of 1790

January and February of 1790 saw the first municipal elections of the new era. Already shaken by the municipal revolution of 1789, the old political class was quickly swept aside.

IN LILLE, IMMEDIATE EVICTION BY THE BUSINESS BOURGEOISIE

On 26 January the 5,461 active citizens of Lille were called on to elect the first mayor chosen under the 'regime of liberty'. Louis Vanhoenacker, the quintessential Lillois bourgeois merchant, gained 56 per cent of the votes, despite lacking political sparkle worthy of his integrity.[20] On 10 and 19 February came the election of the 17 officers and 38 notables in which Lille was entitled under the municipal law. The list of winners shows the strong push of members of the Chamber of Commerce and the equally striking absence of former officials. Only Squire Arnould Vandercruisse de Waziers, alderman from 1782 to 1785, made it to the Council. It may be added that he resigned as early as November and then emigrated. Clearly, Lille represents an extreme case of abrupt discontinuity between the old and new.

GRADUAL RETREAT IN VALENCIENNES AND DOUAI

In the case of Valenciennes it is possible to look at both the social condition and the family connections of the new men elected in February 1790. The new team comprised prosperous merchants (five out of eleven officers) as well as rather more modestly situated men of law. Yet it may be noted that the new mayor, Pierre Le Hardy de la Loge, belonged to a lineage often represented in the *ancien régime* magistrature, while his only serious competition came from Pujol de Mortry, the former provost. Yet one should not overestimate the survival of former officials. Only those who, like Le Hardy, had clearly indicated their conversion to the new order were able to escape the débâcle. Even the half-dozen survivors had gained only a temporary respite. Le Hardy resigned on 7 November, quickly followed by two others, while a fourth lost out in a draw by lots. The discontinuity in Valenciennes came in November 1790.

The families traditionally supplying aldermen held out best in Douai. Three of the ten municipal officers elected in January were from the old Council, as were the solicitor and *syndic*. When one returnee, Briffault, was chosen by lot to step down in November, he stood again and was elected in the first round. The former political class of Douai did well because the business bourgeoisie put up such weak resistance; it took popular action to shake the old structure. On 16 and 17 March a riot, henceforth known as the *émeute des goulottes*, caused the National Assembly to dissolve the municipal government.[21] Of the eight commissioners then named by the Nord's departmental administrators, two were merchants and one was a goldsmith.

To summarize, the business class took on the task of burying the old political groups. Although the expression 'bourgeois revolution' may be overused, it can properly be applied at least to the cases of Lille and Valenciennes. In Douai, to be sure, it took a systematic ouster of the old aldermanic families to give merchants a larger political role.

Belgium: French conquest and the political rise of the business class

The Belgian provinces experienced an 'estates revolution' (November 1789–December 1790)—called the Brabantine but improperly so, since it went beyond that province—whose traditionalism and attachment to Trentine Catholicism was incompatible with liberal values. As one would expect, therefore, the municipal governments which emerged involved no social renewal.[22] Despite a considerable turnover of personnel, aristocrats and lawyers continued in power stronger than ever.[23] The disaster—from the point of view of political oligarchies of the *ancient régime*—awaited the first French occupation (November 1792–March 1793).

MONS: FIRST BELGIAN CITY TO HAVE NEW MUNICIPAL AUTHORITIES
The French national assembly voted almost unanimously on 20 April 1792 to declare war on the 'King of Bohemia and Hungary'. France was embarking on a crusade to liberate the peoples of Europe. On 26 October Dumouriez sent a manifesto to the 'brave Belgian nation' from Valenciennes. Crossing the border he quickly routed the Austrian forces at Jemappes (6 November). He entered Mons amid great popular rejoicing and signed a second proclamation on 8 November declaring that new institutions must be created by universally elected representatives of the people.[24] Immediately, the members of the Committee of United Belgians and Liégeois organized, in the presence of Danton, the election by voice vote of the twenty-eight interim representatives of the Montois. Save for the former mayor, Bonaventure de Bousies—who resigned as early as December—not a single family from the past found favour with the Jacobins. While lawyers remained in the majority, a few artisans and shopkeepers made their appearance along with three merchants. However, the defeat of Dumouriez at Neerwinden on 18 March 1793 opened the way for an Austrian restoration. Entering Mons once again on 1 July 1794 the French challenged the prevailing institutions. Four elections within a year led to a change in their social make-up. While lawyers retained 40 per cent of seats, more tradesmen and artisans sat alongside them. No longer would lawyers and other men of law, along with *rentiers*, rule unchallenged.

TOURNAI UNDER THE FRENCH: THE INSTANT RISE OF GENUINE
'SELF-MADE MEN'
The first French occupation of Tournai followed the procedure worked out at Mons. Two delegates of the Committee of United Belgians and Liégeois, alongside two members of the Mons municipality, called the sovereign people together to the sound of drums and marched them to the cathedral to 'decide the course of their government'. On 12 November the election took place by acclamation, and the Society of Friends of Liberty and Equality, organized only the day before, managed to have nine of its members chosen among the twenty interim officials.[25]

These elections proved disastrous for the *ancien régime* oligarchy, involving a clearcut social break with the past. Note that ten of the twenty men elected were merchants, a number of them 'self-made men' who had practised divers trades and so accumulated enough to set themselves up in commerce or manufacturing. One example was the former chimney sweep from Savoy, Philibert Paris, who had given up selling needles and notions for the more lucrative line of linen and cotton goods. Having accumulated one of the city's largest fortunes, he was entrusted with a series of posts in the course of the successive French occupations. Another was a former footman of Bishop Laurent Jacqueleu, who sold fats and oils on the main square and bought *biens nationaux* on a large scale. Finally there was Pierre Hayoit, a one-time constable who retired to Tournai and in 1789 bought a soap works and a salt refinery. He was given the honour of being a member of the Belgian delegation that was received by the Convention on 4 December 1792. No further examples are needed to show how successfully the business bourgeoisie made the leap from spectator to dominant force in municipal politics, in Tournai as elsewhere.

From then on events followed the pattern set at Mons, the former notables returning with the second Austrian restoration. When the French returned, on 3 July 1794, Tournai's office-holders were not summarily dismissed; rather, reliable men were assigned to supervise them. On 17 January 1795 a new government was officially invested, half of them merchants. Finally, in April of the same year the old city on the Escaut received a municipal government on the French model, complete with a municipal corps and general council.[26]

By way of conclusion it is worth reflecting on the reasons why the commercial bourgeoisie had such little access to office under the *ancien régime*. Were merchants too taken up with the daily pressure of business to find time for public matters? Although this view cannot be dismissed out of hand, it raises the point that such pressure did not dissuade merchants from public service during the seventeenth century and even more so during the sixteenth century.

Another explanation is the perception that legal training was the proper and necessary preparation for exercising such powers. Indeed, municipal judicial functions were left undiminished by the rise of absolutism, so that businessmen might feel poorly qualified compared with those with a sound legal training. Yet this argument as well can be applied to the earlier era.

Finally, merchants may have felt unwelcome in urban political circles. I consider this the most plausible explanation. Urban policies were by no means primarily dedicated to the service of commercial capitalism. Businessmen who were working to develop rural textile manufacturing could not help clashing with city fathers striving with might and main to confine productive activity within the walls. Among social élites only men of law and aristocrats were of a mind to champion the non-capitalist goals of what I have called the Hispanic-Trentine model of the *bonne ville* or traditional town.

Notes

1. That is the subject of my recent doctoral thesis, on which this chapter draws heavily: *Le pouvoir dans la ville au XVIIIe siècle. Etude comparative de part et d'autre de la frontière 'gallo-belge'*, Lille, 1988. A presentation summary and report of the discussion appeared in *Revue du Nord*, no. 279, October–December 1988: 789–808. See the thesis for archival references omitted in the present text [translator's note].
2. Maurice Braure, *Lille et la Flandre wallonne au XVIIIe siècle*, Lille, 1932: 450.
3. Pierre Goubert, *Cent mille provinciaux au XVIIe siècle. Beauvais et le Beauvaisis de 1600 à 1750*, Paris, Flammarion, 1968: 369.
4. Jean Sentou, *Fortunes et groupes sociaux à Toulouse sous la Révolution*, Toulouse, 1969: 472ff.
5. I compared the list of new aldermen with the names in H. Convain's 'La chambre ou juridiction consulaire de Lille', Lille, thèse de Droit, 1924, 367–71.
6. Note that insisting on these titles avoids the danger of including commoners who own manors and refer to themselves as 'lord of . . .'.
7. I have drawn on the list of accession to nobility in H. Couvreur and M. Montagne, *La noblesse de la châtellenie de Lille à la fin de l'ancien régime*, Lille, 1970: 48–50.
8. Philippe Guignet, *Mines, manufactures et ouvriers du Valenciennois au XVIIIe siècle. Contribution à l'histoire du travail dans l'ancienne France*, Lille, 1976 (New York, 1977): 108–14.
9. Three out of four of the new families are large-scale merchants, the fourth is a lawyer before the *Parlement* but the son of a goldsmith.
10. Only two of the nineteen names on a 1760 'aptitude list' are businessmen.
11. One of the two is seated in second place during Council sessions.
12. One of the latter is Charles-Alexandre de Calonne (1734–1802), who swears the oath at the bar at the age of 20, is elected alderman at 23 and six months later becomes Attorney-General of the Provincial Council of Artois (before serving as Inspector-General of Finances, 1785–87 [Translator's note]).
13. Jean-Michel Lienard and Yves Moret, *Messieurs du Magistrat de Douai. Pouvoir et société dans une ville en mutation de la fin du XVIe siècle à la fin du XVIIe siècle*, Lille, Mémoire de maitrise, 1982: 156.
14. From the first two to the last two decades of the century the proportion of the nobility rose from about 18 per cent to nearly 42 per cent.
15. For some 7 per cent of families it was impossible to determine the social category.
16. J. Gerard, *Journal des troubles des Pays-Bas*, vol. 1: 311.
17. I am grateful to the author for permission to read and cite her unpublished work, deposited in the Mons archives (L'administration communale de Mons', ULB, 1977–8).
18. Michel-Joseph Fonson, *Petit tableau de la ville de Mons*, Mons, 1784: 37.
19. For 1721 and 1722, see Gilles-Joseph de Boussu, *Histoire de Mons*.
20. Louis Bonaventure Vanhoenacker (1734–94) was elected to the Legislative Assembly on 1 September 1791 and served without attracting notice in the Feuillant group. See George Lepreux, *Nos représentants pendant la Révolution*, Lille, 1898.

21. Under pressure from the crowd, the municipal government ordered that the conduits (*goulottes*) used to load wheat on to boats for export from the city be destroyed. The merchant who protested fell victim to popular anger, as did a printer who tried to assist him. Bernard Lefebvre, *Histoire de Douai*, 157.

22. However, in Tournai the oligarchy had to cope with the thirty-six guilds, determined to restore a popular form of the old urban republic complete with the traditional privileges. Ph. Guignet, *Le Pouvoir dans la ville*, 693–9.

23. In Mons, for example, nine out of ten aldermen were lawyers, but seven out of ten had no previous experience.

24. Suzanne Tassier, *Histoire de la Belgique sous l'occupation française en 1792 et 1793*, Brussels, 1934: 102.

25. See H. Vandenbroeck, *La Magistrature tournaisienne (1789–1870)*, Tournai, 1870, 17–18; also the remarkable biographical sketches of Canon Albert Milet, *Tournai et le Tournaisis sous le bonnet rouge (1792–1793)*, Tournai, 1986: 350–64.

26. See H. Vandenbroeck, *op.cit.*: 38–42.

8 Resistance to change: élites, municipal government and the state in the development of the city of Naples (1750–1870)

John A. Davis

Introduction

Until the early twentieth century Naples was the largest city in Italy, and indeed one of the biggest in Mediterranean Europe. Yet ever since the late eighteenth century the city's growth had been considered pathological because of the evident disproportion between its demographic size, urban structures and economic resources.

After reaching an initial ceiling in the early seventeenth century, the city's demographic growth had been interrupted by plague, political upheaval and commercial recession. During the eighteenth century these losses were quickly recouped and under the weight of constant immigration the city's population rose to reach a new peak around 1790 (probably *c*.400,000). The city then experienced a further long period of crisis and stagnation due to the war in the Mediterranean, the disruption of trade, political upheaval and foreign occupation. The continuation of the war at sea throughout the Napoleonic period — when Naples and the southern mainland (Mezzogiorno) were absorbed into the Empire — contributed to a slight fall in population. After the Restoration of the Bourbon monarchy in 1815 demographic growth resumed at a slower pace. Yet despite the high mortality caused by cholera, which first struck the city in 1834, the city's population continued to rise and by the time of Unification had reached about 450,000. Thereafter there was little expansion, and although Naples remained the largest single city in the new Italian state it was gradually overtaken by the rapidly expanding industrial cities of the north at the turn of the century (Aliberti 1974, Beloch 1937–61, De Seta 1981, Martuscelli 1979, Petraccone 1975, Pilati 1978).

Demography does not tell the whole story, but it does indicate one of the central issues in the city's history throughout this period — its size, the density of its population, its vulnerability to subsistence crises and epidemics, and the inadequacies of its administrative, economic and urban structures. The idea that Naples was a 'problem', indeed one of the central problems of the southern state, was already firmly established in the writings of the Neapolitan economists of the reform era in the second half of the eighteenth century. They depicted the city as a swollen head that lived parasitically off the lifeblood of its provinces.

A series of attempts were made in the last quarter of the eighteenth century to change this situation, to reduce the city's privileged position and to establish a more balanced relationship between the capital and the provinces, but they proved unsuccessful. The same was true of the more coherent and energetic measures introduced by the city's Napoleonic rulers, and again of the initiatives taken by the last Bourbon rulers after 1820. The reasons for this owed at least as much to the working of the 'visible hand' and to human agency as to market forces and other purely economic or structural constraints, although the ways in which the 'visible hand' operated were often curiously opaque.

The eighteenth century

The dangers posed by the city's apparently uncontrollable demographic expansion were first brought home by the famine of 1764, which caused massive mortality in Naples and throughout the provinces of Southern Italy (Venturi 1973, 394–472). The famine aroused fears of a popular revolt comparable to that led a century earlier by Masaniello, but it also revealed the 'structural' nature of the mechanism that fuelled the city's demographic expansion.

Naples was privileged because it was the capital of the Kingdom. As a result, the lion's share of public revenues and administration, of public and royal expenditure was concentrated in the city. It was also the preferred residence of the landed classes, the feudal aristocracy and the higher clergy. These advantages were increased by the desire of the new Bourbon rulers of Naples (after 1734) to turn the city into a showpiece of the new dynasty— huge investments went into building new palaces and triumphal *piazze*. Royal extravagance was imitated, albeit in lesser key, by the nobility who strove to keep up with the tastes of the court and *fare figura*.

The population of Naples enjoyed other privileges too. Its citizens were exempt from many taxes and were not subject to conscription, but most important of all were the regulations which provisioned the city with food supplies directly at the cost of the rest of the Kingdom. By means of a system of price-fixing in the provinces and privileged requisitioning of grain (known as the *annona*) the city was guaranteed cheap bread. Throughout the Kingdom supplies of grain at fixed prices were sent to the capital to meet its needs, and in times of shortages these quotas were imposed by force.

Similar regulations existed in other parts of Europe—notably at Rome, Palermo and Madrid (D.R. Ringrose 1983). However, the regulations subsidized the urban consumer by discriminating against the agricultural producers who were forced to part with their crops at prices fixed in the capital. This was the principal reason for the ever-growing flow of immigrants into the city, and in times of subsistence crisis the flow became an uncontrollable flood.

The famine of 1764 revealed the ways in which these mechanisms worked, but attempts to remedy them were unsuccessful for political reasons. The city's privileged status was firmly embedded in the political as well as the economic structures of the *ancien régime*. Indeed, the monarchy's power to intervene in the administration of the city was severely limited since Naples constituted a semi-autonomous corporation, within which different jurisdictions shared or struggled for power. Any attempt to re-organize the city involved challenging the power of the noble patriciate who governed the city.

Naples was divided into twenty-nine districts or *contrade*, each of which was administered by a *capitano del popolo* on behalf of the King and chosen normally from the guilds or the professional classes. Overall administration of the city was the responsibility of the *Tribunale di San Lorenzo*, at which the Crown was represented by a single magistrate: all the other members came from the noble *Sedili*, the five corporations to which all the noble families of the Kingdom belonged (even the so-called *Piazza del Popolo* was always represented by a nobleman). The *Tribunale di San Lorenzo* appointed six *Eletti* who were responsible for the day-to-day running of the city. They were noblemen, and they met twice a week to set taxes, the prices of foodstuffs on sale in the city and also the prices at which grain would be purchased in the provinces for the *annona* (G. M. Galanti, 185–8).

The power of the urban patriciate reflected the great autonomy which the Neapolitan feudatories had acquired during the years of Spanish rule. Yet it would be wrong to assume that the feudal aristocracy had the city in their hands. They had considerable autonomy with respect to the Crown, but they had in turn to deal with other powerful political and social forces in the city—the church, the wealthy religious houses, the urban guilds and corporations.

The city in reality embraced a network of interlocking, adjacent, official and unofficial corporate authorities and this was reflected in the highly decentralized structures of this vast metropolis. Shortly after Unification the historian Pasquale Villani wrote of Naples:

The inhabitants of one district pass much of their lives without ever entering another. Ways of life, ways of behaving and ways of thinking vary from one quarter to another as from one country to another, and as a result there is little contact between them.

Claudia Petraccone has demonstrated how the separateness of the different *quartieri* was reflected in demographic patterns too, and well into the nineteenth century each district of the city recruited its new immigrants from specific rural areas (like all other European cities, the demographic surplus in Naples was, of course, always a product of immigration, not of natural increase—within the city mortality rates remained catastrophically high, especially amongst infants) (Petraccone 1975).

As in other eighteenth-century cities, the collective identities of the different *quartieri* were often determined by occupational specializations: fishing in Santa Lucia, stevedores and dock workers in Porto, petty commerce in Mercato, a wide variety of industries and trades in the popular districts of Pendino, Vicaria and Santa Lorenzo. Yet although the monarchy and the aristocracy were beginning to build sumptuous new palaces both outside the city and on the perimeter of the 'old city'—on the Riviera di Chiaia, for example—Naples did not acquire 'residential districts' until the nineteenth century. Most of the nobility and the wealthier classes still lived in *palazzi* in the old *quartieri* of the city, occupying the middle and upper floors and leasing the less sought-after ground floor and the basements (*bassi*) to poorer families. This inhibited the development of horizontal social divisions amongst the different *quartieri*, while the presence of occupational and religious institutions—the guilds, parish churches, monasteries and the lay confraternities as well as devotional cults—all served to reinforce the vertical social structure of the *quartieri*.

These structures, combined with the highly precarious nature of its economy (most economic activity revolved around supplying the needs of the wealthier classes), were conducive to the development of powerful systems of patronage and clientism. The weak needed protection, preferment and support, and the provision of employment or charity constituted the means, within each *quartieri*, by which the wealthier families could establish influence and a following.

This meant that the *Eletti* who administered the city had to do so by negotiation rather than fiat. It was very easy for public protest to be mobilized and few things touched more directly on the interest of Neapolitans than food prices and the city's collective privileges. Any attack on those privileges, therefore, threatened the consensus that underpinned the autonomy of the city's aristocratic administration.

Attempts to challenge this autonomy in the late eighteenth century were uncertain. In 1775 the first detailed map of the city and its neighbourhood was produced by Giovanni Carafa, Duke of Noja and indicated an awareness of the need for better control. The introduction of twelve new administrative districts in 1775 pointed in the same direction, while the King's minister Tanucci even considered plans for the forcible resettlement of half the city's population. In practical terms, however, nothing changed, since the city embodied all the obstacles which eighteenth-century feudalism posed to effective state intervention (De Seta 1981, 191–2).

Then came the Revolution in France which brought the Bourbon monarchy in Naples to the verge of bankruptcy. Faced by a major subsistence crisis in 1793–4, the government took unprecedented radical measures. Fearing revolt in the provinces, the policy of requisitioning was abandoned and the city authorities were authorized to buy grain on the market; to meet the costs, new urban consumption taxes were introduced (L. De Rosa 1959, 3). As a result the prices of food and other necessities in the capital rose fast, while the war in the Mediterranean brought the city's port and commercial life to a standstill.

These changes played an important role in fuelling the popular discontent that exploded in the terrible uprisings that took place in the city in 1799. Yet popular discontent was mingled with the more opaque resistance of a wide cross-section of those with vested interests in the maintenance of the old urban order. When a French invasion in 1799 precipitated the fall of the monarchy, there was a move by certain sections of the nobility to create a form of aristocratic republic based on the old city government. However, when Ferdinand IV re-entered the city later in the year one of his early actions was to abolish the nobility's monopoly over the administration of the city.

The French reforms (1806–14)

Following the chaotic events of 1799 which had undermined the fiscal and juridical privileges of the *ancien régime* capital, the short decade of French rule in Naples that began in 1806 offers an ideal opportunity for exploring the working of the 'visible hand'. The French rulers (Joseph Bonaparte, 1806–8; Joachim Murat, 1808–14) attempted to realise a broad and coherent programme of reforms which were designed to transform the city and its relations with the rest of the Kingdom.

The French administrators threw up their hands in horror when they arrived in Naples:

. . . le spectacle de l'indigence qu'offre le Royaume de Naples semble faire que le Religion et la Philosophie ont été parcimonieuses envers l'Humanité. Le Tableau de la Pauvreté est effroyable si on le considère dans les rues de Naples. Les cris lamentables, la Nudité, les plaies, les déformités sur lesquelles la vision ne peut s'empêcher de s'arrêter, rendent dégoûtante cette grande Ville. (Miot de Melito 4.7. 1806)

(. . . the spectacle of destitution offered by the Kingdom of Naples makes it seem as if Religion and Philosophy have been grudging towards Humanity. The Picture of Poverty is appalling if one studies it in the streets of Naples. The pitiful cries, the Nudity, the sores, the deformities, which one cannot help seeing, make this City disgusting.)

The remedies they proposed were simple but coherent: the introduction of centralized bureaucratic administration on the model of French urban administration and the abolition of economic and administrative privileges in order to establish a more balanced relationship between the city and the provinces.

A new centralized system of policing was imposed on Naples on the day when the French entered the city. In the past, policing had been carried out by the city's principal courts which were authorities unto themselves. Police *commissari* were appointed in each district, and a volunteer City Guard was also established in which the propertied classes were expected to serve. The reorganization of policing was accompanied by the first attempts to apply the principles of registration and control typical of the new administrative mentalities that had emerged from the Revolution in France. Streets were named, houses numbered, new regulations were introduced (regarding burial grounds, the location of markets and the movement of livestock within the city). The marginal and precarious sections of Neapolitan society were the object of particularly close control, and the police became solely responsible for issuing licences to pedlars and street vendors, prostitutes, lodging-house keepers, tavern owners and so forth (Davis 1987, 327–54).

The city's administration was also radically changed. Naples lost its remaining financial autonomy and its revenues reverted to the state (law of 1 October 1806). A new municipal body—the *Corpo della Città*—was created consisting of thirty *Decurioni* appointed by the government and a *Sindaco* (mayor) for each of the city's twelve *quartieri* (law of 8 August 1806). Unlike the old patrician city government, the *Corpo della Città* was a purely bureaucratic body, whose task was simply to implement the instructions of the Ministry of the Interior.

The city's economic privileges proved more difficult to destroy. In some cases the obstacles were technical, but more often they were political. This was evident when the *ancien régime* tribunals were abolished, causing heavy unemployment amongst the professional classes and many ancillary groups (clerks, janitors, cleaners, etc.). The government was not slow to understand the danger and in 1811 Murat expressed his fears very explicitly to Napoleon:

Je ne dois pas dissimuler a V.M. que tandis j'ai 10,000 emplois à mon service, la plupart Romains, Toscans ou Italiens, les Napolitains sont sans emploi et meurent de faim et demandent le pain que mangent les Etrangers. Sire, il y eut sous Charles III une révolte à Naples pour le même objet, et je dois prévoir le même événement. (Murat 18.1.1810)

I ought not to conceal from V. M. that while I have 10,000 employees at my service, mostly Romans, Tuscans or Italians, the Neopolitans are unemployed, dying of hunger and asking for the bread which is being eaten by the Foreigners. Sire, under Charles III there was a revolt in Naples for the same reason, and I must predict the same occurence.)

Measures were taken to give Neapolitans jobs in preference to foreigners (including the French who had poured into the Kingdom in search of preferment), and many earlier decisions were reversed in order to preserve jobs in the city.

In practice there was little decentralization of the bureaucracy away from Naples because of the political dangers this presented. Yet unemployment amongst the professional middle classes was not the only source of political danger for the French rulers. Given the high levels of unemployment, any measures designed to reduce the city's commercial or economic privileges were likely to incite political hostility. In fact, the government's initial attempts to open up the city's economy to market forces exposed many sections of the working population to unemployment and disaster. The abolition of the craft guilds, for example, threatened institutions which played a critical role in the provision of welfare in this vast city and provided forms of regulation and control that were not easily replaced: for that reason they were allowed to survive (Min. Interior (2) f.5068).

An even greater reversal of policy occurred when Naples was struck by famine in 1809–10. The government's response was again shaped primarily by political considerations and the fear of popular revolt. Murat's government first incurred the Emperor's fury by purchasing grain from the Allies, but the government then reversed one of the fundamental pillars of their reform programme by abandoning the free trade policies introduced by Joseph Bonaparte.

The change was fundamental. Joseph's free trade legislation had been designed to reduce the capital's economic privileges and establish a more open equilibrium between the capital and the provinces. However, the regulations introduced in 1810, which remained in force until 1860, reversed this. They did not reinstate the old *annona*, but the effect was similar: exports were permitted only when the home supply was assured, in other words in times of plenty when prices were low; when the harvest was scarce, on the other hand, imports were immediately permitted. This advantaged the urban consumer directly at the cost of agricultural producers since the regulations were designed to keep prices low. The export regulations prevented farmers from taking advantage of higher prices on foreign markets and deprived them of commercial incentives, and not surprisingly became a major bone of contention between the government and the landowners.

The French rulers also took more direct measures to bolster the flagging economy of their capital. Like their Bourbon predecessors they wished to turn Naples into a showpiece and it was here that the bulk of public and private expenditure on building and public works was concentrated. New roads were also built to enable troops to enter the popular *quartieri* more easily. All this served to provide work for the poor as well as jobs for the professional classes—architects, engineers and administrators—but the city's most obvious defects, notably the lack of housing and the inadequacies of its infrastructures, were left untouched.

The limitations of the achievements of the 'visible hand' can also be clearly seen in the attempts to reorganize urban welfare institutions. Although the Bourbon rulers had provided Naples with the largest poorhouse in Europe (the *Albergo dei Poveri*) in the late eighteenth century, the inadequacy of the city's welfare institutions were only too evident. However, the reform of the administration of welfare institutions was halfhearted, not least because they continued to be seen as a reserve of bureaucratic employment and patronage. At the same time, the suppression of religious houses reduced the supply of charity and also the revenues of those institutions—such as the *Ospedale degli Incurabili* and the *Ospedale dell'Annunziata*—which survived (Valenzi 1987).

Given the failure of attempts to remedy the economic causes of urban poverty, the French authorities relied increasingly on administrative and police measures to control the consequences, and these were directed above all against the 'marginal' or 'floating' sections of the population. The introduction of much more severe controls on immigrants, for example, compensated for the failure to reverse the economic imbalance between the city and the provinces.

The reforms effected, attempted and abandoned by the French adminis-tration in Naples in these years reveal the difficulty of restructuring the *ancien régime* city. The French *decennio* modified rather than transformed the city's economic and political role, but its administration was more radically changed. This had important consequences, especially for the relations between the government and the urban élites. The new municipal govern-ment, the *Corpo della Città* exercised no independent power, although it did confer considerable patronage and hence influence on its members. Yet access to the government and to individual ministers was now a *sine qua non* for those who wished to exercise patronage and influence. Hence the urban élites had now to reach an accommodation with the state: they could not, as in the past, set themselves up in opposition to it.

Opportunities to exercise power through patronage also grew because the competition for jobs was greater than ever before, while the growth in the state bureaucracy offered new and wider opportunities for building patronage networks and clientist followings. These were to be the political foundations of the new urban élites which took shape in the early nineteenth century.

The last years of Bourbon Naples 1815–60

It was during the final years of Bourbon rule in Naples that the social and economic changes that had begun to emerge during the brief decade of French administration were consolidated. Symptomatic of these changes was the changing composition and interests of the élites, which vividly illustrate the broader character of the city's development in this period.

After 1815, the political power and the corporate solidarity of the noble urban patriciate was destroyed. Their successors were still noblemen rather than bourgeois, but their power owed more to individual position, talent, favour and contacts than to estate. The composition of the new Neapolitan urban élites is not easy to pinpoint precisely, but one thing is certain: the urban patriciate did not become a commercial or entrepreneurial élite in these years. The 1845 census listed some 300 bankers, wholesale merchants, corn–brokers and manufacturers out of a total population of over 400,000: less than 0.07 per cent of the population of the city as a whole but—even more important—less than 2 per cent of the propertied classes of the city, of whom over 25 per cent were lawyers and doctors, and the overwhelming majority were simply landowners (David 1981, 9). If eighteenth century Naples had been a city of noblemen and lawyers ('*togati*'), in the nineteenth century, it was still a city in which the nobility had a very high profile, but they were now accompanied by a much broader stratum of landowners, *rentiers* and professional classes (especially lawyers, but with many new professions as well).

The two developments were closely linked. The sales of Crown and church lands during the French *decennio* had created a new open market in land and urban properties, which had inevitably broadened the social background of the propertied classes. Most important of all, however, the abolition of feudal entails (*maggioraschi*) had—nearly all contemporary observers were agreed—destroyed the great aristocratic patrimonies which had held the great noble families of the past together. Throughout Italy the great symbols of the noble clans or *casate*, the huge family palaces which accommodated various branches of a single family living together with poorer relatives and retainers, began to become a thing of the past (Barbagli 1984).

The social differences between the new and old sections of the urban élites were considerable, but their economic interests were more similar. The breakup of the old noble patrimonies, the appearance of new groups of smaller but independent landowners (many of whom were former feudatories and noblemen) had profound effects on the city. Throughout most of the period after 1815 the conditions of the Kingdom's agricultural economy were poor, with the result that more and more landowners moved into the capital from the provinces, not only because the life there had more to offer but also because they needed some other source of revenue. They—or more often their sons—looked for jobs in public administration or the professions (hence the tremendous pressure on the colleges, schools and University of the capital). Their daughters looked for husbands amongst the professional and propertied classes. Increasingly landowners were also looking to invest in urban property which gave spectacularly better returns than rural assets. The fact that residential rents in Naples were already amongst the highest in Europe indicates the force of attraction (De Seta 1981, 235–7).

The rapid growth in the ownership of property in Naples is clearly shown by tax registers and other sources (Aliberti 1975, 101–2; De Seta 1981, 252–8). In some cases this took the form of building new houses, but more generally—in this period—of converting or extending existing buildings to maximize rented accommodation. These speculative investments brought increasing chaos to the city's urban structures, but it was not until after the cholera epidemic of 1834 that a *Consiglio Edilizio* was created to establish and enforce building regulations.

Although the Council denounced the activities of speculative builders and investors, they proved unable to check them. The cholera epidemic revealed the extent to which the 'invisible hand' dominated the city, and the fears which it aroused in the authorities led to new attempts to impose the visible hand of public intervention and control. However, the Bourbon state in Naples lacked the political will and the financial resources to intervene. The single most costly state-funded project in Naples in this period was the monumental church of San Francesco di Paolo opposite the royal palace, which was built to celebrate the Restoration of the dynasty in 1815. Fittingly this project was unfinished when Bourbon rule in Naples came to an end in 1860, and it remains to the present an eloquent monument to the priorities of urban development in this period.

The continuing absence of sewers and clean water supplies was not only a consequence of the religious devotion of the last Bourbon rulers. The precarious state of public finances meant that the government had to finance public works projects either from private bankers (from the Rothschilds, for example, who in 1821 purchased the Kingdom's Public Debt outright) or from the Kingdom's propertied élites. Urban improvement projects attracted neither, unlike speculative investment in the shortage of housing and accommodation.

Hence the progressive deterioration of the structures of the city and the conditions of those who lived in it. This also contributed to a gradual change in the social composition of the different *quartieri*, as the professional and *rentier* classes moved away into the new residential districts that were taking shape in Chiaia, San Ferdinando, Montecalvario, Avvocato, Stella, San Carlo all'Arena and San Giuseppe (Petraccone 1974, 213). Yet these developments changed rather than undermined the social ties which had played a critical role in establishing hierarchical structures of power within this potentially anarchical metropolis in the previous century. One reason was that the separation of social classes was never complete, and while the old nobility remained in the historical *quartieri* they were joined by many of the new notables. As a result, the paternalistic and populist ethos of the Neapolitan aristocracy (at the court of Ferdinand IV it was fashionable to talk in the dialect of the fishermen of Santa Lucia) was adopted by the new urban élites. The self-conscious romanticization of the Neapolitan poor dates back to this period and is in itself evidence of the attempts to recreate the vertical social bonds of the past (E. Cione).

More direct measures also reinforced the existing stratification of the urban poor. After 1822, for example, the government became committed to building up the Kingdom's industrial and manufacturing capacity, but great care was taken to ensure that the new industrial enterprises were located away from the capital in order not to challenge its old artisan industries and trades. Tariff protection against imported goods served the same purpose, and it was significant that the first major signs of labour unrest in the city did not come until after the British had forced the Neapolitans to abandon their protectionist policies (Davis 1988, 102–4).

Government policy in these years sought as far as possible to preserve the city's economic and social structures from change. However, there were other 'visible hands' at work, even though they were often well shrouded. The Bourbon rulers of Naples, like their French predecessors, preferred wherever possible not to interfere with the 'self-regulating' institutions of Neapolitan life. Policing continued to be directed against the most marginal sections of the population, against immigrants, itinerant salesmen, vagrants and prostitutes. Yet in the city's settled communities, the police were less likely to interfere, and by and large these communities were left to regulate their own affairs. In most cases the old guild corporations—although in theory abolished—continued, and regulated entry into trades, production and prices. When disputes occurred, each occupational group or locality would have intermediaries to settle such matters—the parish priest, a local notable or some other respected figure.

In certain cases these community-based systems of regulation could and did take on a more aggressive character—and this was the case of the *camorra*. Although it ultimately became a purely criminal phenomenon, *camorra* originally grew out of the conditions of the unskilled workers in the city's docks and markets. Because these jobs were unskilled, the monopolies that particular communities and localities established over work in these areas had to be defended, often by force, against outsiders who attempted to muscle in. At a second stage such informal monopolies might become little more than protection rackets: merchants using the docks and Customs warehouses, for example, paid 'tips' to the porters to ensure that their goods were not 'lost' or damaged. The wholesale and retail trades through which the city was supplied with foodstuffs provided similar opportunities to establish monopolies by force, and these affected not only the retailers but also the urban suppliers as well (De Bourcard 1853–84; Marmo 1990)

The existence of informal monopoly structures like *the camorra*—which unlike the Sicilian *mafia* has a well documented history well before Unification—grew out of the self-regulation of particular groups and communities within the city and thrived on the inadequacies of the urban economy which could be exploited through monopolizing those opportunities which did exist. Such structures provided a critical foundation for the expanding patronage and clientist networks of the urban élites.

However, it is not necessary to descend into the murky criminal world of the *camorra* to understand how the urban élites established networks of social and economic patronage in the city in these years. Although they no longer enjoyed the political power of the past, their economic power was growing, and their activities were increasingly dependent on meeting the various needs of the state—for credit, for public works and other services. It was that which enabled sections of the élites to act as intermediaries, and to secure advancement for their clients and followers.

In other words, the mechanisms of patronage were reconstituted in ways that were different from the past but no less powerful. Since the interests of the élites lay primarily in preserving intact as far as possible the status quo in order to exploit the needs of the city and its rulers, the 'visible hand' continued to be a major force which perpetuated the poverty of the city and the social and economic deprivation of the majority of its inhabitants.

Unification

The collapse of the Bourbon state in 1860 and annexation to the new Kingdom of Italy once again faced Naples with apparently overwhelming economic and commercial problems. The failure of the French attempts to generate a self-sustaining economic base for the city meant that dependence on its role as state capital and royal residence had continued—the loss of both those functions in 1860 was therefore little short of a calamity.

The damage was aggravated by the emancipation of the provinces, which were now free to act without reference to Naples. The first railway line to the south, for example, would link the cereal plans of Apulia to the north, depriving Naples of its function as the commercial entrepôt of the Mezzogiorno. Even those industries that had grown up around the capital in response to Bourbon protectionism—the Pietrarsa shipyard a short distance along the coast, which was the single largest industrial workshop in the whole of Italy; the engineering and textile factories which had grown up in the suburbs of the city—were swept away when Piedmontese free trade was brusquely extended to the south in 1861.

These economic and commercial blows reinforced the tertiary and *rentier* character of the city, and recent research has demonstrated how the transfer of wealth from land into urban property accelerated in this period (Macry 1990). The prevailing conditions of under employment and inadequate welfare institutions meant that the structures of patronage remained unchanged, although the introduction of representative government and the ballot box added new dimensions of political power to the hierarchies of clientism and patronage.

The terrible cholera epidemic of 1884 gave a further massive extension to these systems of power. Following the epidemic the government voted special funds for the extensive rebuilding of the historic centre of the city, and the 'Disembowelling of Naples' (*Lo Sventramento*) which followed opened the way to a massive speculative bonanza.

It is not possible to describe these developments in detail, except to say that the extensive reconstruction operations of the 1880s provide the logical conclusion to this chapter. This was the moment when the tendencies which had been evident from much earlier in the century were consolidated. The urban élites had become progressively more dependent on exploiting the commercial and financial opportunities provided by the needs of the city—not to overcome them, but more simply to profit from them. In fact, from the start of the century Naples had been the focus of a steady conversion of wealth from agriculture into urban property. The prevailing conditions of under employment and precariousness amongst the city's middle classes, the degradation of the older parts of the city and the rapid development of new residential regions with little regard to principles of urban planning or aesthetics, and above all the appalling poverty of the vast majority of the population constituted the basis of the power of the élites. Those élites had a powerful vested interest in maintaining those conditions, and by the nature of their power were able to gain control over the working of the 'visible hand': public and private power were directed to the same end.

References

Aliberti, G. (1974), 'La città dolente', in A. Mozzillo, (ed.) *La dorata menzogna*, Naples.

Barbagli, M. (1984), *Sotto lo stesso tetto: mutamenti della famiglia in Italia dal xv al xix secolo*, Bologna, Il Mulino.

Beloch, K.J. (1937–61), *Bevolkerungsgeschichte Italiens*, Volume 3, Berlin.

Cione, E. (1938), *Napoli romantica*, Naples.

Davis, J.A. (1988), *Conflict and control: law and order in 19th century Italy, London*, Macmillan.

Davis, J.A. (1987), 'Naples during the French *decennio*: a problem unresolved', in *Villes et territoire pendant la période napoléonienne*, Rome; École Française de Rome 96: 327–54.

Davis, J.A. (1981), *Merchants, monopolists and contractors*, New York, Arno Press.

De Bourcard, F. (1853–84), *Usi e costumi di Napoli e contorni*, Naples.

De Nicola, C. (1909), 'Diario napoletano', in *Archivio Storico per le Provincie Napoletane 1899–1905*, vol.27, 9 April.

De Rosa, L. (1959), *'Il debito pubblico della città di Napoli e le riforme di Giuseppe Bonaparte'*, in *Archivio Storico del Banco di Napoli*.

De Seta, C. (1981), *La città nella storia d'Italia—Napoli*, Bari.

Galanti, G.M. (1792), *Breve descrizione di Napoli e dei suo contorno*, Napoli.

Galasso, G. (1987), *Napoli*, Bari.

Macry, P. (1990), 'La città e la società urbana', in P. Macry and P. Vallani (eds) *La Campania*, Turin Einaudi: 93–183.

Marmo, M. (1990), 'Tra le carceri e mercati. Spazi e modelli storici del fenomeno camorrista', in P. Macry and P. Vallani (eds) *La Campania*, Turin, Einaudi: 691–732.

Martuscelli, S. (1979), *La popolazione del regno di Napoli nella statistica murattiana*, Napoli, Guida.

Petraccone, C. (1975), *Napoli dal '500 all' 800. Problemi di storia demografica e sociale*, Napoli, Guida.

Pilati, R. (1978), 'La popolazione di Napoli dal 1770 al 1820', in P. Villani (ed.) *Studi sulla società meridionale*, Napoli, Guida.

Ringrose, D.R. (1983), *Madrid and the Spanish Economy*, Berkeley, London, University of California Press.

Valenzi, L. (1987), 'La povertà a Napoli e l'intervento del governo francese', in A. Lepre, (ed.) *Il regno di Napoli durante il decennio francese*, Napoli, Liguori.

Venturi, F. (1973), '1764: Napoli nell'anno della fame', *Riv. Stor. Ital.*: 394–472

Venturi, F. (1973), 'Roma negli anni della fame', *Riv. Stor. Ital.*

9 Fingerprints of an urban élite: the case of a Dutch city in the nineteenth century

Pim Kooij

The aim of this chapter is to evaluate the occupations of the Municipal Council in a Dutch city during the nineteenth century. This city is Groningen in the north, which was at that time the fifth city of the Netherlands. Groningen was rather peripherally situated. It should therefore be easier to make a distinction between influences from within and those from outside the city.

The questions posed are (1) Which groups were particularly represented in the urban government? (2) To what extent were these groups able to serve their own interests and to have their mark on the city?

In this respect one has to take into account that during the nineteenth century many major tasks were taken over or initiated by the central government. This reduced the possibilities of the leading groups in the cities. So we have to see which matters they managed to keep in their own hands, by tracing the fingerprints they have left in the archives and on the urban environment.

The urban electoral system

During the first half of the nineteenth century the Dutch electoral system was very complicated (Blok 1987). According to the constitution of the newly formed Kingdom of the Netherlands (1815), the members of the Second Chamber of the states general were elected by the members of the provincial states. The Second Chamber was the main representative body, though it was in a way controlled by the First Chamber, which consisted of noblemen, appointed by the king. The provincial states in their turn contained the representatives of three orders: the nobility, the towns and the countryside. The number of representatives differed per order per province.

The Netherlands—excluding the future Belgium—comprised eighty-two, later eighty-seven, cities. This distinction was not based on formal criteria. Size, historical development and central functions were the main factors. According to regulations outlined by the central government, cities were to be governed by a municipal council headed four mayors. In 1824 some revisions were made. The number of mayors was reduced to one, henceforward assisted by aldermen.

The right to elect or to be elected was the privilege of only part of the population: men above a given age, mostly 23, who met certain financial qualifications. One had to pay a certain amount of direct taxes, the 'census'. The taxes specified by regulations of 1816 and 1824, were those on land and wealth. The latter was mainly based on the value of one's residence and its contents (Blok and de Meere 1978, 175–92; De Vries 1986, 21). The third existing direct tax, the patent tax, which was to be paid by most people who had their own business, was excluded from the calculations.

It is obvious that the electoral system favoured people who acquired their incomes from rent, including the old urban élites with their traditional display of wealth. The main aim of the census indeed was to restrict electoral power to people who could 'bear the responsibilities'. This was also effectuated by a system of indirect elections. In the towns and in the country election councils were created to elect the members of the municipal councils. The census required to be eligible in these councils was higher. In Groningen, for instance, in 1824 one had to pay 30 guilders in direct taxes to be entitled to a vote, and 50 guilders to be elected. Only people from the latter category could become a member of the Municipal Council. As Table 9.1 shows, only a small section of the population met those qualifications.

Table 9.1 Voters and eligible men in the city of Groningen

Year	1816	1830	1852	1870	1890	1910
Number of inhabitants	27,824	30,260	31,577	38,528	56,038	74,613
Number of men qualified to vote		1,089	1,734	1,925	2,917	9,093
As a percentage of the population		3.6	5.5	5.0	5.2	12.2
Number of members Municipal Council	17	16	21	35	30	33
Census voter threshold (guilders)	20	30	25	25	10	10
Census threshold for eligible persons	35	50				

Sources: Blok 1987, 299; provincial almanacs; Archives of the Municipality (275); Census.

The members of the municipal council were chosen for life, those of the election councils for nine years[1]. The representatives of the city in the provincial states were appointed by the municipal council.

The revision of the constitution in 1848 brought major changes. The system of indirect elections was abolished.[2] The election councils disappeared, but the census remained as well as its regional and local variations. An important alteration was the inclusion of the patent tax which augmented the opportunities for businessmen. The census for the Second

Chamber was fixed twice as high as the census for the municipal council. There was no extra threshold for candidacy. The urban government was specifically regulated by the Local Government Act of 1851, abolishing the political distinction between town and country. A term of five years was introduced for the members of the municipal council and re-election was possible.

After 1848 the election system remained unchanged for the rest of the nineteenth century. In 1887, however, the census was lowered and it became possible to admit people with a certain status and abilities to the elections, for instance from the field of education. This was extended in 1896. All these reforms led to a rise in the number of electors. Let us see now what this meant for representation on the local level.

Representatives and representation

Table 9.1 gives some evidence on Groningen voters and eligible candidates. Unfortunately, in the first half of the nineteenth century the registration of electors was not very accurate. We have only some totals, but a number of lists still exist with the names of the men who qualified for the election council. These lists contain the names of about two-thirds of the potential voters. From 1852 there are complete lists of electors for every year.

Since, after the proclamation of the regulations in 1816 and 1824, the members of the municipal councils were appointed by the king, the elections gained importance only during the 1830s. Table 9.2 gives a classification of the occupations of the potential members of the election council in 1830. A comparison with other large cities is impossible, because of the lack of data.[3] However, since we have reconstructed the occupational structure of Groningen in 1830, it is possible to give some evaluations.

As Table 9.3 shows, there was a strong overrepresentation of the services and the Civil Service among the potential members of the election council and underrepresentation of industry. This is because Groningen had a long tradition as a regional political and service centre (Kooij 1988, 361). Many Civil Servants derived their wealth from the land, while in services many fortunes had been made, often displayed in expensive houses. In 1830 most of the industrial sector consisted of very small-scale firms and was mainly focused on the local market. Most bakers, butchers, carpenters, tailors, coachbuilders, etc. occupied small houses and therefore paid a low property tax. Even when their business flourished, they ploughed their profits back into the business instead of living in lavish style. The traditional producers of glue, soap, ropes, oil, textiles, and so forth, had a larger service area and do figure on the list, as well as the chemists and most of the gold and silvermiths, who had the farmers in the countryside as their customers.

It is probable that a number of craftsmen had voting power but were not eligible. More artisans, however, had to wait until 1851. Even then it was the service sector which profited most. The lowering of the census and the inclusion of the patent tax resulted in an increase in the number of electors of the Municipal Council from 1,007 in 1850 to 1,734 in 1852. Of this total,

Table 9.2 Occupations of potential members of the election council in 1830 (%)

Agriculture (1.3)	
farmers	1.3
Industry (24.7)	
owners of factories (*fabrikeurs*)	1.3
pharmacists	2.5
artisans:	
building (carpenters, painters . . .)	2.5
food (bakers, butchers . . .)	5.1
gold and silversmiths	2.8
metal, wood, leather (smiths, shoemakers, joiners)	5.4
textiles (dyers, tailors, weavers . . .)	2.6
others (printers, manufacturers of soap, glue, oil)	2.6
Services (44.8)	
merchants (no specification given)	25.7
wholesale merchants (wood, textiles, iron, stone)	2.5
booksellers, winesellers	2.1
other shopkeepers	1.8
shopservants, valets	1.1
bookkeepers, clerks	0.8
traffic (boatmen, wagoners)	1.8
hotel and catering industry	4.2
the professions (doctors, notaries, lawyers)	5.0
Civil Services (14.2)	
top civil servants	7.4
civil servants (teachers, corn-measurers . . .)	2.9
military officers	1.1
professors	2.8
Religious Services (2.6)	
clergymen, priests . . .	2.6
Others	
without occupation (including students)	9.3
unknown	3.1

(N = 612)

Sources: Municipal Archives (275/8–880), the Groningen register.

312 people passed the census threshold owing to the inclusion of the patent tax. Among them were fifty-one boatmen, who were not assessed for other direct taxes.[4]

At the municipal level, exclusivity in voting disappeared after 1851. In fact, only the lowest class, consisting of labourers and small artisans, were excluded. This is shown in Table 9.4 in which an income stratification of the Groningen heads of households, based on a local poll-tax, is compared with the percentage of electors among men of 23 years and over.

Even between 1824 and 1852, when the census was at its highest level, some members of the lower middle class had the right to vote (see also the

Table 9.3 Electors and the occupational structure in 1830

Potential members election council		Heads of households
Agriculture	1.3	2.9
Industry	24.7	36.1
Services	44.8	25.4
Civil Service	14.2	4.1
Religious service	2.6	0.3
Free labour	–	6.1
Without and unknown	12.4	25.0

Sources: Table 9.2. Sample from the Groningen register of population 1830 (n=653).

occupations mentioned in Table 9.2). In 1852 the number of voters already exceeded the number of heads of households in the income groups 1–4. Besides, about 17–20 per cent of the heads of households were women, mostly widows who had a low income, and 1–2 per cent of the heads of households were under 23. The percentage of the heads of households entitled to vote did not change very much in 1887. It was the revision of 1896 which mobilized electors within the lowest stratum. However, electoral power for many groups did not automatically mean that they were also represented in the Municipal Council.

The members of the Municipal Council

In the first half of the nineteenth century the Groningen electors had hardly any opportunity to exercise their rights. Almost all of the first members of the Municipal Council held their appointments for life. So it is not surprising that there was not much interest in the periodical elections for the election council, charged with filling vacancies. In 1830 only 40 per cent of the members returned their ballots and most votes were in favour of the retiring members. The election council was scarcely larger than the Municipal Council—thirty-two members—all the members of the Municipal Council were included in it, and new councillors were elected from the membership.

In fact, Groningen at that time had an oligarchy of allied distinguished families who, before and during the French occupation, had already formed the local government. Table 9.5 contains a survey. One has to bear in mind that relatives in the first and second degree were not allowed to be members at the same time.

Only by 1850 were some outsiders admitted, like the merchant J. Slot, who was born in Koog aan de Zaan. He became mayor afterwards, but was dismissed for incompetence and continued as a common member. The first elections according to the Local Administration Act caused an important change. The number of seats was increased and ten new members were elected. Among them were two shopkeepers, which extended the range of represented occupations.

Table 9.4 Income stratification of the Groningen heads of households (%)

Income	1830	1850	1870	1890	1910	Specification
1. ƒ4,000	2.3	2.0	1.6	4.3	3.3	the élite: top civil servants, top professional men, top wholesale merchants, industrialists
2. ƒ2,000–ƒ4,000			3.8	3.2	5.5	the sub-élite: high civil servants, important manufacturers and merchants
	7.0	9.3				
3. ƒ1,000–ƒ2,000			7.3	5.8	11.4	the upper middle class: trained executives, important tradesmen, teachers (sec.school)
4. ƒ500–ƒ1,000	14.1	16.1	10.9	16.7	31.7	lower middle class: shopkeepers civil servants, tradesmen
5. Modal ƒ500						artisans, small shopkeepers, small tradesmen
	76.6	72.6	76.4	70.0	48.0	
6. Exclusively ƒ500						labourers, servants, small artisans
% of men of 23 and over with voting power	15.9	21*	20.7	23.4	54.2	*=1852

Sources: Kooij 1987, 39–49; sample from the Groningen register of population 1830 and 1850; poll tax, register of real property.

Explanation: The stratification for 1870–1910 is based on the Hoofdelijke Omslag, a local poll tax, which was set up in 1856. For the first ten years it was based on the value of houses, thereafter on income. For the 1850 stratification the data on house values from 1856 to 1859 have been used. This stratification could be linked to the stratifications of 1870 and later years by comparing the data for 1865 (on house values) and 1866 (on incomes). The values for 1830 are derived from the register of real property and linked to the 1856 data.

No deflator has been used. The only deflator available for the whole period is the index of wholesale prices (Van Stuijvenberg 1982). The index numbers for 1830 etc. are respectively 100, 105, 125, 99 and 103.

Table 9.6 shows that in 1816 judges had the strongest position in the Council. In the following years this was taken over by lawyers and some notaries. Since some lawyers were also aldermen, it is obvious that until 1850 the Municipal Council was dominated by people who were paid by the local or central government. This was still the case in the new Council of 1852, but then there was an important rise in the number of representatives from trade and industry. As we have seen, members of the middle class could in theory elect their own representatives. Among the newly elected

Table 9.5   Families in the Groningen Municipal Council

	Number of members	Period	Related to
Civil services/professions			
1. Busch/Geertsema	3	1816–62	7
2. Cremers	2	1816–82	13
3. Van Iddekinge*	3	1816–50/1873–82	6,8,14
4. De Savornin Lohman*	4	1816–56/1883–95	6,10,11
5. Trip*	2	1816–64	8
6. Quintus*	4	1816–73/1880–92	3, 4, 7, 9, 10, 14
7. Feith*	4	1828–1910	1, 6
8. Van Imhoff*/			
Van Swinderen*	5	1828–47/50–1900	3, 5, 11
9. Rengers*/De Sitter	2	1844–74	6
10. Baart de la Faille	2	1851–95	4, 6, 11
11. Modderman/Sijmons	2	1865–1910	4, 8, 10
12. Tjarda van Starkenborg			
Stachouwer*	2	1867–1910	
13. Tellegen	2	1869–83/98–1908	2
14. Wijckerheld Bisdom/	2	1870–1910	3, 6, 8
De Marees van Swinderen*			
Trade and industry			
15. Van Olst/Van Calcar	3	1816–52/1882–7	
16. Homan/Thieme	2	1835–49/1876–83	
17. Roelfsema	3	1852–59/1873–6/	19
		1882–1910	
18. Van Houten/			
Blaupot ten Cate	5	1852–69/1872–83/	19
		1888–1905	
19. Mesdag	2	1854–68/1882–5	17, 18
20. Bennema/Sissingh	2	1884–1901/1908–10	
21. Smith	2	1893–1910	

Sources: Almanacs, genealogies, register of population.

Explanation: * means nobility; Column 1 contains relations of the first and second degree (including sons-in-law), column 4 contains relations of the third and fourth degree and also brothers-in-law.

wholesale merchants, there were indeed at least three who belonged to the upper middle class (category 3), and a producer of tobacco as well. Yet they could not challenge the dominance of the wealth categories 1 and 2.

Even in 1870, eighteen of the twenty-five members belonged to the highest class, and fourteen of them were extremely wealthy (Kooij 1987, 64). The other members, with only one exception, belonged to category 2. As expected, given the information about electors in the preceding section, the reform of 1887 did not alter the situation much. In 1890, twenty-five of the thirty members belonged to the élite (category 1). However, in 1898 the first workers' representative was elected, the painter J.H. Schaper. In 1901

Table 9.6 Occupations of the members of the Municipal Council

	1816	1830	1850	1852	1870	1890	1910
Doctors	–	1	–	–	1	1	2
Lawyers, notaries	1	5	4	6	8	8	5
Top civil servants	2	1	5	3	3	3	3
Judges, prosecutors	7	2	3	2	2	4	–
Professors	–	–	1	1	–	1	1
Clergymen	–	–	–	–	2	–	–
Factory owners	1	2	1	2	2	3	5
Wholesale traders	4	3	1	5	3	4	3
Shopkeepers	–	–	–	2	2	3	3
Bankers	–	–	–	–	1	2	2
Others	–	1	1	–	–	1	9
None	2	1	–	–	1	–	–
Total	17	16	16	21	25	30	33

Sources: Almanacs; the Groningen register of population.

he was joined by a second representative of the SDAP, the socialist party founded in 1894. This number was doubled as a result of the revision of the election law in 1907.

In 1910 therefore, the occupations of the members of the Council were more differentiated and included the lower strata (tailor, typographer). This diversification was also caused by the emergence of two Christian parties since the end of the 1880s: the 'Anti Revolutionaire Partij' and the 'Christelijk Historische Unie'. The first party claimed to represent the Christian members of the middle classes. For instance, in 1910 two journalists were member of the Municipal Council on behalf of the ARP. The first ARP members, by the way, was jhr. mr. W.N. de Savornin Lohman, who after 1900 joined the CHU.

None the less, the members of the Municipal Council still did not reflect the composition of the electorate. Twenty-two out of the thirty-three still belonged to the élite, and fifteen even to the top élite, who were at least twice as rich. Of the eleven non-élite members, two belonged to category 2 and three to category 3 (Kooij 1987, 64). During the whole nineteenth century Groningen was therefore ruled by members of the élite, who also enjoyed the confidence of the lower strata. Old and often noble families continued to send their representatives, and the ties between them remained close. A truly central position was taken by mr. S.M.S. Modderman, who started as an alderman in 1865 and was mayor from 1893 until his death in 1900. Most dynasties consisted of lawyers, judges and top Civil Servants, but there were some clans of merchants and industrialists as well. The most important was a group of Mennonite wood-sellers, corn-traders, traditional manufacturers of liqueur and paper, and bankers. The Van Calcar, van Houten, and Mesdag families belonged to that group, but in the end almost all Baptist members of the Council—Helder, Hesselink, Schilthuis and Wouters—were related.

By the end of the century the presence of the old noble families diminished in favour of more commercial and industrial interests. However, some noblemen had already made the switch to that sector and founded the leading banking-houses 'Geertsema, Feith en Co' and 'Van Vierssen Trip, Feith en Co' which partly arranged the issue of loans by the local government.

The composition of the Groningen Municipal Council in some ways resembled that of The Hague, although its status was somewhat lower (Stokvis 1987, 320). In The Hague between 1889 and 1919, 82 per cent belonged to the highest class, compared with 67 per cent in Groningen in 1910. Besides, in The Hague there were very few factory-owners and no representatives of the labouring class. Yet in The Hague as well as in Groningen, the share of the nobility and *haute bourgeoisie* was high, though in Groningen somewhat lower: 31 per cent between 1889 and 1919 in the royal residence, against 26 per cent.[5] There are no exact data available for Amsterdam and Rotterdam, but Van Dijk points out that in Rotterdam there was not much continuity (Van Dijk 1986, 146). The old élite only partly returned after 1813. Migration to The Hague, the seat of the national government, was one reason for that. So already in the first half of the century the Municipal Council was dominated by the interests of new tradesmen.

At the end of the century in the industrializing city of Delft, only three of the traditional ruling families still had seats on the Council. They were replaced by representatives of the traditional trades who still belonged to the élite (De Jonge 1974, 190). The modern industrialists did not show much interest in local administration. This was also the case in Groningen, where the most important industrialist, Jan Evert Scholten, a producer of potato flour, paper and sugar, occupied his seat for only three years. He considered the First Chamber more fitting for his status and a better place to defend his interests. This indicates the political as well as the economic unification in the Netherlands during the nineteenth century (Kooij 1988). As we will see in the next section, this unification also affected the local Groningen élite, which before the nineteenth century had been rather autonomous in decision-making.

The élite and the local government: a financial survey

The records of local government policy in the first half of the nineteenth century are very skimpy. Only after 1851 do the minutes of the Municipal Council give some insight into the involvement of individual members in different projects. The Municipal Accounts, however, offer some indicators for the preoccupations of the ruling élite.

Figures 9.1 and 9.2 contain a survey of revenues and expenditures. The enormous influence of the Municipal Administration Act of 1851 becomes clear at first sight. This Act urged an increase of expenditures. As the figures show, the revenues were more or less adjusted by taxes, but as we shall see, mostly by loans. The credit balance in most years is artificial. Particular expenditures, which did not figure in the budget, had to be transferred to the accounts of the next year.

The peaks reflect some dramatic episodes in local and national history as well as new local initiatives. In 1826/7 for instance, there was a mysterious epidemic, called the Groningen disease, which might have been some kind of malaria. This enforced expensive preventive measures and support for broken families. This was financed by a loan advanced by the central government. Groningen was affected as well by the riots and disturbances of 1848, which pushed the expenditures for public safety and the relief of the poor to a higher level.

The rise after 1851 was mainly due to an extension of the tasks of the municipal government in the fields of poor relief (Poor Law 1854) and education (Public Education Law 1857). But it also concerned public works and the foundation of public utilities. So the peaks after 1853 were caused by the construction of the local gas works, around 1860 by the building of schools, and in 1865 by the construction of the Corn Exchange and the extension of the gas works.

After 1874 most extra expenditures were made to finance the construction of new waterways, roads, squares and parks after the removal of the fortifications. The removal itself was financed by the state. Around 1900 the construction of a new hospital laid a heavy burden on the local treasury as did the founding of a power-station. Several years later it was the electric tramway which had to be financed. The enormous peaks in 1881, 1887 and 1895 were caused by debt conversion.

Table 9.7 offers some insight into the composition of the Municipal Accounts. During the whole period public works were a major budget item. Part of the public works is also included in the item 'particular expenditures', as will be mentioned below. Table 9.7 also reflects the growth of the urban bureaucracy (item administration), while the reason for the rise of the expenditures for education and poor relief has already been mentioned.

Compared with the cities in the west of the Netherlands, Groningen had high costs for poor relief at the end of the century. This was due to the agrarian depression which struck Groningen as the centre of an agrarian hinterland. The expenditures for health care, placed between brackets, are hidden in the items 'public safety', 'education', 'poor relief' and 'particular expenditures' (Kooij 1987, 266–7).

The most interesting items in the context of this article are 'particular expenditures' and 'interests and discharges'. Here it is possible to trace the fingerprints the urban élite left on their town. The item 'particular expenditures' contains all the unique undertakings of the municipal government, most of which were not financed by the normal means. Here the local élite could make its own decisions, even though these expenditures had to be approved by the king and later on by the provincial aldermen. Most of the time, however, these authorities did not make any trouble. Almost all of the infrastructural works mentioned above figure in this item.

These particular expenditures were usually financed by loans. There was a long tradition of borrowing in Groningen. The city emerged from the

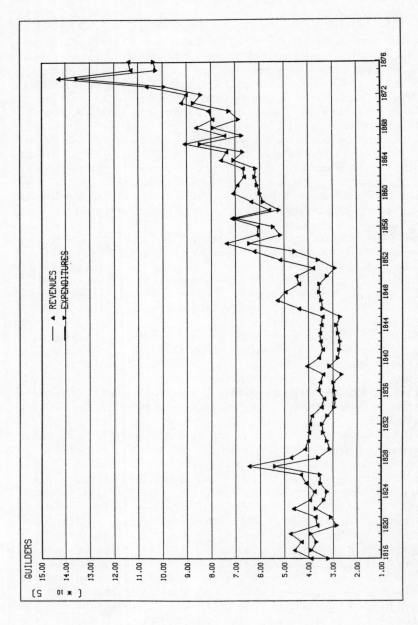

Figure 9.1 Municipal accounts, Groningen, 1816–76

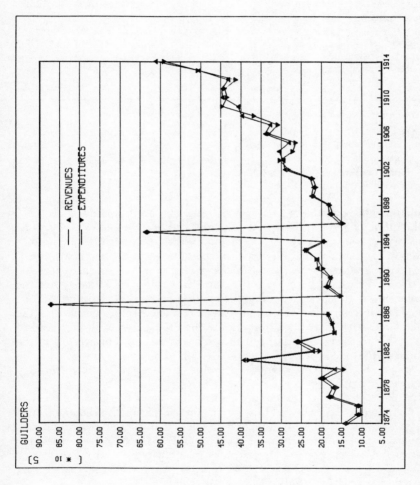

Figure 9.2 Municipal accounts, Groningen, 1874–1914

114 *Pim Kooij*

Table 9.7 Municipal expenditures (x £.1000)

	1816	1830	1850	1870	1890	1910
Administration★	27	25	29	60	87	121
Public works inside the city★	51	60	47	111	168	282
Public works outside the city★				44	67	143
Public safety★	13	23	31	43	89	172
(Health care★)				(33)	(64)	(122)
Public lighting★	10	11	16	..	41	63
Education★	1	10	18	77	336	617
Poor relief★	12	36	53	82	146	258
Interests and discharges	62	78	63	117	443	598
Particular expenditures	5	65	30	116	119	1,056
Total	181	308	287	...	1,496	3,310

Sources: Municipal accounts.

Specification: 1830 = the average of 1829–31 etc. For 1870 the costs of public lighting are hidden in the total costs of the gas works.

★ = including salaries. Money advanced which was paid back during the same year is not included (this is not the case in Figures 9.1 and 9.2.

Napoleonic era with a debt of 1,139,992 guilders, accumulated since 1630. Yet the money had been used well. The city had bought and exploited vast areas in the Province of Groningen, most of which, before the foundation of the Republic of the United Netherlands, belonged to Catholic institutions. Most of the estates were situated in the peat area in the south-east of the province, which was therefore called the Peat Colonies. The city left the exploitation of the peat to companies and others. But Groningen constructed an infrastructure of canals, with lucrative tolls, and leased the levelled land. The Groningen household refuse and night-soil were sold to this area for fertilizer. In addition, the city owned some properties in the clay area in the north of the province. In 1855 the net revenue of all these areas was ƒ.250,000- which was 50 per cent of all the revenues of the city (Sybenga 1916, 5).

While cities like The Hague and Delft started to take loans only after 1851, Groningen had followed this practice in the first half of the nineteenth century. Table 9.8 offers a complete list. These loans became a real burden for the local government. Since the rents in the Peat Colonies were fixed for centuries, known as *beklemming* revenues from that area did not rise very fast. The other revenues came from indirect taxes while a smaller part consisted of surcharges on direct taxes.

In 1855 indirect taxes were partly, and in 1865 completely abolished. They were replaced with 80 per cent of the local revenues of the direct taxes, plus surcharges. The cities were also allowed to raise school fees (Meijer 1971, 29–45). Besides, cities had the opportunity to create a poll-tax, the

Table 9.8 Loans taken by the Groningen Municipal Council

1827	ƒ 150,000	4¹/₂%	–	Groningen disease
1832	ƒ 55,000	4¹/₂%	–	Poor relief; citizen soldiery
1833	ƒ 55,000	4¹/₂%	–	Poor relief; repercussions of the Belgian war
1838	ƒ 50,000	4%	–	Discharge debt of 1827
1846	ƒ 180,000	4%	–	University building; poor relief; public works
1850	ƒ 55,000	4%	–	Budgetary deficit
1853	ƒ 250,000	4%	–	Gas works
1854	ƒ 100,000	4%	–	Gas works
1857	ƒ 38,000	4¹/₂%	–	Gas works
1859	ƒ 115,000	4%	–	Building of schools (Public Education Act)
1860	ƒ 100,000	4%	–	Building of schools
1862	ƒ 47,500	4%	–	Participation in the construction of a canal
1864	ƒ 108,000	4¹/₂%	–	Secondary schools; public works
1865	ƒ 30,000	4¹/₂%	–	Corn exchange; secondary schools
1866	ƒ 125,000	5%	–	Discharge old debts; gas works; canal
1867	ƒ 40,000	5%	–	Roads
1868	ƒ 63,000	5%	–	Road to Hanover
1873	ƒ 185,000	4¹/₂%	–	Streets
1874	ƒ 196,000	4¹/₂%	–	Streets; public works in the Peat Colonies
1874	ƒ 167,000	4¹/₂%	–	Public works; school
1876	ƒ 103,000	4¹/₂%	–	Public works
1877	ƒ 65,500	4¹/₂%	–	Public works
1878	ƒ 188,000	4%	–	Streets; harbour; schools
1879	ƒ 740,000	4¹/₂%	–	Bridges and other public works; schools
1880	ƒ 326,000	4%	–	Public works (initially refused by the Province)
1881	ƒ 348,000	4%	–	Conversion loan
1882	ƒ 423,000	4%	–	Public works
1883	ƒ 982,000	4%	–	Conversion loan
1884	ƒ 130,000	4%	–	Schools; harbour; roads; fire brigade
1885	ƒ 216,000	4%	–	Public works
1886	ƒ 180,000	3¹/₂%	–	Sewage works; planting; bridge; school; gas works
1887	ƒ4585,000	3¹/₂%	–	Conversion loan
1889	ƒ 331,000	3¹/₂%	–	Conversion loan; public works
1891	ƒ 309,400	3¹/₂%	–	Cattle market; gas works
1893	ƒ 107,000	3¹/₂%	–	Public works
1894	ƒ 64,000	3¹/₂%	–	Public works
1895	ƒ 270,780	3%	–	Gas works
1895	ƒ4792,200	3%	–	Conversion loan
1897	ƒ 105,000	3¹/₂%	–	Abattoir; public works
1899	ƒ 839,800	3¹/₂%	–	Hospital; abattoir; sewerage; theatre; gas works
1902	ƒ 900,000	4%	–	Hospital; power-station
1904	ƒ 500,000	3¹/₂%	–	Power-station; water works; police station
1906	ƒ 900,000	3¹/₂%	–	Power-station; tramway; public works
1907	ƒ 490,000	4%	–	Hospital; gas works; public works
1908	ƒ1053,000	4%	–	Hospital; gas works; public works
1910	ƒ1000,000	3¹/₂%	–	Tramway
1911	ƒ 900,000	4%	–	Power-station; water works
1912	ƒ1200,000	4%	–	Gas works; public works
1913	ƒ5000,000	4¹/₂%	–	Gas works; power-station; public works
1914	ƒ 500,000	4¹/₂%	–	Public works

Sources: Minutes of the Council; Resolutions of the Municipality, municipal accounts.

Hoofdelijke Omslag. However, its level was kept very low for a long time. Most élite members of the Municipal Council were in favour of this limitation. Their main argument was, as in other cities, that a high poll-tax might drive away the wealthiest inhabitants to neighbouring villages, where those taxes did not exist or were at a much lower level (Kooij 1987, Appendix B). So the city had to borrow, and since the terms were rather long, sometimes even ninety years, and repayments were small, they had to borrow again or to sell some city properties to pay the interest.

In 1900 the city already had a debt of about ƒ.5,200,000.-, which was ƒ.78.- per inhabitant. In The Hague in that year the debt burden per inhabitant was ƒ.113.51 (amount of the debt ƒ.23,386,000.-); in Rotterdam ƒ.73.42 (amount ƒ.47,636,000.-); and in Delft ƒ.63.31 (amount ƒ.2,000,000.-).[6]

As indicated above, the Municipal Council of The Hague was the most aristocratic one, while in Rotterdam and Delft commercial and industrial interests prevailed. In Groningen these two intermixed. So it seems as if there was some correlation between the level of aristocracy in the Municipal Council and the level of the debt. Indeed the old aristocracy had interests in loans, as private persons and as administrators of orphanages, of homes for the old and infirm, and other institutions, which were important creditors. There was much opposition from that quarter whenever the mayor and his aldermen proposed to convert old loans into loans with a lower interest rate. On the other hand, the élite did not have scruples about withdrawing their money when the rate of interest rose. This happened for instance in 1864, when 75 per cent of the $3^{1}/_{2}$–4 per cent terminable debt, dating from the *ancien régime*, was withdrawn. The ruling élite then decided to issue a new non-withdrawable loan at $4^{1}/_{2}$ per cent interest.[7]

The municipal loans were therefore partly used by the local élite to improve their financial position. They also kept the direct-tax burden rather low. In 1902 it was ƒ.6.50 per inhabitant. Compared with other large cities, this was lower than in Amsterdam (ƒ.9.91), The Hague (ƒ.8.34), Haarlem (ƒ.8.61) and Arnhem (ƒ.7.68) but higher than in Rotterdam (ƒ.5.82), Utrecht (ƒ.6.27) and Leiden (ƒ.5.24) (Messing 1972, 127). Of course these amounts are related not only to politics, but also to prosperity and social structure. Leiden, for instance, was a poor city with relatively high unemployment, while the non-paying working class in Rotterdam, Groningen, and perhaps also in Utrecht was large. The Hague and Arnhem were primarily residential cities with a larger upper class.

In the 1890s and especially after 1900, the debt of Groningen rose considerably to hfl.11,000,000.- in 1916, and the financial situation became rather critical. Groningen was not exceptional. The debt of The Hague, for instance, rose to 73 million guilders in 1914 and that of Rotterdam to 106 million, while there was not much inflation at that time. Most of the profits of the public utilities had to be used for interest and amortization. The debts would have been even larger if the national government had not given some subsidies from time to time for specific tasks, which were partly mandated by new laws such as the Health Care Act and the Housing Act of 1901.

Still, it was not until 1915 that the provincial aldermen raised questions about the Groningen habit of borrowing for every expenditure that in some way was unusual (Sybenga 1916, 23). Until then, only in 1880 was a loan refused, because the purposes were not indicated at all (Geertsema 1895, 47). So the urban élite had a free hand in spending money on matters they deemed important.

When we take into account the list of loans, it is apparent, that the urban élite liked to spend primarily in two areas: the urban environment and public utilities. There was also some preoccupation with education, but this was mainly enforced by the central government, which for instance ordered the institution of at least one secondary school in cities of more than 10,000 inhabitants. In this field, it was above all the university which captured the attention of the urban élite. In 1876 a serious threat arose that this institution might be closed, but the efforts of Groningen members of the central government and of the Second Chamber avoided the worst. Large loans were also made for health care, most of them for the construction of a new hospital.

A better view of the policy of the urban élite can be derived from an analysis of the decision-making on matters mentioned above. This will be done for some cases in the next section.

Some cases

Politics in the province and city of Groningen was characterized and complicated by a mixture of cleavages. First, there was the old animosity between town and country. The Groningen hinterland frequently tried to eradicate the city's domination. At first this movement was headed by the gentry, but in the nineteenth century the liberal farmers took the lead.

Second, there was the opposition against the central government. For a long time Groningen claimed to be an independent city-state and tried to remain as autonomous as possible within the Dutch Republic. This was frustrated by Napoleon and the formation of the Kingdom of the Netherlands with a strong central power. The Groningen farmers took advantage of this movement and especially advocated the constitutional reform of 1848 to slacken the domination of the city. In some ways, the provincial government at that time acted as an extension of the central government, with the Governor, after 1848 called Commissioner of the King, as a viceroy. On the other hand, however, many members of the urban élite families participated in the provincial government. Before he became a mayor, for instance, De Sitter was a provincial as well as a Groningen alderman who completed his career as a member of the Second Chamber in The Hague.

Structural antitheses were also traversed by personal loyalties. This complicated structure resulted in a range of *ad hoc* coalitions dependent on the issue at stake. When, for instance, the province forbade the city to extend the cattle market, the city called in the assistance of the Minister of Internal Affairs, at that time a member of the Groningen family De Savornin Lohman. He was not the only Groningen person who became a member of the central government. Of course the urban élite tried to take advantage of that.

Within the city itself an antithesis of a somewhat different character divided the old élite and *homines novi*. As a result of the economic integration of the Netherlands, Groningen combined its functions as a centre for its region with a position in a national urban network based on specialization (Kooij 1988, 365–9). At least four industrial sectors obtained national importance: the printing-industry, the food and allied products industry, the manufacture of ready-made clothing and the production of bicycles.

This development brought wealth to people who had other interests than the establishment. As mentioned before, these *nouveaux riches* seldom became members of the Municipal Council, partly because they did not aspire to office, but also partly because membership was given to natives in the first place. Many owners of the new factories originated from outside the city, some even from Germany. However, the new economic orientation in Groningen also influenced the traditional wholesale trade, which became more and more (inter)national. The grain trade is a good example. This sector was indeed represented in the Council.

There was almost no intermarriage between the old noble families and members of the élite from trade and industry. Yet in administration there was always a mixture of aldermen from both sides. The centralizing policy of *The Hague* sometimes resulted in the appointment of a mayor from elsewhere, but they were not very successful. J. Slot (1853–62) has already been mentioned. B. van Royen (1872–80), born in Zwolle (also the birthplace of Prime Minister Thorbecke), suddenly resigned 'longing for a quieter life' and J.N.A. Bucaille (1883–93) from Voorburg near The Hague suffered from dementia.

The complicated mixture of different interests can be demonstrated by the three major issues in municipal politics, which took the greater part of the special expenditures.

Public utilities

The municipal interest in public utilities started with the construction of the gas works, which opened in 1854. The coincidence with the new composition of the Municipal Council is striking, but this was partly accidental. The aristocrat De Sitter was an advocate as well as the retired mayor Baron van Imhoff. The argument that the city should be the first beneficiary, however, was originally put forward by the new members from trade and industry, already before 1851. The decision not to give a concession to private firms but have the city operate the works was taken as early as 1845. However, the King refused consent for strategic reasons. This enforced the unity in the Groningen Council, which even sent a delegation to The Hague. However, they had to await the revision of the constitution, until the new King accepted.

The financial success of this enterprise encouraged the Council to create other public utilities. The initiatives were taken by representatives and aldermen from trade and industry, but the old families readily agreed. Together they frustrated initiatives by individual members of the Council or other members of the élite. Thus in 1895 Jan Evert Scholten, by far the richest man in the city, did not gain a concession to construct a power-station (Kooij 1972, 278). A municipal station started in 1902. Apart from the profit motive, the main argument was that the élite wanted this luxurious and efficient method of illumination for themselves, their shops and their city, in that order. They took example from the 'luxurious city', The Hague, and hired an adviser from that city. Even the councillors from trade and industry did not speak about the electric motor, which was to be extremely important for the small-scale Groningen industry (Kooij 1972).

The corn exchange (1865), cattle market (1892) and the slaughterhouse (1900) for which a concession was refused to some Belgians, were established as municipal enterprises. The horsedrawn tramway was left at first to private exploitation. It started as a Belgian enterprise, and in 1896 was taken over by some locals, among them J.E. Scholten and the former member of the Council, jhr. W.C.A. Alberda van Ekenstein. However, as the Council had expected, the large profits failed to come. The tramway was eventually taken over by the city and transformed into an electric system (1910). This was especially advocated by the socialist members of the Council. The top élite retained their carriages.

The waterworks (1878) were the most important public utility in private hands. The concession was granted by a one-vote majority to two doctors from Leeuwarden. One of them was M.E. Baart de la Faille, who got the support of his Groningen relative in the Council, who, however, abstained from voting.[8] When the enterprise proved to be profitable, the municipality tried to take it over. In 1912 it eventually succeeded, after some lawsuits. According to probate inventories, many members of the Council were shareholders, the former member R. Feith was even director. The minutes of the Council do not reveal whether and how they served their own interests.

In the case of public utilities it is obvious that the élite members of the Council were motivated by the interests of their own group in the first place. In a way, they also considered the public utilities as their own firms. This is not surprising: their terms were very long, which enlarged their commitment.

Town planning

In 1874, when Groningen was allowed to demolish its fortifications, a conflict arose between the municipality and the state on the ownership of the land. Groningen did not dare to take legal action, which testifies to the relationship.

The central government were to level and prepare the ramparts. However, the municipality stipulated it was to develop the area. Therefore a specialist was hired, Bert Brouwer, again from The Hague. The Minister had no difficulty with this, all the more because the plans had to be conspicuous, which caused the prices of the lots for sale to rise. Town planning now became the first indulgence of the ruling élite and they borrowed huge amounts to create for themselves a suitable environment.

First, the ramparts in the north of the city were bought and transformed into a park. An additional argument was put forward, that the moat could be used by woodsellers for storage. Most of the levelled land in the west and the east remained the property of the state. Eventually large university buildings were to be constructed here, like the new hospital.

Most attention was paid to the area in the south, near the new railway station. Beautiful boulevards and squares were constructed here. The Groningen élite bought parcels of lands for the construction of villas. At least seventeen members of the Municipal Council moved to that area between 1880 and 1910. The members from trade and industry were underrepresented. For the greater part they went on living near their enterprises and shops. In the neighbourhood of the boulevards expensive schools were constructed, and a new museum as well as a fire-station, and a campaign was started to move prostitution from that area.

Commercial interests were also taken into account. For instance two new harbours were constructed. One of them was situated at the end of the Eemskanaal (1876), which became the new connection with the sea. This canal was financed by the province to stimulate the building of larger ships. The urban members of the provincial estates advocated the construction of the canal to support the aspirations of the city as a sea port. This did not work out very well (Kooij 1987, 360).

The close attention paid by the élite to their own immediate surroundings provided a violent contrast to their involvement in the construction of working-class houses. This was left mainly to landowners, who were allowed to divide their properties into small lots, provided that these houses were out of sight. However, a number of the Council's members were involved in the three housing associations existing before 1900, either as a board member or as a shareholder. Nevertheless, they withdrew their money, when the dividend was fixed too low. These associations usually let their houses to members of the lower middle class (Kooij 1987, 216–27).

In the 1870s only three members of the Council pleaded for an overall view on town planning. This was enforced by the Housing Act (1901). An extension plan was made by city architect Mulock Houwer. Then again the Council did not allow individual members of the élite to pursue their own interests. They protested in vain against the planning of a road on their land instead of lucrative houses.[9]

The Hospital

At all government levels there was a keen interest in the replacement of the ramshackle municipal and academic hospital with a modern one. The ruling élite in the city needed it for poor relief and to keep those suffering from contagious diseases out of their way. The province wanted a central facility for health care, which could cope with the growing demand. Also, the state wanted to provide the university with a modern hospital.

In 1872 the municipality already tried to obtain subsidies from the state. They gained the co-operation of the Minister of Internal Affairs, J.H. Geertsema, who once was a member of the Groningen Municipal Council. Unfortunately he had to leave and his successor postponed the decision because of the bleak prospects of the university.

Once this was settled, the parties involved discussed their financial contributions for twenty years. The Professor of Surgery, Koch, even took a seat in the Municipal Council to accelerate decision-making. Eventually the terms of the city were accepted. The amount to be paid by the state, in years to come, was to exceed that of the construction costs lent by the city, including interests (Kooij 1987, 270). This was advanced because the Minister involved in the final negotiations was A.F. de Savornin Lohman.

The Groningen élite could afford to wait. The university was an impatient interested party. Moreover, in the meantime a Protestant and a Catholic hospital were founded, where the élite preferred to be nursed. Of course one of these hospitals was situated along a boulevard in the south of the city.

Conclusion

Already in the first half of the nineteenth century, taking Groningen as an example, some members of the middle classes had the right to elect members of the Municipal Council. After 1851 only the lowest stratum was excluded. This did not result in proportional representation. During the whole century the Municipal Council was dominated by the local élite. The margins of the policy of this élite were defined by higher political institutions. Yet they had a relatively free hand in the creation of public utilities and in town planning. Their actions in these fields were financed by loans.

The policy of the élite was in the first place inspired by the interests of their own group. Councillors from the Civil Service and the professions worked together most of the time with those from trade and industry, though public utilities were initiated by the second group. The fortune of the city was translated into the fortune of the élite and the success of their administration. This view was reinforced by the long terms of the councillors and the continuity in representation of the established families, related to a relatively low geographical mobility within the leading group.

Acknowledgement

I wish to thank Daan van der Haer, Anneke ten Koppel, Harmina Tasma and Rolf van der Woude for their assistance.

Notes

1. Before 1824 the term was three years. Since that year every three years a third had to step down, but could stand again.
2. There was one exception: the First Chamber of the states general was elected by the members of the provincial states.
3. Some data are available for Utrecht (1830), Haarlem (1842) and Delft (1842) but these concern all electors while the classification used is uncomparable. (Blok 1979, 401; Blok 1987, 302.)
4. This is shown by a comparison of the lists of electors of 1850 and 1852 (Municipal Archives Groningen).
5. According to the criterion of being mentioned in the red and blue books: *Nederlands Adelsboek* and *Nederlands Patriciaat*.
6. Estimated from *Geschiedkundig overzicht van de wijze van dekking der buitengewone uitgaven van de gemeente s'Gravenhage*, The Hague, 1916; Berends, R.E. *De ontwikkeling der Rotterdamsche gemeenteschuld van het jaar 1851 af tot den wereldoorlog*, Arnhem, 1932; De Jonge 1974.
7. Minutes of the Municipal Council, 1864/5.
8. Minutes of the Municipal Council, 12 January 1878.
9. Minutes of the Municipal Council, March/April 1904.

References

Blok, L. (1979), 'Van eene wettelijke fictie tot eene waarheid. Beschouwingen over kiesstelsel en kiesrecht in Nederland in de eerste helft van de negentiende eeuw'. *Tijdschrift voor geschiedenis*, 92: 391–413.

Blok, L. (1987), *Stemmen en kiezen. Het kiesstelsel in Nederland in de periode 1814–1850*, Groningen, Wolters-Noordhoff.

Blok, L. and J.M.M. de Meere (1978), 'Welstand, ongelijkheid in welstand en, censuskiesrecht in Nederland omstreeks het midden van de 19e eeuw'. *Economisch-en Sociaalhistorisch Jaarboek*, 41: 175–92.

Dijk, H. van (1986), 'Het negentiende-eeuwse stadsbestuur. Continuïteit of verandering', in P.B.M. Blaas and J. van Herwaarden, *Stedelijke naijver*, The Hague VUGA: 128–50.

Geertsema, J.H. (1895). *De geldleeningen der gemeente Groningen*.

Jonge, J.A. de (1974). Delft in de 19e eeuw. Van stille nette plaats tot centrum van industrie, *Economisch- en Sociaalhistorisch Jaarboek*, 37: 145–248.

Kooij, P. (1972). De eerste verbruikers van electriciteit in de gemeente Groningen 1895–1912, *Economisch- en Sociaalhistorisch Jaarboek*, 35: 274–303.

Kooij, P. (1987). *Groningen 1870–1914. Sociale verandering en economische ontwikkeling in een regionaal centrum.* Assen/Maastricht, Van Gorcum publishers.

Kooij, Pim (1988). 'Peripheral cities and their regions in the Dutch urban system until 1900'. *The Journal of Economic History*, 48: 357–71.

Meijer, W. a.o. (1971). 'De financiën van de Nederlandse provinciën en gemeenten in de periode 1850–1914'. *Economisch- en Sociaalhistorisch Jaarboek*, 33: 27–67.

Messing, F.A.M. (1972). *Werken en leven in Haarlem 1850–1914*. Amsterdam.

Stokvis, P.R.D. (1987). *De wording van modern Den Haag*. Zwolle, Waanders.

Stuijvenberg, J.H. van and J.E.J. de Vrijer (1982). 'Prices, population and national income in the Netherlands 1620–1978'. *Journal of European economic history*, 11: 699–711.

Sybenga, S. (1916). *Geldleeningen en schulden der gemeente Groningen*, Groningen.

Vries, Boudien de (1986). *Electoraat en elite. Sociale structuur en sociale mobiliteit in Amsterdam 1850–1895*, Amsterdam.

Vries, Joh. de (1971). Het censuskiesrecht en de welvaart in Nederland 1850–1917. *Economisch- en Sociaalhistorisch Jaarboek*, 34: 178–232.

10 Foresight is not the essence of government

Jan van den Noort

Nineteenth-century Rotterdam was a city of drastic changes.[1] Demographic, geographical and economic factors put immense strains on the City Council. In the last three decades of the nineteenth century Rotterdam faced a growth of the city population of almost 170 per cent. Due to annexations the territory of the city, in the same period, increased to eight times its original size. Moreover, the digging of the Nieuwe Waterweg, a new mouth for the river Rhine, improved the geographical position of Rotterdam and made it very sensitive to signals from the industrializing Ruhr region.

In the second half of the nineteenth century the City Council of Rotterdam took several decisions concerning the extension of the city on Feijenoord on the south bank of the river (Figure 10.1). The construction of a bridge was considered but the cost involved created an effective barrier. The involvement of private and state capital supplied sufficient pressure to proceed with the plans. Three contracts, one with the Dutch state, signed in 1869, the other two, concluded in 1872 and 1882, with the private Rotterdamsche Handelsvereeniging (RHV), will be analysed to show the interaction between these three parties and the division of labour that resulted.

Cart or bark

Whether an open bridge is open to ships or to land traffic is a confusing question. Whatever the answer, bridges can be a time-consuming barrier to water and land traffic. To W.N. Rose, former surveyor of Rotterdam Public Works and influential adviser to the city council, the bridge connecting Rotterdam with Feijenoord should form a permanent link with the other side. In his view the successful development of the new territory on the left bank depended to a great extent on the sort of bridge that was built. He stressed the need for a fixed bridge, because a bridge that had to be lifted to let tall ships pass would hamper road traffic too much. The large number of ships which had to pass would cause the bridge to be open too often. This way Feijenoord could turn into a separate city. Some day the merchants and manufacturers on Feijenoord

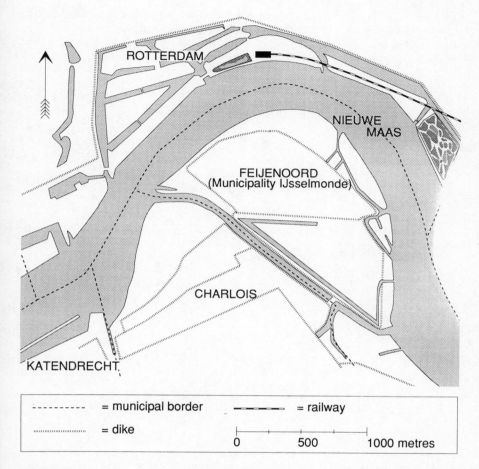

Figure 10.1 Feijenoord in 1869. The Meuse forms a part of the Dutch river delta. Rhine and Meuse merge east of Rotterdam and its combined waters are called Nieuwe Maas as they pass the city. For the extension of Rotterdam on the island Feijenoord a bridge crossing the Nieuwe Maas was considered indispensable. In 1870 Feijenoord and parts of the villages Katendrecht and Charlois were annexed.

Source: GAR, Library, XII B 36.

might even like to have their own exchange as well, Rose argued, and then separation would be complete.[2]

However, a fixed bridge is a barrier to water traffic and without an alternative route the drastic plan of Rose had no chance of being accepted. Although his Feijenoord plan of 1862/3 provided for two canals, the Oosterkanaal and the Westerkanaal, and two docks, the Noorderhaven and the Zuiderhaven, his plan was in essence meant to fulfil Rotterdam's need for building land (Figure 10.2). By digging the canals and the docks he provided sufficient material to elevate the ground above the highest flood level.[3] The interests of road traffic were well looked after by Rose. On the basis of his plan the Council decided in 1863 to extend Rotterdam on the other bank of the river and to that end to annex the villages in that area.[4]

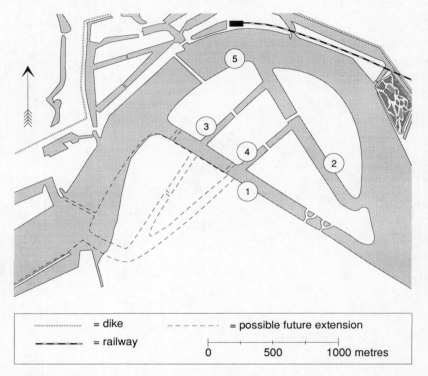

Figure 10.2   The Rose Plan for the extension of Rotterdam on Feijenoord (1862/3). 1. Westerkanaal 2. Oosterkanaal 3. Noorderhaven 4. Zuiderhaven 5. The south bank of the river was projected northward to increase the velocity of the river and thereby its depth. The second bridge and the part west of the Westerkanaal were intended as a possible future extension of the project.

Source: GAR, Library, XII B 35.

The interests of water traffic were better looked after by central government and by the Rotterdam Chamber of Commerce. The latter hammered on the necessity to provide more docks,[5] especially in deep water, not only for loading and unloading ships, but equally important, to protect the substantial capital invested in the vessels from severe winters. Nowadays ice hardly has a chance to influence river navigation on the Dutch section of the Rhine, and it is hard to imagine sliding and piling ice floes crushing everything that is in their way. Nineteenth-century shipping, however, was hazardous without protection from the elements.[6] Yet the main concern of central government was not the construction of docks, but the control of the river. It kept the river free from obstacles like bridges and dams, and, more cautiously it tried to relieve river traffic from the unnecessary burden of duties.[7]

Flood control was the basis for central government authority over the river. Up till then, however, the fight against the dangers of flooding rivers was in a way counterproductive. Vulnerable areas were protected by dikes, and if there was a surplus of water it was drained by overflows into less vulnerable areas. Through this system the main flow of the river decreased in velocity and as a consequence reduced its capacity to transport mud. The mud accumulated on the river bed and hindered the navigability of the river as well as its capacity to hold water. More flooding was the result. The authoritative report of L.J.A. van der Kun and J.H. Ferrand from 1850 reversed cause and consequence and supplied a new revolutionary concept to the control of rivers. Van der Kun and Ferrand stressed the importance of the normalization of the rivers. By damming up river arms the velocity of the mainstream could be increased. The depth of the rivers and their capacity to transport water would improve dramatically. Less flooding and a better navigability would result. It was indeed a radical, and what is more, a successful scheme for the control of Dutch rivers.[8] The new scheme had its consequences. It was recognized that anything happening upstream had an immediate effect downstream. Central and provincial government therefore gradually took over control from the polder boards.[9] Navigability, besides safety, was given a greater priority. The construction of the Nieuwe Waterweg, a new mouth for the Rhine Meuse delta that gave Rotterdam direct access to the North Sea, formed an extra impetus for centralization. The new canal to the sea was important for Rotterdam economically, but it also had some serious administrative drawbacks. The project could be successful only if several requirements were fulfilled upstream. Therefore the digging of docks and canals could not be left under the control of local governments any more.[10] The wish to maintain good relations with the neighbours was a strong incentive for the Dutch government to put the River Rhine under central government control. Prussia and the other states on the Rhine watched closely to see that their umbilical cord was well cared for. In 1868 they agreed on the Deed of Mannheim,[11] an international treaty liberalizing the navigation on this important international transportation route. Among other things the treaty obliged the Dutch government to supply an alternative canal if it was to bridge the River Rhine at Rotterdam. The Council of Rotterdam, eager to supply the city with new building-land, hesitated to spend a lot of money on a bridge providing communications with the new territory. Furthermore, a city bridge was strongly opposed by the Chamber of Commerce and central government, which did not intend to give planning permission, unless a solution was found for the passage of ships. Rose's plan offered a bridge and an alternative canal, but the costs involved were, too high to convince the City Council and execution of the plan seemed far away (Figure 10.2).

The arm or the head

The River Rhine divides the Netherlands into north and south. For most of the nineteenth century no bridges connected the banks, thus limiting nineteenth-century communication and condemning the two Netherlands to live separate lives. The construction of Dutch railroads faced the same problem, and two separate networks of railways emerged: the southern and northern systems. In 1860, however, central government decided to connect the two systems. One of the connections was planned near Rotterdam, but where exactly the bridge was to be constructed remained a matter of dispute.[12] Several plans were reviewed, from a low bridge west of the city to a very high bridge several miles east of Rotterdam. In the end the only acceptable solution was a bridge right in front of the city, passing through Feijenoord. This way, it was argued, the inland navigation and the sea-going vessels would be the least disrupted in their activities, because the boundary between their lines of traffic was located there.[13]

The City Council of Rotterdam did not easily agree on the railway bridge spoiling the look of its pretty quay. Together with the Chamber of Commerce they protested against this barrier for river navigation, but in the end gave way. The location in front of the city had too many advantages. It connected Feijenoord, where central government had planned the construction of a station and a railway dock, with the two local railway stations. In addition it was thought that the railway bridge could easily be extended to serve as a bridge for normal traffic as well. The cost of such an extension would be 'infinitely' lower than that of building a separate bridge.[14]

The Rotterdam Council offered their co-operation in a strange way, though. In their session of 21 January 1865 they voted against building a bridge over the river and suggested a terminal station on Feijenoord. Rotterdam would, however, co-operate if the connection was sought in the interest of the country. L. Pincoffs,[15] member of the Council, explained this contradictory decision as follows:

When a stronger person came to a weaker person and wanted to take away his arm or head, and the answer of the weaker that he rather wanted to keep both, was not enough for him, in that case forced by superior power, the weaker person would most certainly rather have his arm chopped off than his head and to that end even very politely file a request.[16]

The Chamber of Commerce supported the idea of the terminal station on Feijenoord and suggested a horse tram connection with the city.[17] The Rotterdam Council played a very clever game. They did not offend the Minister of the Interior and they improved their position in the negotiations. For what was constructed in the interest of the country could not be charged to the city, especially when it was not in the favour of Rotterdam. The Minister of the Interior, Heemskerk, however, managed to turn the situation to his advantage quite easily. The newly appointed mayor of Rotterdam, Joost van Vollenhoven, was informed about a sudden change of the railway plans in 1867. He had much trouble finding out that central government now planned to cross the river east of Rotterdam.[18] For the time being the existing railway station east of Rotterdam served as the destination of the new line.[19] The railway dock was projected north of that station instead of on Feijenoord. The Council was shocked by the plans, the Chamber of Commerce recorded their deep disappointment.[20]

A delegation from Rotterdam headed by its mayor tried to convince the minister to reconsider his plans. Heemskerk showed his willingness to do so, but he also had a special request. He was prepared to take up the plans for a bridge in front of the city, connecting Rotterdam with Feijenoord, if Rotterdam granted him the building land he needed for the railway line through Rotterdam. The Council hastily consented, but Heemskerk wanted more. He suggested that he might reconsider the Feijenoord line if Rotterdam would build him a new post office. The old one would have to be pulled down if the Feijenoord line was chosen.[21]

This time Rotterdam was lucky. Before it could react to Heemskerk's second request, the minister had to abdicate. To the new Minister of the Interior, Thorbecke, Rotterdam stated that it could hardly imagine that Heemskerk's suggestions were to be taken seriously.[22] Again the Council pleaded for a terminal station at Feijenoord and objected to the Heemskerk agreement to supply the state with the necessary building land. Thorbecke agreed to the latter and in 1869 finally reached and signed an agreement with Rotterdam.[23] The state initiative to bridge the river was the main impulse for Rotterdam to start seriously the Feijenoord development.

Cart, bark and train

The contract signed was quite different from the original plan Rose made in 1863. Let us have a closer look at the changes and their causes. As discussed, central government was heavily involved with the development of Feijenoord and took part of the responsibility for it by appointing government engineers specially for that area, who took over control from city government. The engineers found themselves in the difficult position of having to consider the interests of both the inland navigation and of Rotterdam. The demands posed by the construction of the Nieuwe Waterweg did not make the job easier.

The shipping trade protested against the alternatives Rose offered to ships that could not pass under the bridge. Shipping experts considered Rose's canals through Feijenoord as a hindrance and to a certain extent dangerous. The width of Rose's main alternative, the 100 metre-wide Westerkanaal (Figure 10.2.1), should at least be 150 metres.[24] The Chamber of Commerce supported this view.[25] The engineers were prepared to accommodate the wishes of the shipping trade and widen the Westerkanaal to 150 metres (Figure 10.3.1) and the Zuiderhaven to 100 metres (Figure 10.3.4). However, to prevent the canals from drawing too much water from the river, the mouths of the Westerkanaal and the Oosterkanaal had to be combined and furnished with thresholds (Figure 10.3.2). In his plan Rose

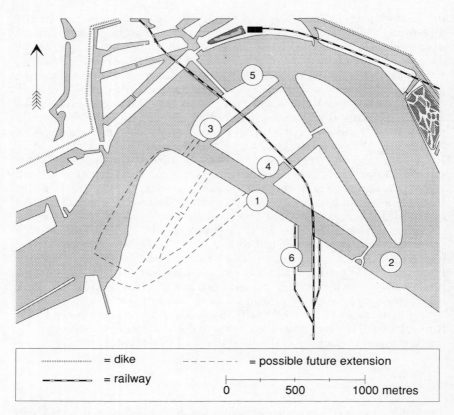

Figure 10.3   Amended Rose Plan (1865) 1. Westerkanaal now 150 metres wide 2. Oosterkanaal and Westerkanaal united 3. Noorderhaven moved northward 4. Zuiderhaven now 100 metres wide 5. Width of the river maintained 6. Railway dock.

Source: GAR, Library, XII B 35.

had moved the south bank forward, with the intention of increasing the velocity of the flow, thereby deepening the water in front of the city and making the city quay better suited for ocean-going vessels (Figure 10.2.5). His design was tackled by the engineers. A gradual widening of the river was considered better for the river as a whole (Figure 10.3.5).[26] A year later the engineers designed an improved passage through Feijenoord by moving the Noorderhaven further to the north (Figure 10.3.3). This way ships could cut their routes short and would avoid extra bridges.[27] Originally the railway dock was planned west of the Westerkanaal (Figure 10.3.6), but the surveyor of Rotterdam Public Works, Van der Tak, proposed another plan: a canal open on one side and closed on the other, almost at the same place as the Westerkanaal (Figure 10.4.1). The railway could then be constructed in a straight line and the expensive bridge over the Westerkanaal could be replaced with a smaller one, thus offering financial advantages for central government (Figure 10.4.2). The expensive Westerkanaal and the Zuiderhaven were abandoned as well, which meant a saving for local finance.[28] The Noorderhaven replaced the Westerkanaal as the main alternative to river navigation and, after protests by the Chamber of Commerce, was widened to 150 metres (Figure 10.4.3).[29] The westerly approaches of the Noorderhaven were extended to prevent a possible silting–up of its south bank.[30] The mouths of the Noorderhaven and the railway dock were combined to ease the navigation of sailing ships (Figure 10.4.4).

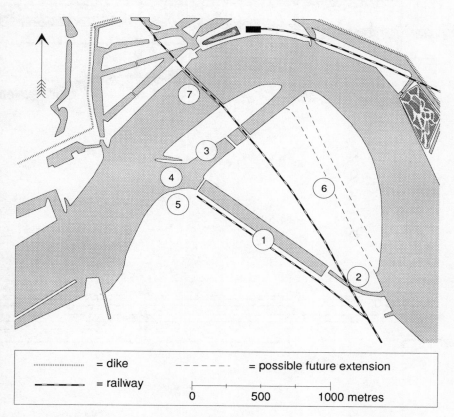

⸱⸱⸱⸱⸱⸱⸱⸱⸱⸱⸱⸱⸱ = dike	‐ ‐ ‐ ‐ ‐ ‐ = possible future extension
—·—·— = railway	0 500 1000 metres

Figure 10.4 Plan Van der Tak (1868) 1. The railway dock replaces the Westerkanaal 2. The railway line can be straightened and the expensive bridge over the Westerkanaal is no longer necessary anymore 3. The Noorderhaven takes over the role of the Westerkanaal. 4. The mouths of the railway dock and the Noorderhaven are combined 5. The western extension that Rose planned is no longer possible 6. The Zuiderhaven has been left out of the plan, the Oosterkanaal is a possible option. 7. The railway bridge includes footbridges.

Source: GAR, Handelingen van de Raad 1868, 122).

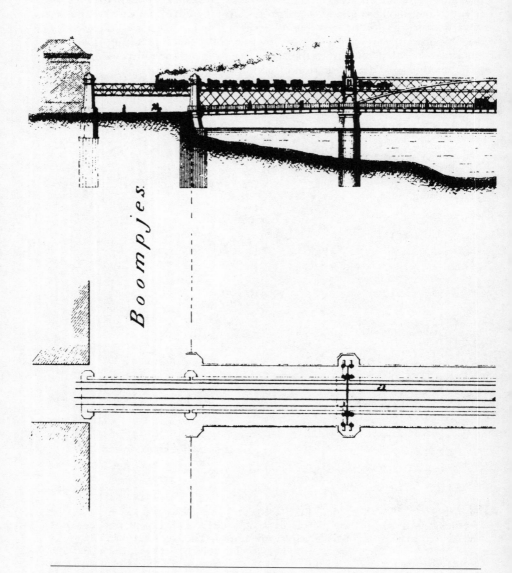

Plate 10.1   The combined rail and road bridge as designed by the surveyor of Rotterdam Public Works Van der Tak in 1865

Source: GAR, Library, XII B 35.

The combination of the mouths provided Rotterdam with another opportunity to cut expenses. Central government was invited to make a contribution to the excavation of the combined mouths. They were prepared to pay for their share of the construction, but accepted no responsibility for the maintenance of the Noorderhaven. Instead they limited their contribution to a single payment of Dfl. 100,000. —[31] Central government reconsidered their decision in 1878 after international protest over the insufficient depth of the Noorderhaven. Central government had often complained to Rotterdam about it, but with no success. As soon as they took over the maintenance, however, the tables were turned and the state now found Rotterdam complaining about insufficient maintenance.[32]

By moving the mouth of the Noorderhaven, Rose's plans for the westward extension of Feijenoord had to be abandoned (Figure 10.4.5). In a later phase another approach was taken. The villages of IJsselmonde, Katendrecht and Charlois who were losing part of their territory to the expanding Rotterdam complained, but the power of Rotterdam, working closely together with central government to make the Feijenoord extension, was superior. In 1869 central government formally confirmed the annexation (Figure 10.1 and 10.5).[33]

One of the advantages of planning the railway bridge in front of the city was the possibility to construct a cheaper city bridge suspended underneath for normal traffic to Feijenoord. This option was soon considered to be too expensive for Rotterdam as well.[34] Moreover, the engineers designing the railway bridge were not very happy with the appendix they had to construct. The necessary strengthening of the pillars would lessen the financial advantage over the building of a separate city bridge.[35] Rotterdam was not prepared to invest in a costly bridge over the river, and in 1868 confined the passage to two footbridges each two metres wide, attached to the railway bridge (Figure 10.4.7). The future city bridge, it was hoped, could, in this way be limited to 8 metres.[36]

In 1870 however Van der Tak advised the Council to forget about the footbridges and make a separate city bridge to the west of the railway bridge after all. Initially the city bridge was planned eastward of the railway bridge, but it soon became clear that the foundation of the pillars of the latter reached too far and would hinder the construction of the city bridge. It therefore was decided to place the bridge to the west of the railway bridge, a location favoured by Van der Tak (Figure 10.7.6). In this way, Van der Tak argued, the bridge would be safer and better protected against water and ice than to the east of the railway bridge. The latter would serve as an ice-breaker.[37] The change of the position of the bridge had its consequences for Feijenoord, for with the bridge the centre of development was moved to the west as well.

Despite the high cost of constructing the bridge only two members of the Council voted against the long-awaited bridging of the river.[38] It is, however, doubtful if the city bridge would have materialized without pressure from outside. The pressure was put on by a consortium of private financiers interested in the extension of Rotterdam on Feijenoord. They were prepared to invest their capital in a well-connected Feijenoord and considered

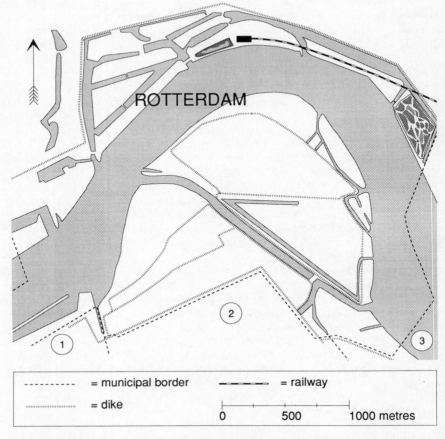

Figure 10.5   The borders of Rotterdam in 1870. Through the annexation of parts of the villages 1. Katendrecht 2. Charlois and 3. IJsselmonde, Rotterdam obtained the jurisdiction over the south bank of the river.

Source: J. Kuyper, Gemeenteatlas van de provincie Zuid–Holland naar officieele bronnen bewerkt (Leeuwarden 1869).

the city bridge as indispensable for a safe investment. In the actual decision to build the bridge the demands of private interest weighed heavily, as did the critical remarks made by the engineer of the consortium about the design of the bridge.[39]

A change of scene

In 1868 the Council decided to finance the extension of Feijenoord by raising taxes and harbour duties. The returns were expected to cover most of the expenses: Dfl. 1 million for Feijenoord and another Dfl. 2 million to build the bridge.[40] It was not realized that the figures were very provisional and the 1870 estimate therefore caused quite a shock. Van der Tak estimated a requirement of just under Dfl. 9 million for the project. The first phase would cost Dfl. 4.6 million.[41] The finance committee of the Council could not solve the problem, and feared for the health of city finance.[42]

L. Pincoffs, member of the Council and the finance committee, came up with a solution. Thanks to his mediation three financiers, who called themselves the Combination, presented themselves to city government: the Rotterdamsche Bank, the Commanditaire Bankvereeniging Rensburg & Van Witsen and a private person, Marten Mees, member of the finance firm R. Mees & Zoonen.[43]

Their engineer, the well-known ir. Th.J. Stieltjes had made a plan for the arrangement of docks and building land, the latter taking a greater part than in the city plans.[44] Obviously the Combination saw a safer perspective in the exploitation of building land than in that of docks. There is another clear indication that the Combination initially had its eye mainly on the selling of building land and not on the exploitation of docks. Stieltjes had planned sluices in the canals to protect Feijenoord against high water. In so doing he could avoid the costly raising of the ground level, but undoubtedly hindered the shipping trade tremendously (figure 10.6).

In its contact with central government Rotterdam defended territorial interests, but in its negotiations with the Combination it set itself up as a defender of the water interest. Local government insisted on extending the dock capacity and, to avoid sluices, stressed the necessity to raise the ground above flood level. The Combination agreed, as it did on many demands from city government, and planned the Binnenhaven (figure 10.7.2). The prospects for mercantile docks were good. ToeWater, local inspector of taxes, presented himself as the first customer of the Combination. He saw possibilities for a bonded warehouse on Feijenoord and planned to rent dock facilities.[45]

In the negotiations Rotterdam was obviously the stronger party, the Combination having to give in to many demands. They were prepared to change the location of the planned docks and accepted the preference of the government to sell the building land; they also agreed to a long lease for the dock area. This way a double agreement was reached: one for the building land, some 160,000 m^2, and one for the dock area, 240,000 m^2. Furthermore, Rotterdam found the Combination prepared to share their profits with the city.[46]

Although the three financiers were very willing they aborted negotiations in October 1872. The same company stayed at the conference table, but Pincoffs, who until then attended the meetings as a mediator, now became the leading man. His Rotterdamsche Handelsvereeniging (RHV), founded seven weeks earlier, took over the role of the Combination as a financier and exploiter of Feijenoord. The Combination excused their withdrawal by pointing at the financial situation in Germany, but a look at the origin of the capital of the Rotterdamsche Handelsvereeniging, predominantly Frankfurt am Main, makes this argument less convincing.[47] There is more reason to

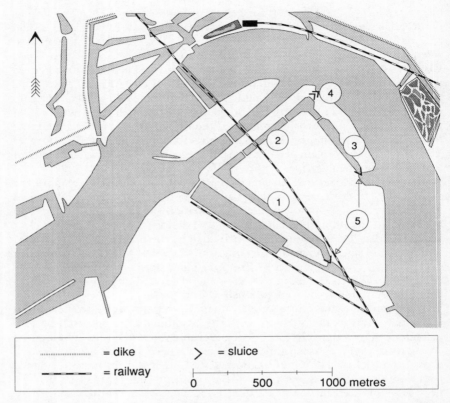

Figure 10.6 Second plan of Stieltjes (1871). In this plan some of the critical remarks of local government are reflected. More docks are planned: 1. Wester Binnenhaven 2. Kleine or Binnen Noorderhaven and 3. Oosterhaven. The sluices, however, remain: 4. Lift lock 5. Other sluices.

Source: GAR, Rotonde Port. GIIE no. 58a.

believe that the change of trade caused the change of scene. As long as the main aim, was to buy and sell land– a reasonably easy and safe undertaking –the financial construction could be quite simple. The exploitation of docks, however, a risky and complicated affair, needed limited liability and an organization with a director at its head. The Rotterdamsche Handelsvereeniging was that organization and Pincoffs acted as its president. The members of the Combination remained at the conference table but from that moment acted as commissioners of the RHV.

Pincoffs stressed the risk of the undertaking and demanded to give as much publicity as possible to the negotiations. Everyone able to offer better conditions should say so, he said, for the RHV would gladly leave the big risk to them. Local government would rather have Public Works construct the docks, quays and bridges and consequently charge the RHV for it,

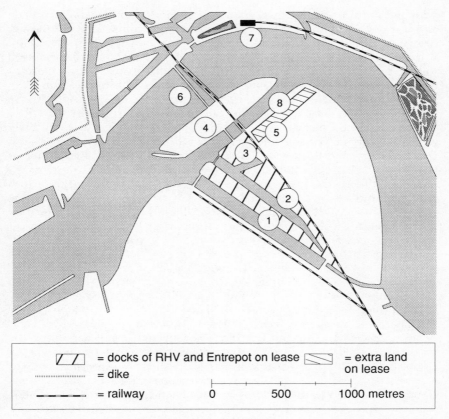

Figure 10.7 The extension of Rotterdam on Feijenoord according to the contracts with the RHV (1872 and 1873). 1. Railway dock 2. Binnenhaven 3. Entrepothaven 4. Noordereiland, main stretch of RHV building land 5. Location of the stretch of land of RHV leased to avoid competition 6. The city bridge is now projected west of the railway bridge 7. The railway station of the Nederlandsche Rhijnspoorwegmaat-schappij 8. The RHV landing-stages in the Noorderhaven.

Source: GAR, Library, XII B 36.

rather than letting the RHV construct the docks themselves. Pincoffs went a step further by asking Rotterdam to take care of all the works, including the raising of the ground level. Pincoffs considered the bridging of the railway dock as essential and therefore suggested a financial contribution from the RHV to let Public Works construct it, adding the condition that the share of Rotterdam in the RHV profits should then be expunged from the contract. Like the Combination he stressed the necessity to protect the RHV against possible competition and therefore claimed the lease of the southern quay of the Noorderhaven eastward from the projected railway (Figure 10.7.5). He also seized the opportunity to apply for local government support for his efforts to obtain a central government concession for a railway line parallel with and north of the Nieuwe Waterweg to Hoek van Holland. His main aim was not to exploit that line, but to prevent his competitor, the railway company Rhijnspoorwegmaatschappij (Figure 10.7.7), from doing so. Rotterdam feared the monopoly of the railway company as well and agreed to talk to the Minister of the Interior about this matter. The minister's reassuring words were sufficient for Pincoffs to drop his reservations.[48]

One month after the change of scene the draft of the contract was presented to the City Council. Instead of a budgetary deficit of Dfl. 1 million the project had a surplus of Dfl. 500,000. — and had an even wider scope. Proudly mayor and aldermen stated that no loans were necessary.[49] On the other hand Rotterdam lost the possession of some 400,000 m^2 of land. Although private initiative was welcomed to lighten Rotterdam's financial burden, the involvement of the RHV did not contribute to a reduction of the deficit. The RHV invested in extra provisions and left the basic investment to Rotterdam. The RHV did meet the need for capital by advancing loans to Rotterdam,[50] but on the other hand local government had to accept extra obligations that exceeded the initial budgetary deficit. It had to construct extra quays for almost Dfl. 1 million and the figures for pavement, sewers and maintenance were higher as well. On balance the contract was no solution but gave extra financial problems. For Alderman Hoffmann this formed the stumbling-block. He therefore insisted on delaying the project for a number of years.[51] The RHV, however, was in a hurry and gave the Council only fourteen days to decide about the contract.

The proposal of mayor and aldermen to lay the future of Feijenoord in the hands of the RHV caused some excitement inside as well as outside the Council. The political association Burgerpligt called for a special meeting to hear the pros and cons.[52] Advocates and adversaries sent letters to the Council,[53] and articles in the local newspapers helped to provoke a public ferment. Feijenoord was given away for a trifle and would be exploited by a sheer monopoly.[54] In a number of crowded meetings, which despite the winter cold took place in a heated atmosphere, the contract was discussed point by point.[55] Besides a rather unfruitful discussion over the price level, the criticism centred on the attempts of the RHV to exclude future competition on the eastern part of Feijenoord by leasing a strip of land along the Noorderhaven (Figure 10.7.5). Though the RHV claimed that it leased the strip to protect its interests in the selling of building-land on Feijenoord, critics saw it as an attempt to monopolize the RHV trading interests on the south bank.

After two long days of debate the decision to sign the contract was taken, the opponents gaining only minor victories: the RHV was kindly requested to reconsider the lease of land along the Noorderhaven. The RHV did not agree, but had to show its goodwill and officially stated that it was prepared to drop the lease if others were prepared to buy the RHV building-land on Feijenoord. In this way the protection of that interest was no longer necessary.[56] A group of well-known citizens, with connections in the opposition, reacted immediately and, like the RHV, deposited an official statement at the office of a solicitor. They offered to take over the RHV building-land for the same price, that the RHV would pay for it. This, however, was not the intention of the RHV and they manoeuvred to reject the offer without losing face. In their letter to the Council the RHV juggled with figures to demonstrate that the price offered was unrealistic. To the regret of the potential buyers and the opposition in the Council the boldness of the RHV had no consequences. The Council did not revert to the subject and considered the case closed.[57] One could easily have the impression that the RHV were determined to gain as much as possible at the lowest possible price; the construction of the docks and the layout of the building–land could, however, stand the test. Local government were consulted about the layout of the building land north of the Noorderhaven and the result of their co-operative effort had the approval of the city council.[58] The construction of the docks is a fine example of the willingness of the RHV to pay more and acquire the best. It designed a Binnenhaven with steep quays to facilitate the handling of cargo (Figure 10.7.2). Instead of putting cargo on the landing–stage first, the ship could be loaded directly from the trains. Local government constructed cheaper oblique quays, but were encouraged by the RHV to design steep quays as well, the RHV being prepared to pay two-thirds of the extra cost involved.

The quay of the eastern part of the railway dock was constructed under these conditions (Figure 10.7.1), but as far as the Noorderhaven was concerned the council reached other conclusions. A recent collapse of the steep Entrepothaven quay (Figure 10.7.3) obviously contributed to the attitude of the council.[59]

Table 10.1 Prices for the construction of quays at Feijenoord (prices in Dfl. per metre run)

docks	oblique	steep
RHV docks		Dfl. 600.–
Railway dock		Dfl. 700.–
Noorderhaven	Dfl. 145.–	Dfl. 450.–

Source: Directeur Gemeentewerken-Commissie Plaatselijke Werken 29 November 1874, GAR, NSA, Rb. 1875: 123.

Municipal after all

On 24 October 1878 a procession of coaches carrying the mayor and his aldermen and the other members of the Council visited Feijenoord to celebrate the completion of the task of local government in the project. Rotterdam had kept its part of the bargain: a bridge connected Feijenoord with Rotterdam and the Noorderhaven was ready and bridged as well. The co-operative and flexible attitude of the RHV was a sufficient guarantee that they would keep their side of the bargain.

On 14 May 1879 the president of the RHV, Pincoffs, completely unexpectedly left the country in a hurry. Afraid that the administrative malpractice with one of his other companies, the Afrikaansche Handelsvereeniging (AHV), would become known, and convinced that he could no longer count on the support of his colleagues, he fled to America. The AHV was a commercial disaster, which Pincoffs tried to camouflage by manipulating the books, thereby using funds from other companies, including the RHV. The relationship between local government and the RHV, which flourished during the project on Feijenoord was given a severe blow by Pincoffs' flight.[60] The president of the Chamber of Commerce, together with a prominent Rotterdam businessman, formed the new board of the RHV. They were appointed to prevent the potentially profitable RHV from going bankrupt along with the AHV. Without the completion of the project on Feijenoord the RHV could not collect the fruits of their work, but the money to complete it was not available. Pincoffs' juggling of the AHV accounts had also cast a shadow over the RHV. Thanks to a loan from the Nederlandsche Handel-Maatschappij (NHM) and an agreement with the creditors to postpone payment on debts, the RHV, for the time being, survived and completed the project.[61]

The profitability of the RHV did not materialize, however, because the ultra-modern docks remained almost empty. To stay in the RHV docks ships were obliged to pay harbour dues to the RHV and to local government as well. The city harbour master considered this to be the main reason for the low performance of the RHV.[62]

The greater activity on the river again stressed the need for protection from the elements in winter. In emergencies local government were forced to remit ships to the railway dock. The Binnenhaven was also regularly used for that purpose. In 1881 the RHV announced that ships seeking protection would be charged half the local harbour dues. On the outcry of indignation by local government the RHV stressed that it regarded the charge as legitimate, nevertheless it decided to postpone the introduction: The city obtained other landing-stages by cancelling the RHV concessions for landing-stages in the Noorderhaven and convinced the RHV of the necessity to take a more humble stand (Figure 10.7.8). The RHV management requested local government to continue the concession for the Noorderhaven landing-stages, which were important for the company. To their 'satisfaction' the commissioners of the RHV had authorized them to permit ships free of charge in the Binnenhaven.[63]

The problematic relationship between Rotterdam and the RHV was not limited to the Binnenhaven. The railway dock also played a role in spoiling the atmosphere. From central government Rotterdam obtained the right to exploit the eastern side of the railway dock. Rotterdam agreed on the construction of modern quays there and its exploitation by the RHV from their adjacent territory. The RHV soon made agreements with the railway company that exploited the west side of the dock and together they ruled the railway dock, to the dissatisfaction of local government. Central government intervened, placed the railway dock under central government control and appointed a state harbour master.[64] Rotterdam could send ships to the railway dock, but without the permission of the RHV they were not allowed to use the RHV quay for loading and unloading goods. Using an anchor and loading onto other ships would be the solution, but central government regulations for the railway dock forbade the use of anchors.[65] The problems increased as central government came in conflict with the railway company. The latter exploited the western quay of the railway dock, and according to its contract with the state, it would be obliged only to the maintenance of the quay if the state did not impose harbour dues. Stopping the imposition of harbour dues would, however, create a strange anomaly, and was considered unacceptable.[66]

The city was confronted with a shortage of landing-stages, while the ultra-modern docks on Feijenoord remained empty. Because its jurisdiction was limited, it couldn't solve the problem in an easy way. The number of ships visiting Rotterdam increased steadily and a solution had to be found. The new surveyor of Rotterdam Public Works, De Jongh, was asked to investigate the possibility of constructing a breakwater west of Feijenoord and using it as a landing stage. De Jongh, however, conceived his task to be much wider and designed a 30-hectare dock, in which the construction of a breakwater was the first step to take.[67] The decision to build the dock gave local government room to breathe, but a solution for the inconvenient situation on Feijenoord still had to be found.

Despite the loan of the Nederlandsche Handel-Maatschappij and the creditor's restraint the future of the RHV was precarious. The completion of the Nieuwe Waterweg would certainly have contributed to a more optimistic outlook, but the project to connect Rotterdam with the sea was suffering some very severe setbacks and these cast a doubt on the viability of the RHV. Even its first customer had to face the facts. The result of the entrepôt remained poor, and it was thus unable to pay its rent.[68] The RHV management was fighting hard to survive and on several occasions asked local government for support. A consortium headed by the Banque Centrale Anversoise was prepared to supply the RHV a loan of Dfl. 6.5 million, but found it safer to use Rotterdam as an intermediary. Local government turned down the request.[69] M. Mainz jr from Frankfurt am Main on behalf of a number of banks offered to supply Dfl. 7 million to Rotterdam to buy out the RHV. This offer fitted in the RHV option to sell the docks and to rent them from Rotterdam, but city government again turned down the proposal. Wiser by experience they accepted only complete local control in the Feijenoord docks.[70]

In the negotiations that followed the RHV agreed on selling its assets for Dfl. 4.5 million. Rotterdam, however, offered only Dfl. 3.5 million. At that moment eight members of the City Council intervened and proposed to offer Dfl. 4 million to prevent a probable stalemate.[71] Council and RHV agreed to the price and signed an agreement (1882),[72] thereby bringing a short but emotional private interlude in the history of the dock development of Rotterdam to a conclusion. The building-land owned by the RHV was not included in the sale, but came under control of a new company. For every RHV share of Dfl. 250.—the shareholders received a share in the new company worth Dfl. 12.50.[73]

The essence

For Rotterdam the extension of Feijenoord obviously was an increase in local government activities. We can hardly say that the City Council freely chose to do so, central government forced Rotterdam to start the project. Nor can we say that Rotterdam hesitated to extend the city on the left bank because of ideological, *laissez-faire* reasons. Rotterdam was reluctant to do so simply for financial reasons. Rotterdam put a lot of energy in finding someone else to pay the bill and central government were obviously candidate to finance the project. To a certain extent Rotterdam succeeded in doing so, for the construction of the railway dock—the Westerkanaal in Rose's plan—and the maintenance of the Noorderhaven were financed by the state and for the westerly extension of the Noorderhaven central government paid their share. The main expenditure, however, the bridge, was to be paid by Rotterdam alone. A postponement of the construction was therefore agreed.

The second candidate to present the bill to was private enterprise. There is no reason to think that Rotterdam had noble, *laissez-faire* reasons to award private enterprise with the extension project. Again financial motives played the leading role. This time, however, Rotterdam did not succeed in its intentions. Pincoffs was an experienced negotiator profiting from his experience in the Council and in its finance committee. Besides, he had an outstanding reputation. He managed to reach a profitable agreement giving him a virtual monopoly on Feijenoord.

In the end, however, things turned out completely different. Pincoffs ran to avoid arrest. He left the Rotterdamsche Handelsvereeniging in trouble, short of financial breath and generating a bad result, caused by double harbour duties and a blocked Nieuwe Waterweg. For three more years the Feijenoord apple was left on the tree. Once ripe it could easily be picked by Rotterdam. An investment of Dfl. 12 million was obtained with Dfl. 4 million, indeed a financial success. Yet this time the buying of the assets of the RHV was not motivated with financial arguments. The problems Rotterdam faced in dealing with the company and the irritation it caused, had taken away Rotterdam's desire to co-operate. Traditionally Rotterdam had been lord and master over the docks and only a few years under RHV rule were sufficient to convince it that this tradition should be maintained. Rotterdam tried hard to balance the budget and to present the bill to someone else, but its opponents tried just as hard to reduce cost. The outcome was therefore hard to predict. The lack of foresight is obvious and it remained but a proverbial wish.

Notes

1. Ravesteyn, 1924, passim, still serves as a good introduction. Also Nieuwenhuis 1955, passim. The archives used are all at the Gemeentelijke Archiefdienst Rotterdam (GAR).
2. W.N. Rose to Commissie Plaatselijke Werken 28 April Raadsbijlage (Rb.) 1861:421.
3. The Rose Plan, 4 February 1862, *Uitbreiding van de gemeente Rotterdam op Feyenoord en de daarmee verband houdende staatsspoorwegverbinding; 1855–1873* (2 volumes) (GAR Library XII B 35). This was an elaborated version of the one he presented in 1847: Cie over stadsgebouwen, eigendommen enz. to Burgemeester & Wethouders (B & W) 15 March 1847, NSA, Ink.nr. B & W 1847:1315.
4. Handelingen van de Raad 12 November 1863, 79.
5. For instance 30 September 1840, 18 November 1841 and 6 September 1845, NSA, Ink.nr. B & W 1840:2175, 2821 and 2799.
6. Woud, van der 1987: 98.
7. The levying of tariffs is not discussed in detail.
8. Lintsen 1980:282.
9. Woud, van der 1987:100–5.
10. Minister of the Interior to B & W 8 January 1868, NSA, Ink.nr. B & W 1868:140.
11. *Staatsblad* 1869:75, pp. 45, 55 and 82.
12. Jonckers Nieboer 1938:90–6.
13. Minister van Binnenlandsche Zaken to B & W 24 December 1863, NSA, Ink.nr. B & W 1863:4249.
14. Commissie Plaatselijke Werken to B & W 8 January 1864, NSA, Ink.nr. B & W 1864:74.
15. Oosterwijk 1979: passim.
16. *Handelingen* 20 January 1865, 7 (Pincoffs).
17. Kamer van Koophandel to Minister van Binnenlandsche Zaken 29 January 1864, *Uitbreiding Rotterdam op Feyenoord*.
18. Burgemeester to B & W 22 June 1867, NSA, Ink.nr. B & W 1867:2765.
19. A future connection with the station north of the city was considered.
20. Kamer van Koophandel to Minister van Binnenlandsche Zaken 7 September 1867, NSA, Ink.nr. B & W 1867:3931.
21. Commissie voor de audiëntie to B & W 27 July 1867, NSA, Ink.nr. B & W 1867:3270. Besloten vergadering van de Raad 3 October 1867 and 10 October 1867, *Handelingen* 9 December 1868, 251–2. Minister van Binnenlandsche Zaken to B & W 7 February 1868, NSA, Ink.nr. B & W 1868:601. B & W to Gemeenteraad 17 August 1868, *Handelingen* 17 August 1868, 117–9.
22. B & W to Minister van Binnenlandsche Zaken 29 June 1868, NSA, Uitg.nr. B & W 1868:837.
23. *Handelingen* 3, 4, 8, 9, 10 and 11 December 1868, 229–76.
24. Dirk Visser to Commissie tot onderzoek der plannen van uitbreiding en verdere bebouwing der stad Rotterdam, April 1862, *Uitbreiding Rotterdam op Feyenoord*. Dirk Visser to Commissie Plaatselijke Werken 3 May 1864, Ibid. Commissie voor de Rhijnvaart te Rotterdam to Minister van Financiën (copy to B & W Rotterdam) ibid.
25. Kamer van Koophandel to B & W 28 August 1868, NSA, Ink.nr. B & W 1868:5.
26. Rapport van de commissie van onderzoek nopens den invloed op de Maas van

eene uitbreiding der gemeente Rotterdam op Feijenoord, 19 February 1863, *Uitbreiding Rotterdam op Feyenoord*. Gewijzigd plan tot uitbreiding der gemeente Rotterdam op Feijenoord 13 September 1864, ibid.

27. Waterstaats-commissie voor de uitbreiding van Rotterdam op Feijenoord (Conrad, J.A. Beyerinck and P. Caland) to B & W 19 November 1864, *Uitbreiding Rotterdam op Feyenoord*.
28. Rose and Van der Tak to Commissie Plaatselijke Werken 30 November 1867, *Handelingen* 17 August 1868, 119–20.
29. Kamer van Koophandel to B & W 28 August 1868, Rb.1868:464. *Handelingen* 10 December 1868, 263.
30. In this Rotterdam followed the advice of the Minister of the Interior: Minister van Binnenlandse Zaken to B & W 7 February 1868, NSA, Ink.nr. B & W 1868:601. Commissie Plaatselijke Werken to B & W 27 March 1868, NSA, Ink.nr. B & W 1868:1440.
31. Minister van Binnenlandse Zaken to B & W 15 July 1868 and 22 January 1869, NSA, Ink.nr. B & W 1868:3222 and 351.
32. Minister van Binnenlandse zaken to B & W 14 February 1877, 31 May 1877, 6 August 1877, NSA, Ink.nr. B & W 1877:785, 2906, 3877. B & W to Minister van Binnenlandse zaken 13 August 1877, NSA, Uitg.nr. B & W 1877:1171. *Handelingen* 7 February 1879. Commissie Plaatselijke Werken to B & W, NSA, Ink.nr. B & W 1878:5381.
33. *Handelingen* 9 December 1868, 248. Law of 15 July 1869, *Staatsblad* no. 128.
34. Besloten vergadering van de raadscommissie Financiën 4 October 1867 and 30 November 1867.
35. Rose and Van der Tak to Commissie Plaatselijke Werken 31 August 1869, NSA, Ink.nr. B & W 1869:3679.
36. *Handelingen* 9 December 1868, 249. Geschreven Notulen van de Raad 25 November 1869.
37. V.d. Tak (co-signed by Rose) to Commissie Plaatselijke Werken 15 December 1870, *Uitbreiding Rotterdam op Feyenoord*.
38. *Handelingen* 27 October 1870, 111–13. Ibid. 1 February 1872.
39. T.J. Stieltjes to B & W 28 August 1876, appendix to *Handelingen* 21 September 1876, 81–2. Ibid. 21 March 1878.
40. B & W to Raad 18 November 1868, appendix to *Handelingen* 19 November 1868, 189–92.
41. V.d. Tak (co-signed by Rose) to Commissie Plaatselijke Werken 15 December 1870, *Uitbreiding Rotterdam op Feyenoord*. B & W to Commissie Plaatselijke Werken 17 March 1871, NSA, Uitg.nr. B & W 1871:348. Directeur Gemeentewerken to Commissie Plaatselijke Werken 29 March 1871, appendix of *Handelingen* 1 June 1871, 76.
42. Commissie voor de Financiën to B & W 17 May 1871, Rb.1871:2980. *Handelingen* 22 June 1871.
43. Mees 1946: passim.
44. Rose, Van der Tak and Stieltjes to B & W 28 July 1871, NSA, Ink.nr. B & W 1871:3679.
45. ToeWater to B & W 13 June 1871 and 20 November 1871, *Uitbreiding Rotterdam op Feyenoord*.
46. Commissie Plaatselijke Werken to B & W 4 May 1872, NSA, Ink.nr. B & W 1872:1964. Appendix 1a and 1b to Notulen B & W 1872–1875, NSA:1221.
47. Notulen B & W 1 November 1872, NSA:1221. Handschriften:3268–3272.
48. Notulen B & W 1 November 1872, NSA:1221. *Handelingen* 7 April 1873, 45–6.
49. *Handelingen* 11 December 1872, 116–20.

50. An advance in the form of a 5 per cent loan of Dfl. 1 million in the fourth and fifth year of construction.
51. *Handelingen* 27 December 1872, 138.
52. *Rotterdamsche Courant* 22 December 1872.
53. *Handelingen* 27 December 1872, 127.
54. *Rotterdamsche Courant* 22 and 27 December 1872. *Nieuwe Rotterdamsche Courant* 28 December 1872.
55. *Handelingen* 27 and 28 December 1872, 127–50.
56. RHV to B & W, appendix to *Handelingen* 2 January 1873.
57. *Handelingen* 16 January 1873, 5–8. Ibid. 23 January 1873, 10–12.
58. GAR Library *Verzamelingen* 1880:1. *Handelingen* 5 February 1880, 17–23. *Ibid.* 4 March 1880, 30–3.
59. *Handelingen* 20 August 1874, 64–5. Ibid. 27 August 1874, 72–5. Ibid. 25 March 1875, 31–3. Ibid. 8 April 1875, 35–8. B & W to Raad 4 March 1875, Rb.1875:123.
60. *Weekblad van het Regt* 12 January 1880 and 13 January 1880. Oosterwijk 1979: passim.
61. GAR Library *Verzamelingen* 1879:28. The city of Rotterdam was also a creditor of the RHV.
62. Havenmeester to Burgemeester 14 August 1880, NSA, Ink.nr. B & W 1880:4272.
63. RHV to B & W 26 April 1881, 28 April 1881 and 17 May 1881, NSA, Ink.nr. B & W 1881:2241, 2297 and 2647. B & W to RHV 27 April 1881, NSA, Uitg.nr. B & W 1881:0562.
64. *Handelingen* 30 December 1880, 226. B & W to Minister van Waterstaat Handel en Nijverheid 2 May 1881, 28 January 1882 and 23 February 1882, NSA, Uitg.nr. B & W 1881:591, 1882:152 and 298. Ministerie van Waterstaat Handel en Nijverheid to B & W 17 January 1882, 4 February 1882 and 3 March 1882, NSA, Ink.nr. B & W 1882:286, 636 and 1125.
65. Reglement voor de Spoorweghaven 8 December 1878 *Staatsblad* 1878:176.
66. B & W to Minister van Waterstaat Handel en Nijverheid 2 May 1881, NSA, Uitg.nr. B & W 1881:591.
67. Commissie Plaatselijke Werken to B & W 3 June 1881 and 17 February 1882, NSA, Ink.nr. B & W 1881:2992 and 927.
68. B & W to Raad 20 December 1880, *Verzamelingen* 1880:45, 322.
69. Rb.1880:730. *Verzamelingen* 1880:45. *Handelingen* 30 December 1880, 225–32. Ibid. 31 December 1880, 233–8.
70. M. Mainz jr to B & W 9 March 1881 and 24 April 1881, NSA, Ink.nr. B & W 1881:1535 and 2223. B & W to M. Mainz jr, 24 April 1881, NSA, Ink.nr. B & W 1881:354.
71. *Handelingen* 25 April 1882, 45–51.
72. *Handelingen* 8 and 29 June 1882. GAR Library *Verz.* 1882:19 and 20.
73. Final report of the RHV 1882, GAR Bedrijfsarchief Mees, 636. Maatschappij tot verkoop en bebouwing van gronden op Feijenoord te Rotterdam founded 1882, *Staatscourant* 11 November 1882.

Bibliography

Anonymous (1839), *Betoog van de noodzakelijkheid eener vereeniging van het Eiland Feijenoord met de stad Rotterdam ook in het belang van de algemeene welvaart*, The Hague.

Anonymous (1928), *Kamer van Koophandel en Fabrieken 1803–1928*, Rotterdam.

Beyerinck, J.A. (1849), 'Verhandeling over de indijking en uitbreiding der stad Rotterdam', *Nieuwe Verhandelingen v. h. Bataafsch Genootschap voor Proefondervindelijk wijsbegeerte*, Volume IX, 2nd part.

Edzes, H. (1879), *100,150 jaar Vrij Entrepot, 'n stukje geschiedenis van Rotterdam*, Rotterdam.

Es, F.N. van (1972), *De ontwikkeling van de Rotterdamse haven in de periode 1850–1914*. Rotterdam.

Fritschy, Wantje (1983), 'Spoorwegaanleg in Nederland van 1831 tot 1845 en de rol van de staat', *ESHJ*, 46: 180–227.

Hansen, G., B. Jacobson and S. Meester (1980), *De uitleg van Rotterdam-Zuid 1880–1980*, Utrecht.

Hazewinkel, H.C. (1937), 'Feijenoord', *Rotterdamsch Jaarboekje*, 4th series 5: 1–46.

Hogesteeger, G. (1977), *De verbinding van Rotterdam met zee in de tweede helft van de negentiende eeuw*, Rotterdam.

Jonckers Nieboer, J.H. (1938), *Geschiedenis der Nederlandsche Spoorwegen 1832–1938*, reprint, Rotterdam.

Lintsen, H.W. (1980), *Ingenieurs in Nederland, een streven naar erkenning en macht*, The Hague.

Mees, W.C. (1946), *Man van de daad, Mr. Marten Mees en de opkomst van Rotterdam*, Rotterdam.

Nieuwenhuis, J. (1955), *Mensen maken een stad 1855–1955, Uit de geschiedenis van de Dienst van Gemeentewerken te Rotterdam*, Rotterdam.

Noort, Jan van den (1990), *Pion of pionier, Rotterdam-gemeentelÿke debzijvigheid in de nogentiende eeuw*, Rotterdam.

Oosterwijk, Bram (1979), *Vlucht na victorie, Lodewijk Pincoffs (1827–1911)*, Rotterdam.

Pincoffs, Adolph L. (1927), 'Lodewijk Pincoffs door zijn zoon Adolph L. Pincoffs' *Rotterdamsch Jaarboekje*, 3rd series 5: 68–74.

Prak, N.L. (1986), 'De oorspronkelijke bebouwing van het Eerste Nieuwe Werk te Rotterdam', *Bulletin KNOB* 85: 57–71.

Ravesteyn, L.J.C.J. van (1924), *Rotterdam in de negentiende eeuw, de ontwikkeling der stad*. Rotterdam, reprint Schiedam 1974.

Rogier, L.J. (1953), *Rotterdam tegen het midden van de negentiende eeuw*, Rotterdam.

Rogier, L.J. (1953), *Rotterdam in het derde kwart van de negentiende eeuw*, Rotterdam.

Stieltjes, T.J. and A.W. Mees (1876), *De werken der Rotterdamsche Handelsvereeniging op Feijenoord. Atlas*. Rotterdam.

Woud, A. van der (1987), *Het lege land, de ruimtelijke orde van Nederland 1798–1848*, Amsterdam.

Wijtvliet, C.A.M. (1989), 'De Nederlandse Handel-Maatschappij; van handelsonderneming naar bankbedrijf', *Jaarboek voor de Geschiedenis van Bedrijf en Techniek*, 6: 96–118.

IJsselsteyn, H.A. van (1900), *De haven van Rotterdam*, Rotterdam.

IJsselsteyn, H.A. van (1907), 'De haven van Rotterdam', *Rotterdam in de loop der eeuwen*, Rotterdam.

11 The city council and the economic élite: Haarlem 1890–1920

Boudien de Vries

Introduction

The population of Dutch cities grew incredibly fast between the 1880s and 1920. A combination of natural population growth and migration from the country to the city was responsible for the steady and rapid increase in the number of inhabitants. In this way Amsterdam's population increased from more than 300,000 inhabitants to more than 500,000. In the same period Rotterdam doubled its population from 150,000 to 300,000 and The Hague had gained almost 100,000 inhabitants. Smaller cities too—Arnhem, Groningen, Nijmegen and Haarlem—showed high population growth rates until the turn of the century. In comparison with the modest increase of the urban population in previous decades this development had a spectacular character.

The urban expansion forced local authorities to take decisions regarding town planning, sanitation and infrastructure. The official *laissez-faire* policy held that the government was to interfere as little as possible with the economic process, in order to make 'the invisible hand' function at its maximum effectiveness. Nevertheless the city authorities were forced to interfere because chaos had to be prevented at all costs. The planning of new residential quarters had to be initiated, likewise the building of streets and bridges and the dismantling of old city walls. The attention of the city authorities was also drawn to building sewerage and waterworks, to licences for abattoirs and to grants for gas works and power-stations. It was imperative also (most of the time at the instigation of the national government) to put more energy into health services, education, administration of the population and into the tapping of municipal sources of revenue, such as local taxes. None of these areas of government interference was entirely new, but the increasing number of people forced the urban authorities to face an accomplished fact: a more active attitude had become imperative. In their daily lives, the citizens were increasingly confronted with the government's 'visible hand'.

Yet where was the limit? How far would this government interference reach? It is clear that at the end of the nineteenth century urban authorities began to feel responsible (in principle) for 'the infrastructural well-being' of the individual citizen. A residential quarter needed paved roads, safety was served by street lighting, sewerage and waterworks prevented outbreaks of contagious diseases. In practice sanitary conditions above all were deplorable in the fast-growing cities and housing was purely a private affair before the turn of the century, almost without any government regulation.

What was in fact the policy as far as *economic* infrastructure was concerned? Did the City Council feel that it was up to them to encourage trade and industry by the construction of, for instance, factory sites, harbours loading docks warehouses? The construction of such infrastructural provisions is very expensive; therefore it is hardly possible to leave it to private initiative. Moreover, these projects do not lend themselves to financing by means of the issue of shares and bonds; for instance, hardly any profit is to be expected from railway enterprises. Profit is to be found in an improvement of the climate for investment: a sound economic infrastructure stimulates both the extension of existing enterprises and the founding of new ones. Direct profits for the government by means of harbour dues etc., are few. Indirectly, an increase of general welfare will possibly ensue in the course of time, entailing an increase of tax revenues.

Unlike the social infrastructure, the economic area does not generally force the City Council to take measures. There is rather the possibility of choice in this area either to start projects or not. This raises the question of which factors influence this kind of choice. Under what circumstances does the government abandon the *laissez-faire* policy and start to take active steps to promote the economic infrastructure? Undoubtedly, the composition of the City Council is an important factor. Would it be too cynical to suppose that some members of this Council would welcome projects with reference to the common good, the more so as their own interest would be served by them? We may expect that those city councillors who themselves have interests in trade and industry will advocate the improvement of the economic infrastructure. In other words, it depends only on the capability of any local economic élite to influence the decisions of the council. This influence may be exercised either directly (members of the economic élite are councillors themselves) or indirectly: interest groups belonging to the economic élite may exercise pressure on councillors to take certain decisions. As the economic élite rarely had the majority in the local corporations at the end of the nineteenth century, a combination of both direct and indirect influences would have presented itself most of the time.

The previous paragraph is, of course, an extreme simplification. Members of the economic élite have different interests; therefore they will be divided regarding the desirability of certain projects. Councillors who have no immediate interest in a proposal might fervently support it for political reasons. Infrastructural projects of other cities may evoke feelings of envy and a sense of retardation on the part of the councillors; in this way the general mood may be influenced. The economic tide may work either favourably or unfavourably, etc. An accurate investigation of the discussions about *one* specific project serves better, therefore, to provide insight into the decision-making mechanisms and the factors influencing these mechanisms, than the rough general picture drawn above. To put it briefly, the balance of power between the conservative forces which disapprove of any government interference on the one hand, and the progressive movement which actually attributes the area of economic infrastructure to the government on the other hand, becomes clear in this way.

In this chapter we shall concentrate on the dispute about the building of a railway harbour in Haarlem between 1890 and 1920. Haarlem, a city 25 kilometres west of Amsterdam, had at the end of the nineteenth century a fast-growing population. Between 1890 and 1920 the population grew from 50,000 to 80,000 inhabitants, which made Haarlem the fifth largest city in the Netherlands. The most important expanding branches of industry were metals, building and graphics. Famous metal companies were the Koninklijke Fabriek van Rijtuigen en Spoorwegwagons (Royal Factory of Carriages and Railway carriages) of J.J.F. Beynes, the engineering works of the Figee Brothers and the Conrad shipyard. As far as graphics industry was concerned, the company of Joh. Enschedé en Zonen was by far the biggest and most modern firm.

The building of a railway harbour was an urgent wish of Haarlem industrialists. The fulfilment of this wish, however, was hampered by the attitude of the municipality; the local authorities hesitated and acted very slowly. Between 1890 and 1920 the building of a harbour was frequently the subject of heated arguments in which the Court of Mayor and Aldermen was alternately for or against the project. The Council too, changed its ground continually. This causes the Haarlem harbour to be a highly interesting subject of investigation. Was the changing view of the urban authorities related to a changing composition of the Court of Mayor and Aldermen? To what extent could the industrial élite penetrate the Council or Court? What other opportunities did the industrial élite have to raise its voice, apart from representation in the Council?

The harbour project is also worthy of investigation because it concerns a strictly local matter. The building of a railway section too, will, on a local level, involve discussions about the desirability of improving the infrastructure; in this case, however, scope for decision-making is constrained by regional or national corporations.

In the subsequent part of this chapter attention is paid first to the composition of the Council between 1890 and 1920. Professions and incomes of the councillors are, where possible, compared with those of the electorate and the entire Haarlem population. This comparison is preceded by a brief survey of the electoral system. Second, we shall investigate the party which is most directly concerned: the Haarlem Chamber of Commerce and Manufacture, which addressed the Council many times. Finally, we shall concentrate on the lengthy affair of the railway harbour.

Electors and the elect

At the end of the nineteenth century the Netherlands had, like so many
West European countries, a system of direct elections for the national
Parliament, the regional corporations, and the city councils. The vote,
however, was as elsewhere, reserved for a small section of the population,
who alone possessed the right to express their opinion about the constitution of the councils, boards or chambers which exercised political power.
Although the electoral system varied from country to country, landed
property and overall wealth constituted the most important criteria everywhere for the right to vote. Only wealthy citizens were considered to be
able to elect the proper representatives in the corporations. Political power
was to be acquired by those people who would defend the interests of the
propertied classes, thus in practice securing peace and tranquillity. The
influence of the majority of the population on local and national government was nil.

Between 1851 and 1887, 5 per cent of the entire Dutch population were
enfranchised for the City Council, only 3 per cent for the national
Parliament (De Vries 1971, 184). One had to pay a certain amount of tax to
qualify for the vote. This poll-access tax was linked to the number of
inhabitants in a municipality. For the poll three different kinds of taxes were
taken into account: land tax, a levy on real estate; inhabited house duty,
imposed on outward signs of wealth such as the rentable, value of the house
one occupied, the value of the furniture and the number of residential
servants, etc.; and the licence fee for the exercise of a profession or the
running of a business. In Haarlem *f*25 in taxes qualified to vote for the City
Council; twice this amount was required for the grant of voting rights for
the Second Chamber. This put Haarlem in the same category as cities like
Groningen and Leiden (De Vries 1971, 228). In cities of such a size the
minimum tax level was so high that only a small proportion of the population acquired the right to vote, the more so because there was still another
restriction which at the time was so much taken for granted that it was not
even mentioned in the electoral law: women, though they might meet the
tax requirements, had no voting rights. In this respect the Dutch situation
was, of course, not at all exceptional.

At that time 4.5 per cent of the entire Haarlem population had voting
rights for the City Council, that is, 20 per cent of the adult male population.
In absolute numbers it meant 1,238 electors in 1851 and 2,119 electors in
1886 (Messing 1972, 140; Gemeenteverslag 1886). For the Second Chamber
the percentage of adult males entitled to vote was even lower (12 per cent).
This does not, however, comprise only the élite either here or in Groningen
which had a similar proportion of voters.[1] A section of the middle classes—
shopkeepers, artisans and minor Civil Servants—also qualified.[2] The power
to influence the composition of the City Council existed in theory, but
practice there was little interest in the elections: scarcely 50 per cent of the
electorate actually voted. Time and again they chose the same representatives in the Council. The councillors' average term of office was at least
nineteen to twenty years (Messing 1972, 141). All twenty-five councillors

belonged to the category of the town notability with the highest incomes (Messing 1972, 282). The City Council was controlled by prominent judges and solicitors, rich bankers, wealthy merchants, gentlemen of leisure and some entrepreneurs. The Council constituted a conservative–liberal stronghold, set against every form of government interference in the economic area.

The far-reaching restriction of voting rights in the period before 1887 was inspired by the thought that only a high poll-tax could guarantee the exclusion of unfit or unworthy electors. On the part of the conservatives and liberals especially, all were fiercely opposed to extending the electorate by lowering the poll-tax. The conservatives taking the lead in the national Parliament in the 1860s and 1870s knew how to check reforms successfully. The call for voting rights grew louder, however, first in progressive liberal circles, later on also in socialist circles. Change had become inevitable in the 1880s.

The first step was taken with the 1887 revision of the constitution. The difference between the poll-tax for the Second Chamber and for the City Council was dropped; the poll-tax itself was lowered a little, but the link with the number of inhabitants in a municipality continued to exist. In Haarlem the right to vote was extended to anyone who had a house with a rentable value of *f*55 or more and was thus assessed for inhabited house duty, or anyone who paid *f*10 land tax. Consequently the Haarlem electorate grew from over 600 to 2,781 in 1889, that is, 25 per cent of the adult male population (Messing 1972, 140).

This first reform was modest, but the new election law of 1896 made the circle of electors considerably wider. The social tide, which no longer allowed that only a small group should possess political rights, was not to be turned back now. Yet fear of electors from the lower classes continued to exist. Certain tax criteria continued in force, although the minimum required amounts were drastically lowered. The election law mentioned other criteria also, such as a certain income or pension, or some 'skill' proved by the possession of certificates. The election system was complicated, to put it mildly, and it gave the municipalities much administrative trouble. The number of electors, however, grew steadily, in absolute numbers as well as in percentages of the population. The gradual expansion of the electorate culminated in 1917, when universal suffrage for men was introduced. Two years later women also received voting rights. Table 11.1 summarizes the growth in the number of electors during the period 1859–1920.

Though this steadily increasing electorate had the possibility, in principle, of influencing the composition of the City Council, people took little interest in the elections. Compulsory voting did not exist until 1917; usually, only half of the electorate took the trouble to fill in the voting-paper (Messing 1972, 140). Only the elections for the Second Chamber aroused somewhat more interest. The composition of the electorate, however, changed as the poll-tax threshold fell. How far did the City Council reflect this change? Did the élite, which had a firm control over everything at the time of limited voting rights, have to give up its power? Did industrializa-

Table 11.1   Electors and the City Council, 1859–1920

Year	Number of electors	Population	a	b
1859	1,238	27,719	4.5	19
1879	1,684	36,976	4.5	20
1889	2,781	50,500	5.5	25
1899	5,724	64,079	8.9	43
1909	9,314	69,410	13.4	52
1918	16,417	74,816	22.0	100
1920	38,042	76,302	49.8	–

a = share of total population
b = share of adult male population

Sources: Messing 1972, 2 and 140; *Census* 1899 and 1909; *Gemeenteverslag* 1859–1920.

tion show in the City Council through more say for representatives of industrial interests?

In our search for answers we have, in the first place, tax data for the period 1890–1915. Like many other municipalities Haarlem levied a direct local tax. Till 1896 this tax was levied on yearly 'expenses'. Whether the taxpayer spent during the year, either on himself or for his family, qualified as expenses (Verslagen verhandelde 1885, 648 ff.). Householders who spent less than *f*300 (the annual working wage) a year, were exempted from this tax[3], meaning nearly half of all householders.[4] In the period 1897–1915 the tax was levied on income; incomes lower than *f*500 were exempt. In the beginning the number of assessable people decreased somewhat owing to this higher exemption rate. In 1912, however, the rising wages of the first decade of the twentieth century caused more than 80 per cent of householders to be liable.[5] Table 11.2 compares the incomes of all taxpayers and that of the councillors for 1890, 1900 and 1912. Moreover, for 1890 the distribution of incomes of the electorate has been determined. Random samples from the assessment lists of the direct local tax and from the 1890 electoral roll have been taken for this comparison.[6]

It is obvious from this table that around 1890 the councillors' level of spending was way above that of the electorate, the taxpayers in general and the population as a whole. The 1887 Constitutional Amendment Act, which brought about some extension of the electorate, had no effect whatsoever on the composition of the City Council. The Council continued to be a stronghold of the rich and the very rich. Most of the councillors enjoyed incomes of *f*4,000 or more. Many councillors even greatly surpassed this amount, considerable though it was. A few examples are N.G.Cnoop Koopmans, a lawyer who spent *f*13,000 a year, or J.de Clerq van Weel, judge at the district court, who stood registered on the assessment list for an amount no less than *f*17,000. Even the Mayor, E.A. Jordens, was beaten by this huge amount, but he was still good for *f*9,000.

The year 1900 provides us with equally high amounts. At that time income, not yearly spending, constituted the tax basis. The then Mayor,

Table 11.2 Distribution of incomes, Haarlem (%), 1890, 1900 and 1912

tax category (f)	1890			1900		1912	
	t	e	c	t	c	t	c
500–1,000	55	48	0	55	11	67	6
1,000–2,000	27	27	0	26	11	18	16
2,000–4,000	11	18	16	12	14	8	19
>4,000	6	7	84	7	64	7	59
n	436	256	25	750	28	988	32

t = taxpayers
e = electorate
c = councillors

Sources: Kohier 1890, 1900, 1912; *Kiezerslijst* 1890; *Gemeenteverslag* 1890, 1900, 1912.

J.W.G. Boreel van Hogelanden Esq., declared an income of f59,000; this made him the highest assessed person. There are also incomes of, for instance, f26,000 for the banker E.de Lanoy, or f13,500 for the lawyer F.W. van Styrum Esq. Compared with the situation of ten years before, however, the number of councillors with top incomes had obviously decreased. There are indeed a few councillors with a modest income. We are referring now to three socialists who upset upper-class Haarlem by their admission to the Council after the 1899 elections (Nieuwenhuis 1946, 308–9). The incomes of the plumber L. Modoo (f700), the shopkeeper J. Hofland (f750) and the bookseller J.J. Groot (f550) contrasted strongly with the other incomes. By 1912 the relative number of very wealthy councillors had decreased even more in favour of moderate incomes. The right honourable gentlemen, however, continued to be in the majority in the Council. The way in which the incomes were structured in the city council did not remotely reflect the incomes of all taxpayers.

Haarlem's development resembles that of other cities. In Groningen too, where in 1890 the Council consisted mostly of members of the élite, membership became less exclusive in the period 1890–1910. The number of incomes highest on the scale, though, was somewhat larger in Groningen in 1910: 67 per cent as opposed to 59 per cent in Haarlem.[7]

The 1887 revision of the constitution brought little change in the professions of the Haarlem councillors. In Table 11.3 a comparison is made between the professions of the male adult population, those of the electors and those of the councillors.

Considerable continuity characterizes the City Council. The electors, already a select group themselves, chose, just as in the years previous to 1887, mainly councillors who had private means of those who had a profession in the area of services, mainly lawyers and members of the judiciary. The trade and industry sectors were underrepresented. The many shopkeepers who had received voting rights did not have a single representative in the Council in 1890. The same held for the independent artisans, clerks and junior Civil Servants such as teachers. Councillors actually

Table 11.3 Occupational sectors of Haarlem's male adult population, electors and councillors, 1890, in %

	male adult pop.	electors	councillors
Industry	45	27	19
Trade and transportation	24	34	16
Services	11	19	44
Labourers	6	0	0
Agriculture	5	3	0
Without occupation	9	17	20
N/n	10,857	278	25

Sources: Uitkomsten beroepstelling 1889; Kiezerslijst 1890; Adresboek 1890.

engaged in trade or industry belonged to the category of merchants or factory-managers. This situation underwent an important change in the period up to and including 1918, as is shown in Table 11.4. In this table councillors are divided according to three occupational categories; the development of the average income for each category is added. This cannot be accomplished for the year 1918, as there are no income data for that period.

Table 11.4 Occupations and average incomes of Haarlem councillors, 1890–1918

Occupation	Number				Average income (*f*)		
	1890	1900	1912	1918	1890	1900	1912
I	17	15	20	15	8,014	9,427	8,425
II	8	9	6	5	6,250	8,033	16,400
III	0	4	6	13	–	975	1,550
total	25	28	32	33	7,450	7,771	8,631

I   The professions, senior civil servants, persons of independent means
II Merchants, factory-managers
III Artisans, shopkeepers, clerks, skilled labourers

Sources: Kohier 1890, 1900, 1912; Adresboeken 1890–1918.

The extension of the number of councillors chiefly favoured the lower classes: in 1918 they constituted more than one-third of the City Council. It appears that the Council was of a very mixed nature; this may be concluded from the wide gap between the average incomes of the first two categories and the average income of the third. Apart from that, our attention is drawn to the decreasing representation of trade and industry. One would have expected a different result just at the time when industrialization gained momentum in Haarlem. Perhaps the reason was that merchants and manufacturers thought little of the Council's political power, so that they were hardly inclined to be present at endless discussions about predominantly trivial matters. The absence of manufacturers from the local political stage is not peculiar to Haarlem: it was also an established fact in The Hague, Groningen and Delft. Although merchant and manufacturer councillors were decreasing in number, their average income was growing steadily. This growth, however, is caused by the huge income of A. van Rossum, manager-director of the sugar factory in nearby Halfweg, who had an income of ƒ74,500. If we leave him aside, the average income falls to ƒ4,780.

We may conclude that the Haarlem élite, which until the 1890s had governed with a firm hand, survived the expansion of voting rights rather well. After the introduction of universal suffrage for men in 1917, the wealthy still held a large proportion of the available seats. However, the less wealthy, with less distinguished professions, were increasingly elected to the Council. It is also clear that the representatives of trade and industry showed little or no enthusiasm for Council membership. Rather than voicing their opinion directly, they used the Chamber of Commerce and Manufacture, on which we shall now briefly concentrate.

The Chamber of Commerce and Manufacture

In the nineteenth century city of any size possessed a Chamber of Commerce and Manufacture. The main task of these chambers was to give advice (asked and unasked) to the national government, the provincial states and the City Council about trade and industry. Since 1852 members of the Chamber were directly elected by all male adults who, having a business or factory, were assessed a licence fee at a certain minimum. Every city had its own minimum sum according to the number of its inhabitants. Haarlem had a bottom line of ƒ15, a modest sum compared with nearby Amsterdam, where the minimum amounted to ƒ75. This means that in Haarlem many craftsmen and entrepreneurs with small businesses had the right to elect the nine members of the Chamber. Here, the same situation occurred as with the elections of the City Council. Although in the 1890s 600 to 700 residents possessed voting rights, only 100 of them actually voted. Exclusively prominent merchants and entrepreneurs were chosen, and just as with the City Council they kept their seat for years on end. In 1890, for instance, the engineer Th. Figee belonged to the Chamber; also the builder of railway carriages J.J.F. Beynes. Furthermore, J.H. Kersten represented the bulb-growing industry, a very important sector for Haarlem. A member of the family company Enschedé was chairman. Ten years later, the composition of the Chamber had not changed, with the exception of one member.

It is hardly surprising that the members of the Chamber of Commerce belonged to the same top layer as the councillors as regards their income. The average income was, for all years, more than ƒ10,000. However, in sharp contrast to the City Council, the Chamber judged a favourable economic infrastructure to be the responsibility of the municipality and of the national government, arguing that this would naturally encourage private initiative and so the general welfare. The Haarlem Chamber of Commerce emphasized this point with inexhaustible energy in many notes, reports, petitions and addresses, in which its members harassed the national, provincial and local governments. Therefore, the Chamber may be considered as an outstanding exponent of the Haarlem economic élite. Considering the small interest of this group in the Council membership, it is not surprising that the two groups involved, the City Council and the Chamber of Commerce, hardly overlapped. Sometimes one or two members of the Chamber happened to be councillors too, but there were also years in which no double membership occurred. It might have happened, though, that councillors with an industrial or commercial background defended the Chamber's ideas about the task of the government as far as economic infrastructure was concerned. In order to investigate whether the progressive ideas about government interference brought any response from the Council, and to find out what kind of decisions the government eventually took, we shall now turn to the discussions about the Haarlem railway harbour. This was a matter which, between 1890 and 1920, caused many tongues (and pens) to be loosened.

The railway harbour on the Spaarne

About 1890 Haarlem had a favourable position in the national traffic network. The Amsterdam–The Hague–Rotterdam railway ran through Haarlem; the city was connected to the important North Sea Canal by means of the so-called canal C (see Figure 11.1). After a tough fight for years on end on the part of the Chamber of Commerce, the City Council decided in 1892 to build a bigger sluice near Spaarndam, so as to make it possible for seagoing vessels to reach Haarlem via the Spaarne (Messing 1972, 132–4). A railway harbour was still lacking, where goods could be loaded directly from railway carriages into ships, and vice versa. Already as early as 1884 the Chamber of Commerce had made a proposal which provided for a harbour as well as a trans-shipment station at the Noorder Buiten Spaarne. No reaction whatsoever came from City Council. In the following years, however, the Chamber frequently drew the City Council's attention to the importance of this harbour; the Chamber insisted on a decision. In 1892, for instance, the Chamber again put forward a proposal for a harbour. The Chamber offered to contribute ƒ70,000 towards the costs (Mollerus 1927, 31).

As late as 1901, seventeen years after the first proposal, the Council really began to attend to the matter of the trans-shipment station. A necessary change of the railway section caused this change of attitude. The Chamber of Commerce and the Haarlem industrialists and tradesmen began to cherish the hope now for a harbour on the Spaarne. However, to the utter amazement of everyone involved, a proposal was made in which not the Spaarne, but the Westergracht was suggested as the port location (see Figure 11.2). Enterprising Haarlem rightly considered the Westergracht the most inappropriate spot conceivable for a railway harbour: using the canals of the

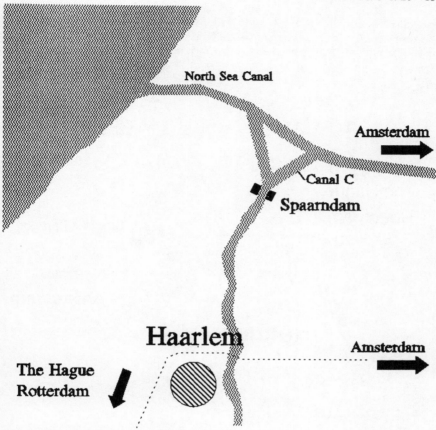

Figure 11.1   Haarlem's railway and waterway connections

town was the only possible way of reaching the Westergracht by water. Nine fixed bridges with small headways spanned the canals. This meant that goods would often have to be transported to the trans-shipment station by horse and wagon. Twenty-seven prominent entrepreneurs, therefore, addressed a written petition to the Court of the Mayor and Aldermen in which they pleaded with forceful arguments for a revision of the plans and for a decision in favour of the Spaarne harbour. The petitioners were supported by the Chamber of Commerce. However, at the Council meeting where this proposal was discussed, only Beynes and the entrepreneur G.J. van Dieren Bijvoet protested; both of them had signed the address. The proposal of the Mayor and Aldermen was accepted without significant objections (Messing 1972, 134–5; Verslagen verhandelde 1901, 288–92; Verslag van de raad 1901, 124). Obviously, the Chamber of Commerce had too little influence with the councillors to convince them of the importance of the Spaarne harbour. Moreover, not every councillor with an industrial or commercial background appeared to support the Spaarne harbour. It is not clear why the Mayor and Aldermen suggested a port on the Westergracht; presumably, they considered the relatively low construction costs of a port on that spot of major importance.

Figure 11.2   The location of the *Westergracht and Spaarne harbour*

The harbour location on the Westergracht was not be suitable, and the Chamber of Commerce was flooded with complaints. In the following decade the Chamber emphasized in every annual report the importance of proper harbour facilities. For a long time their attempts to convince the Mayor and Aldermen failed. We read, thus, in the 1904 report that the Haarlem Cotton Company had informed the Chamber that the transport of goods had become more expensive 'due to the new trans-shipment station on the Leidsche Vaart'. In the following year the Chamber reported that 'lack of sufficient opportunity to supply or to convey goods which have to be forwarded by water or which are to be supplied by train, is felt as a serious omission'. By 1911 the tenor had not changed: 'the unfavourable location of the trans-shipment station gives cause for serious complaints, since the low bridges etc. make the city quite inaccessible'.[8]

Was this unremitting stream of complaints the reason why the Court of Mayor and Aldermen in 1912 proposed to decide (in principle) on the building of 'an open railway and trans-shipment station on the Noorder Buiten Spaarne'? I do not think so, as the complaints had already continued for twenty-five years. We should consider personal factors. In 1912 one of the aldermen was the engineer J.F. Hulswit, a fervent supporter of the Spaarne harbour. The then mayor, Boreel van Hogelanden, was himself not inclined to government interference in the economic area, but he allowed Hulswit to introduce his plan to the City Council. The Council reacted hesitatingly and decided to establish an advisory committee (Verslagen verhandelde 1912, 307–10 and 348). This committee consisted of five councillors who either fervently supported the harbour plan, or fiercely opposed it. Supporters were, naturally, Hulswit, who was also chairman, the major captain of industry Van Rossum, and an architect, J.B. Lasschuit. Fierce opponents were the liqueur-distiller E. Levert and the lawyer J. Spoor, who, after his death, was succeeded by E.H. Krelage, a bulb-grower who, just like Spoor, showed little enthusiasm for the harbour plan. In view of this composition it is not at all surprising that in 1913 the committee presented a report containing much contradictory advice.

The committee's report (Verslagen verhandelde 1913, 1258–67) reflects very well the arguments for and against the building of a harbour, as they emerge, time and again, in later discussions too. The opponents emphasized the fact that Haarlem did not need a railway harbour at all, for this would only attract new industries. The addition of 3,000 labourers, who, in times of need, would call on the public purse would be the result. Haarlem was not a manufacturing town and was not about to become one. Moreover, the expensive harbour plan, the cost of which was rated at half a million guilders, would involve an increase of the tax burden. This in turn would lead to a departure of the more wealthy inhabitants to surrounding munici-palities. Supporters, on the other hand, held the view that the costs of the harbour project would be covered by the revenues, including the sale of industrial sites. In addition, many industries which still caused much incon-venience by their position within city areas would move to the Spaarne banks. In this way, Haarlem would become even more attractive as a residential town for those who wanted to live quietly on their private means. The supporters of the harbour plan also drew attention to other initiatives taken in this area, initiatives taken by comparable cities such as Arnhem and Den Bosch. The instalment of new industries would not only provide for the growth of the number of substantial people such as manu-facturers and engineers, but wages and salaries paid by industry, would, for the most part, be spent again in Haarlem, to the benefit of the middle classes.

The committee's report was not discussed immediately with the City Council, but the Mayor and Aldermen were asked to offer a preliminary judgement. The Court of Mayor and Aldermen took ample time to do this, as two years later the Council had still not heard anything. In April 1915 the committee finally presented a supplementary report (Verslagen verhandelde 1915, 447–62), in which they pressed for urgent action. Contrary to the earlier report, the committee now unanimously agreed on quick construction of the Spaarne harbour, in response to 'the changed circumstances'. In the Council discussions concerning these plans this argument was also heard (Verslagen gesprokene 1915, 267–82). Outspoken opponents, like Krelage, had to admit that at this time of crisis the case had taken a different turn, and that the industrial issue was a general concern. Others pointed out that the damage done to industry, due to the lack of a proper harbour site, was a substantial fact: 'Haarlem should progress toward industry; it should no longer remain a luxury city' (Verslagen gesprokene 1915, 277). Members of the Socialist Party pointed out that the settlement of gentlemen of leisure in the city would not serve the labourers' interests; on the contrary, a flourishing industry was essential. The labourers applauded the harbour plans (Verslagen gesprokene 1915, 272).

The committee's opinion was supported by various addresses to the City Council; one of them, of course, was from the Chamber of Commerce: 'to only be a luxury city is no longer an honourable title' (Verslagen verhandelde 1915, 465). In a previous address the Chamber had already stated that 'being a luxury city was not at all irreconcilable with being an industrial city, as long as these two kinds were clearly separated' (Gedenkboek 1952, 414). In regard to this matter, the Chamber, just like the committee, had in mind the construction of working-class houses near the harbour and the industrial site on the Spaarne. Another address came from seven important entrepreneurs who, once again, pointed out 'the continuing disadvantages caused by the unfavourable position of the trans-shipment station . . ., and by the insufficient equipment for the handling and the transportation of goods'. Moreover, they added 'that the existing situation was extremely unfavourable for Haarlem trade and industry, as it already had occurred, recently, that enterprises wishing to settle there abandoned their plans for those very reasons and went elsewhere' (Verslagen verhandelde 1915, 462–3). In the end, they offered to contribute ƒ60,000 towards the cost of construction, maintenance and exploitation.

The councillors, who all more or less favoured the construction of the harbour, stood this time face to face with a demurring Court of Mayor and Aldermen. Hulswit, who had launched the harbour plans in 1912, no longer belonged to the Court; the attitude of the Court of Mayor and Aldermen was at this time far more conservative than it had been three years earlier. The Court shrank from the high cost of the project. Although the Mayor and Aldermen acknowledged that 'it is generally accepted that the government is also to promote trade and industry', they amplified this statement with an additional remark: 'This is true only if the municipality prospers from the interference, otherwise it is not' (Verslagen gesprokene 1915, 274). According to the Court of Mayor and Aldermen, the high cost was justified only if the municipal boundaries were to be altered considerably. Negotiations should be conducted not only with the border communities Spaarndam and Haarlemmerliede (necessary for the harbour project proper), but other suburbs, too, should be involved in the alterations. This had to be done to provide Haarlem with a stronger fiscal foundation, for the Mayor and Aldermen feared that all the wealthy people employed in industry would settle down outside Haarlem (Verslagen gesprokene 1915, 275).

The councillors quite rightly considered this attitude of Mayor and Aldermen as an attempt to defer the matter indefinitely. An extensive alteration of the municipal boundaries was rather complicated, if the Mayor and Aldermen insisted on making this alteration first, before developing the harbour plan any further, a long delay would be the consequence. The issue dragged on for several more years, until on 1 May 1918 the Council unamimously decided on the plan for the construction of a harbour (Verslagen verhandelde 1918, 337–9).

The Chamber of Commerce dedicated an extra meeting to this joyful event. The members reacted enthusiastibly to the decision which, after too long a prologue, should be carried out quickly: 'for time presses, now that so many people are preparing to set up new industries or to expand existing ones' (Gedenkboek 1952, 420). The construction of a harbour would stimulate employment, and the Chamber presumed that many a councillor had voted in favour of the harbour plan because of the employment factor. Unfortunately, the harbour plan was unanimously agreed upon in the end without any debate, so we are unable to confirm whether this supposition was based on reality.

Now what can we conclude from these developments? Within a short time—sixteen years—the City Council had made a complete turn: no one was interested in 1902 in the development of trade and industry (with the exception of two councillors), yet in 1918 the harbour project was unanimously approved. Of course the expansion of voting rights had brought about changes in the composition of the Council; and we could therefore expect that members who did not belong to the traditional groups in the council would pay more attention to industrial interests. This cannot be the reason, however, for the unanimous consent of 1918, for, as we have seen previously (Table 11.4), the traditional élite were still represented extensively in the Council. Members of this élite had a different attitude now towards economic interference, different in comparison with their attitude at the turn of the century.

It is not possible, either, to ascribe a strong influence to the Chamber of Commerce. The Chamber had inexhaustibly pleaded for the Spaarne harbour, but not until 1915 was any attention given to its views. The economic élite showed little enthusiasm for the City Council; indeed, the influence which the economic élite itself exercised on the Council's decisions was quite negligible. No, we have to explain the reason for this change of attitude as 'the extraordinary circumstances'. The First World War had made government interference necessary in many areas, so traditional ideas about the tasks of the government changed quickly. After the war, a new era would ensue in which trade and industry would flourish again. Here, a task offered itself to the City Council. Haarlem was not to miss the chances it had been offered.

In this way the Haarlem situation is a good illustration of the famous platform theory of Peacock and Wiseman (Peacock and Wiseman 1961). Peacock and Wiseman state that citizens generally resist a rise in government expenditure because this involves a heavier tax burden. However, 'social disturbances', especially wars, necessarily entail a high level of expenditure. After this shock, expenses drop again, but they stabilize at a higher level than before the war. Although the Netherlands did not wage war, the First World War generated indeed a wide consensus about the desirability of an active economic policy. The 'visible hand' was accepted; moreover, it was even considered indispensable for the further economic development of Haarlem.

The First World War is certainly responsible for this difference in outlook, but it did not lead in the end to a fundamental turnaround. This appears from the sequel to this story after the First World War. For many years nothing happened; during the depression of the 1930s, when classical-liberal economists did not tire of condemning any kind of government interference, the harbour project disappeared entirely from the scene. The ambitious harbour project was not executed until after the Second World War, and then only on a very small scale; the trans-shipment station, so fervently wished for, was never realized. The forces which opposed the 'visible hand' in the economy might have been silenced by the shock of the First World War; they had not, however, disappeared.

Acknowledgement

I would like to thank mrs. drs. Judith Eringa for the translation of this chapter into English.

Notes

1. See P. Kooij, Chapter 9 in this volume, Table 9.4.
2. Owing to the lack of stratification data—which were available to Kooij at the time—it is difficult to determine which part this is.
3. Further, each family member was granted a deduction of $f50$. This means that the threshold of the tax is somewhat vague. A family with two children and expenses amounting to $f500$ was still required to pay tax over $f50$: the total tax deduction was $f450$, $f300$ for the householder and three times $f50$ for wife and two children. A family with three children and the same expenses were exempt. Therefore, an unknown number of families with rather low expenses do not appear in the assessment lists. A different story characterizes families with high expenses, for even after a deduction due to the family size, a taxable amount remains. The assessment lists indicate both the expenses and the taxable sum.
4. This is calculated on the basis of the 1889 census, which contains a report of the number of male and female householders, and of the number of one-person male and female households, a total of 11,473 people. The assessment list of 1890 contains the names of more than 6,000 householders and one-person households.
5. Calculated on the basis of the 1899 and 1909 census, which mention the number

of householders and the number of one-person households. These figures can be related to the total number of assessed persons mentioned annually in the council report.

6. For 1890 and 1900 the local direct tax assessments lists are made up for each quarter. It is necessary, therefore, to include the entire assessment list in the random sample. A sample of one in ten was chosen. From the 1890 election roll I also took a random sample of one in ten. The 1912 assessment list is alphabetically arranged; moreover, the people were numbered, a total of 17,078. The random sample consists of the numbers 2,000–2,999. Some people were dropped after having objected to their tax assessment, their names having been crossed off the list. An attempt to determine the income structures of the 1900 and 1912 electorate was abandoned as, due to the lowering of the census criteria in 1896, these income structures were almost identical to the income structure of all taxpayers. The latter was easier to determine.

7. Kooij states in Chapter 9 in this volume that in 1890, of the 30 councillors, 25 had an income of ƒ4000 or more, this means 83 per cent; in 1910 22 out of 33 councillors (67 per cent) had an income of ƒ4000 or more.

8. *Gemeenteverslag*, appendix U: *Verslag van de Kamer van Koophandel* 1904, 58; 1905, 77; and 1911, 81. Apart from this information, the railway harbour committee's Archive (Gemeente-archief Haarlem, Nieuw Archief 181 c, Archief van de commissie tot onderzoek in zake de aanleg van een spoor- en overlaadhaven) presents us with a report which systematically mentions all the complaints of the Chamber of Commerce.

Bibliography

(Haarlem Municipal Archive)

Adresboeken (1890–1918).
Archief van de commissie tot onderzoek in zake de aanleg van een spoor- en overlaadhaven, Nieuw Archief 181c.
Gemeenteverslag (Council reports) (1859–1920).
Kiezerslijst (1890), Nieuw Archief, 52.
Kohieren van de plaatselijke directe belasting der gemeente Haarlem (1890, 1900, 1912), Nieuw Archief, 148.
Verslag van de Kamer van Koophandel (Appendix U of the Council report) (1904, 1905, 1911).
Verslagen van het gesprokene in den gemeenteraad (1915).
Verslagen van de vergaderingen van de raad der gemeente Haarlem (1901).
Verslagen van het verhandelde in de zittingen van den raad der gemeente Haarlem (1885, 1901, 1912, 1913, 1915, 1918).

Other Sources

Census (1899, 1909).
Gedenkboek, samengesteld ter gelegenheid van het honderdjarig bestaan der Kamer. Overzicht van de werkzaamheden over het tijdvak 1852–1952, (1952), Haarlem.
Messing, F.A.M. (1972), *Werken en leven in Haarlem (1850–1914). Een sociaal-economische studie van de stad*, Amsterdam.

Mollerus, J.C. (1927), *Gedenkboek ter herinnering aan het 75-jarig bestaan der Haarlemsche Kamer van Koophandel en Fabrieken*, Haarlem.

Nieuwenhuis, G.M. (1946), *De stad aan het Spaarne in zeven eeuwen*, Amsterdam.

Peacock A.T. and Wiseman, J. (1961), *The growth of public expenditure in the United Kingdom*, London.

Uitkomsten beroepstelling (1889).

Vries, Joh. de (1971), 'Het censuskiesrecht en de welvaart in Nederland 1850–1917', *Economisch- en sociaal-historisch jaarboek*, 34: 178–231.

12 From hidden hand to public intervention: land use and zoning strategies in the liberal and post-liberal city (1875–1914)

Michael Wagenaar

One of the important tasks for local government under the *ancien régime* was planning the spatial order of the city. Urban planning pursued two aims. On the one hand it concerned the planning of urban expansion. On the other it aimed at sorting out or zoning activities which were held to be mutually incompatible.

In the days of the Republic of the United Provinces, cities enjoyed a highly independent status, which they had attained as a result of the rebellion against the Habsburg Empire's centralization and state-building policies. Cities like Amsterdam, Haarlem, Leyden, Delft and Rotterdam were administrative islands, all of which had their paticular laws, charters, weights and measures. Any serious attempts to enhance the central power of the fragmented Republic were effectively thwarted.

In the seventeenth century, Dutch cities had become centres of economic prosperity which attracted numerous migrants. The consequent expansion of urban territory not only provided space for an increasing population and new trades; it also gave local administration the room to move enterprises which hitherto had caused a nuisance in the older built-up areas. In the case of Amsterdam this resulted in a 'stick-and-carrot' policy, whereby each sixteenth or seventeenth-century extension was used to remove undesirable crafts from the older areas and relocate them either at the urban fringe or on the waterfront. There they troubled only the less fortunate members of urban society (Taverne 1978, 112 ff). This resulted in the following pattern of segregation. The mediaeval core and the canal belt (constructed between 1600 and 1680) were cleared of unwanted crafts or industries. Only those forms of employment which by their nature were compatible with a well-to-do residential environment were tolerated: offices, warehouses, shops and the occasional goldsmith's or tailor's workshop. They were allowed premises in the back streets of the prestigious canal district.

Hazardous or polluting manufacturers, whether newcomers or moved out of the old city, were given space in quarters such as the Jordaan, the Eastern and Western Islands (seventeenth-century additions to the water-front), and some isolated areas such as the Noortsche Bos or Roeterseiland. Here, the strict and careful planning procedures which had been applied to the canal belt were ignored. The parcelling of the once agrarian land was left intact. Ditches were filled in and made into streets. Speculators developed high density housing. Land use regulations were absent. The area was intersected by a few canals, unobtrusive copies of the grandeur of the canal belt. Breweries, foundries, tanneries, china works and clay ovens found a niche in these areas. They settled along the ramparts or in the narrow streets which housed the work-force as well — craftsmen, casual labourers and sailors, living in overcrowded mews or courts. Only the small canals with their modest imitations of the merchants' palaces along the main canals were kept free from pollution, fire hazards and overcrowding. They were the domain of petty merchants and successful craftsmen who could not afford the luxury of the main canals but shunned the smaller streets of the area.

The other areas which acted as a refuge for undesirable enterprise had a similar mix of residential and economic functions. The Eastern and Western Islands attracted the port-oriented crafts — the shipyards with their caulkers, the rope-walks and smoking-sheds — and a matching work-force of deck-hands, ship chandlers and stevedores. The Islands were socially mixed as well. Pensioned sea captains occupied the waterfront housing, overlooking the busy port of Amsterdam, while the backstreets were home to the working classes and servants.

Local administration had, in other words, succeeded in zoning environ-mentally undesirable land uses which were removed from the better-off areas of the city. Its strategy had not led, to be sure, to single-function neighbourhoods such as manufacturing districts, nor to purely residential single class areas. The imperative need for every citizen to walk to his work-place excluded such radical segregation. The seventeenth and eighteenth-century solution resulted in mixed neighbourhoods which, as long as local enterprise was of a more hazardous, polluting or noxious nature, were on the average of a lesser residential status than the ones with cleaner forms of employment.

A new political and administrative order (1795–1848)

Under French rule (1795–1815) the Netherlands underwent substantial political, administrative and legal reform. The introduction of the central state, with a national body of laws, rules and criminal procedures, put an end to the fragmented situation of the old Republic. Consequently, it also did away with the urban privilege of local self-government. The Kingdom of the Netherlands, which inherited the central state, initially restored some of the traditional urban privileges, but was careful not to return to the old situation. The liberal revolt of 1848 ended all dreams about restoration of the old urban prerogatives. The new constitution, particularly the Local Government Act of 1851, denied cities the right to issue by-laws, rules or regulations which contradicted national laws or the constitution.

The spirit of this new constitution was truly liberal. Indeed, it was hard to find other continental European nations equally devoted to political and economic liberalism. Next to an ardent faith in free trade, and consequently in the elimination of protectionist barriers, liberalism emphasized the importance of private property. 'The nineteenth century witnessed great advances in individual rights . . . Contemporaries particularly enjoyed the right to acquire, enjoy, and dispose of property freely. Any state interference must be minimal and closely circumscribed by due process' (Hohenberg and Lees 1985, 325–6). The respect for private property, which the Civil Code defined as a 'droit absolu', together with an almost sacred belief in the blessings of the free market as a superior regulatory device, formed two of the pillars of this nineteenth-century *perestroika*.

The 'visible hand' made way for *laissez-faire*. The role of the state was to be limited to providing the essential conditions for the functioning of the free market—the defence of national territory, the protection of private property, the provision of a minimal form of education—but should generally abstain from meddling with society's problems. The inviolable property right was particularly relevant to real estate. It was, from a liberal point of view, unthinkable that a public body lay claims or restrictions on property which it did not legally own. The domain of public law, which was greatly extended in the twentieth-century welfare state, was to be kept minimal.

At the end of the nineteenth-century, however, the dogma of inviolable property rights came under increasing strain. The industrialization of the Netherlands was accompanied by rapid urban growth. The towns of the Western provinces, many of which had experienced almost a century of stagnation or decline, now found themselves growing again. In the 1870s Amsterdam extended its built-up area outside the old ramparts for the first time since 1675.

The problem for the growing cities was that under liberal rule town planning was almost impossible. The respect for landed property prevented any effective control of urban expansion. Within the older built-up areas, the politics of restraint thwarted local government plans for improving the outdated infrastructure. In many cases improvement schemes demanded the demolition of traffic obstacles, requiring much patience when a property-holder refused to co-operate. The final resort lay in compulsory purchase, which, as one would expect from liberal society, was surrounded by many safeguards. Each expropriation required a separate Act of Parliament. When local administration finally obtained permission to evict the owner, it still had to buy him out at current market prices. It was, therefore, not only a long and tiresome business, but also a very costly one, particularly when local authority envisaged large-scale extensions.

The results of nineteenth-century urbanization, the chaotic expansion and congested inner cities, did much to damage the attraction of liberalism as a political and economic doctrine. Around 1900 the political climate began to change, as we shall see. One of the reasons for that change was that liberal ideology faced a paradox it could not solve.

Generally speaking, the paradox was that the liberal's unconditional respect for private property implied that the owner was at liberty to do as he pleased with his property. However, what if his activities were damaging to the quality of the environment, and, consequently, depreciated the property of his neighbours? Were they not property-holders as well? This dilemma became very real as the transition from craft to industry gained momentum. More and more inner-city workshops, such as those mentioned earlier in the Jordaan or other pre-industrial areas, were turned into small factories. The installation of a steam-engine did more than step up production, however. At the same time it had a massive impact on the environment as soot, smog, noise, stench and fire hazards increased. Under current laws it was almost impossible to prevent the owner of the premises from turning his workshop into a small factory.

From craft to industry: a few cases

The consequences of installing a steam-engine in a residential environment were far from hypothetical, as the following cases illustrate.

From the 1870s industrialization in Amsterdam made good progress. Steam-engine capacity rose by more than 50 per cent from 1850 to over 2,000 hp in 1870. After that it almost tripled to 6,324 hp in 1891. In 1910 combined steam capacity passed the 16,700 hp mark (Van Zanden 1987, 131). Much of the heavier equipment was installed in large-scale mills which showed a marked preference for the urban fringe. Here, the major breweries, chemical plants, shipyards and sugar refineries built their factories on a greenfield site.

However, most of the (smaller capacity) steam-engines were installed in the old built-up areas, in many cases as part of the conversion of craft to industry. Blacksmiths, joiners, dairy processers and carpenters joined in the successful application of mechanical power to enhance the volume of production. Around 1875 most steam-engines were situated in the old city. Even in 1914 more than half of all engines stood here. In the meantime, however, the larger plants on what once had been the urban fringe were by now surrounded by residential quarters. The clash of interests between industry and the residential environment had become acute.

What sort of complaints did this *incompatibilité des humeurs* produce? Let us take a look at the consequences of installing a steam-engine within the older built-up district. Many of the registered complaints deal with increased fire hazards, as a result of which insurance premiums were increased. Manifold were the complaints about the emission of smoke and soot. One of the neighbours of a building in the Jordaan resists the opening of a forge next door which

will disturb his tranquillity and will damage his and his family's rest. The blacksmith works from 6 in the morning to 11 at night, during which time one cannot open the windows for ventilation or it will rain blackness and smoke inside. (Municipal Archives Amsterdam, Public Works Dept, 1876, file no. 4483)

Indeed, the long working hours—working days of 12 to 15 hours were not exceptional in the 1870s—aggravated the nuisance considerably. Not only had windows to stay shut, but the emission of soot made the outside drying of laundry impossible as well.

That was one of the many complaints brought in against the proprietor of a diamond-polishing workshop in the Boomstraat, again in the Jordaan area. He wished to install an 1 hp steam-engine in the attic of a (former) residence. Plaintiffs feared 'annoyance from heavy smoke' as well as noise nuisance. As long as the polishing mills were still operated manually, they caused no problems. However, the introduction of steam power in this rickety building gave reasons for serious concern (Municipal Archives Amsterdam, Public Works Dept, 1875, file no. 5371).

Records prove this fear to be far from exaggerated. The neighbour of a mechanized workshop in the inner city (on the Warmoesstraat) complained that the steam-engine recently set up caused

such vibrations . . . and continuous roar that plaintiff can no longer make use of his dwelling; that the premises are deteriorated and downgraded to such an extent that they can no longer be let—while the continuing roar, which often goes on on Sundays from early morning to late at night, causes plaintiff's wife to suffer from nervous disease . . ., [all illustrated by a copy of a medical certificate]. (Municipal Archives Amsterdam, Public Works Dept, 1876, file no. 5180)

Around 1900, complaints were no fewer. By now they were no longer limited to old city areas, as the following case illustrates. The neighbours of a 'Steam factory for Carpentry and Joinery' in the Eastern extension area complained that the discharge of exhaust steam was such that 'it has become impossible to have our doors or windows open'. Visibility on the streets was limited to 3 metres. Sidewalks were constantly blocked by large timber stacks stored in front of the factory, where sawing was incidentally done on the street, and by lorries queuing for delivery.

For the landlord of these premises, his tenants' complaints were reason for serious concern (Municipal Archives Amsterdam, Public Works Dept, 1900, file no. 5180, no. 16). It is easy to understand why. Contrary to the Jordaan or inner city areas, with their predominantly dilapidated, badly maintained housing stock, the Eastern extension area was, around 1900, solid middle-class territory. Landlords took the threat of depreciation of their property very seriously.

Even a prestigious residential area such as the canal belt did not escape industrialization. The area was no exception to the rule that the property-owner could do with his premises whatever he deemed profitable. Local administration had given permission for the construction of a dairy-processing plant at Keizersgracht 371. The residents complained about congestion caused by milkcarts, lorries and farmer's wagons; about the foul smell produced by dumping stale milk and rancid butter in the canal, and finally about the noise produced by the separators (Municipal Archives Amsterdam, Public Works Dept, 1900, file no. 44).

Fire hazards, noise, stench and soot—all were the result of the transition from craft to industry. Manually operated craft shops did produce environmental pollution as well, as the previous pages have made clear. What had changed, however, was the dramatically increased scale of that pollution, the impact of which hit the old city with its high densities particularly hard. That was true for congestion as well. The introduction of a steam-engine considerably increased the input of fuel, raw materials and additives as well as the output of finished goods. The resulting increase in traffic produced serious congestion in an inner city of which the main arteries were waterways. Amsterdam simply was not designed to handle such vast amounts of road haulage. Finally, we should not forget that all factories discharged their exhaust fumes and effluent directly into the canals, which at the same time were the city's main sewers. The putrid smell of the gutters was almost unbearable, and caused many of those who could afford it to leave the city during the summer, when pollution problems were at their worst. Referring to the Jordaan area, van Tijn suggests that

a particular cause for the disgusting condition of the canals was the presence of many factories (sugar refineries, for example) which dumped their exhaust steam into the canals; the consequent heating of the water furthered the decay of litter in the almost dead water. (Van Tijn 1965, 121)

More and more, contemporaries became aware of the *incompatibilité des humeurs* between residence and industry. In a report by a municipal commission focusing on this problem we find that in every expansion area land sold for industrial projects prevented the opportunity for a prestigious residential development. Even the banks of the spacious Amstel river, offering an almost ideal site for high status development, were not safe. Here, 'factories, sometimes of a very perilous and annoying nature, have long foreclosed the construction of modern mansions'. One was powerless, however, 'because in these days no one could prevent factories establishing in areas which had been given a different destination. Nevertheless, the writing was on the wall. In 1900 the local Council commissioned an advisory body on the problems of industrial location. It demonstrated that even hardened liberals were no longer content with matters as they were. The almost unrestricted freedom of location not only jeopardized the residential qualities of the pre-industrial quarters, where the traditional socio-economic mix had now been downgraded to an almost homogeneous poverty, but had become a serious threat to town planning in general, and the creation of elegant residential areas in particular. What could be done?

The Nuisance Act of 1875

On 2 June 1875 a bill was passed, regulating the 'construction of establishments which may cause hindrance, danger or damage', which, since an addition in 1896, has become known as the Nuisance Act. Article 2 of this Act enumerates eighteen relevant categories of enterprise, of which the first (and, we may assume, the most important) is formed by 'steam- or gas-powered establishments'. Where an entrepreneur wished to install such equipment, he was obliged to ask for a permit from the local authority, which could be refused if there was a reasonable chance of

(a) danger; (b) damage to private property, enterprise or health; (c) serious hindrance, including making private dwellings unfit for habitation, the impediment of using premises conforming to the aims to which they were once erected, and the profusion of litter or disgusting smells. (Staatsblad, 95, 1875, 60 ff)

The law gave neighbours a voice to bring their complaints against the intended installation of any such hazardous equipment. A verbatim account of these complaints was drawn up by the Department of Public Works, which also verified the claims. If the entrepreneur or the plaintiff disagreed with the Public Works Department's judgment, they could appeal to the State Council (an administrative appeals body).

On paper this law provided local administration with a powerful instrument in the struggle against industrial pollution. Yet at the same time the law allowed a permissive interpretation. It lacked a precise description of set limits. In addition, it created the arbitrariness so much feared by the liberals. As the municipality was the (first) review body, its political colour was decisive for granting permission.

However, the liberals' main argument, brought forward time and again in political debates—namely, that this Act would serve as a barrier to industrialization—did not come true. Looking back on the first twenty-five years of this Act's jurisprudence, the Liberal Member of Parliament Van Houten's satisfied conclusion was that 'the outstanding manner in which the State Council has treated these matters effectively excluded that the perverted principles of this Law become common practice, and we may safely expect matters to remain this way' (Aalders 1984, 141).

The State Council's sympathy for the protesting entrepreneur was obvious. Complaining neighbours or residents rarely met with success. It is remarkable, by the way, that many objections deal with artisan's workshops, often situated in residential areas. 'What we see here is, besides the effects of an increasing scale . . . the impact of the substitution of manual energy by mechanical or steam-driven power' (Lintsen 1986, 200 ff.). The most common protest dealt with capital losses resulting from real estate depreciation. As a legal instrument, the Nuisance Act was far from effective. The plaintiffs' experiences in Amsterdam are yet further testimony.

All the cases mentioned above deal with entrepreneurs wishing to set up power equipment requiring a permit, or with previously installed engines. None of the complaints was sustained. The Public Works Department rarely refused an entrepreneur his licence. In the single case I found where an entrepreneur was denied such a permit, he successfully appealed to the State Council. He planned to turn an old warehouse, surrounded by a building block, into a chalk mill. Even the Public Works Dept considered this to be too serious a threat to the residential environment. The State Council disagreed (Municipal Archives, Public Works Dept, 1875, file no. 5433).

Was the citizen completely helpless, then? No. Until 1900 he had two alternative options for redress. The first was to take civil action for compensation using article 1401.2 of the Civil Code, or obtaining a ban on causing further harm. Whether this option was widely used, or whether it offered a reasonable chance of success, I do not know.

The second option lay at the urban fringe. One of the problems here was the extremely scattered nature of landownership, a phenomenon common to all the western provinces of the Netherlands. This implied that if a developer bought a few acres from a smallholder to develop for exclusive housing, the neighbouring smallholder could very well sell his plot for industrial development or a working-class housing project. The property structure at the urban fringe almost invited such combined land use, as we saw earlier on.

The only way to prevent this mingling was to form a 'private zoning association'. Wealthy citizens could join to acquire a substantial amount of land with the aim of subdividing it and selling it under stringent land use conditions. The best-known example in Amsterdam is the Vondelpark project. The very well-off initiators desired to create a large park on the south-western urban fringe. They collected sufficient capital to acquire a large number of separate lots until they had assembled a vast contingent stretch of land. Only part of that property was to be turned into a park. The remaining land was sold in building lots, allocated along elegant new streets and avenues. The conditions of sale included zoning regulations ruling out the construction of workshops, factories or warehouses. Combined with a ban on the construction of working-class housing, this was to safeguard the area's development into a prestigious, high status environment (Wagenaar 1984, 157–82).

The development was a great success. The residents were secure from threats so common in the rest of the city, where developers might turn neighbouring property into a factory or an overcrowded boarding-house. It came as no surprise, therefore, that one of the participants in the local Council's debate on the ambitious development plan of 1867 remarked: 'Today, only by association can we accomplish matters, and where in earlier days decrees and charters ruled, we now have to trust the impact of Capital' (Gemeenteblad 1868, I, 113). Until 1900 that statement was correct. Shortly thereafter, however, Parliament passed the Public Housing Act. Combined with the Municipal Leasehold Regulation, Amsterdam's local government now disposed of a set of tools which allowed it to introduce zoning regulations on new land, where from 1900 it could realize the long-cherished goal of an uncontaminated, attractive residential environment.

Towards an industrial location policy (1900–14)

The 'Industry Report' quoted earlier not only offered an interesting analysis of the growing conflicts over land use in the city. It also gave some remarkable recommendations to limit industrial nuisance. The report does not mention the Nuisance Act as a major planning instrument. The most important advice is that the city create a single-purpose factory zone, at some distance from the city but easily accessible. The site favoured by the commission was a stretch of land opposite the water front, on the northern embankment of the Y river. Near the industrial estate, they suggested, should be built working-class housing, since the ferry was unfit for mass commuter transport. Besides, 'Different from the well-to-do, who frequently make use of transport, a location at great distance from the old city is cumbersome to the working classes' (Industry Report, 35).

The authors of the report speculated that the abundance of cheap land next to deep water would induce industry to move away from its old location amidst residential properties. 'As soon as land prices [in the older parts of the city] have risen sufficiently, the factory can be relocated, particularly when it has to be modernised anyway'. The commission even saw opportunities to attract factories from out of town to this site (Industry Report, p.18).

That a number of factories would eventually locate on this site was hardly surprising. It is true that the southern perimeter of the city offered a more attractive site. There, communication with the central city was much easier. Since 1900 however, local administration could successfully prevent the establishment of industry here. The combination of the Housing Act and the local leasehold rule enabled it to pursue a preventive strategy.

The 1901 Housing Act obliged major cities with a certain growth rate to set up a town plan. To be able to realize such a plan the Compulsory Purchase Act had been extended with an article concerning 'expropriation for the sake of public housing'. This paragraph allowed for 'expropriation *par zone*' for the first time in recent Dutch history. 'The municipality can consequently apply for compulsory purchase of *all* the land on which it has planned its expansion' (Delfgaauw 1934, 88). Thus, local authorities could plan the sort of land use they desired. They issued land under a fifty or seventy-five year lease, with strict zoning conditions. When the lease expired they could, if they so wished, alter the plot's usage.

During the the local Council's debate on Berlage's first sketches of the 'southern extension plan'—one of the first town planning achievements based upon the new Housing Law—the alderman concerned left no doubt as to the chances for manufacturing industry in this area. In the plan 'there was room left for light industry only . . ., since it will not cause serious environmental problems' (Gemeenteblad 1905, II, 15). Heavy industry was expected to move to the area north of the waterfront. Without using the term, local authorities pursued an industrial location policy. They relocated potentially polluting industries from both the southern and (later on) western development plan, while offering at the same time sites on the northern embankment. Did their stick-and-carrot policy actually *work*?

Conclusion

On the eve of the First World War the municipal location policy seemed to have produced some results. The number of manufacturing industries north of the Y had increased steadily. Shipyards, wharves and a cable manufacturing plant preferred this peripheral area to the urban fringe, where they would in due course be locked in by other land users. Yet this new factory site hardly succeeded in attracting inner-city firms, which had been one of the principal aims of the 1903 commission. There was only one example of an extremely polluting and hazardous industry, the Ketjen sulphuric acid plant, which twice left its site for the combined reasons of high prices offered for their land, the need to update plant and equipment and because of an increase in legal proceedings in which their neighbours sued them for damages. What finally brought this plant to the northern Y embankment was that local authorities, put under pressure by Ketjen's threat to leave Amsterdam entirely, offered them a leasehold so cheap that the firm could not refuse. The new factory opened in 1900 (Honderd jaar Zwavelzuurfabricatie, 1835–1935).

The Ketjen case undoubtedly fed the hopes of the members of the 1903 commission. Nevertheless, it was to remain an isolated one. The commission itself had already pointed to the exodus of four companies to other towns, a phenomenon which 'should it take place on a broader scale will cause considerable damage to Amsterdam' (Industry Report, 19). Between 1903 and 1914 more companies preferred to leave Amsterdam entirely instead of opting for the new factory zone. One of their main reasons was the lack of cheap, easily accessible sites in Amsterdam. The available sites were expensive. Added to the very high cost of local labour this eroded the competitveness of labour-intensive, space-extensive companies. They left for areas where labour was cheap and land prices were low, either in the suburban hinterland or, after 1918, in the outer provinces of the Netherlands, often maintaining their head office in Amsterdam (Vries, Joh. de 1961, 95 ff.). The considerable increase in mobility allowed for this territorial division of labour between 'head' and 'trunk'.

Over the years an increasingly dense network of trains, trams and, on the eve of the First World War, — buses was woven around Amsterdam. It enlarged the scale of the daily urban system substantially. The introduction of intra-regional telephone lines further added to the territorial division of labour.

Could Amsterdam have prevented this exodus? Some local politicians complained about an 'anti-manufacturing-spirit' in some of the public departments, fed by a growing distaste for industrial waste and pollution (Gemeenteblad 1906, II, 22). The mayor did not refute this. He himself had not mourned it as a great loss when some years earlier another factory had left Amsterdam for a different location, although it had been a major employer (Vries, Joh. de 1961, 44).

Yet one can doubt whether a more stimulative approach would have helped much. The larger companies in particular were increasingly oriented to a regional or national market. Their locational preference became more and more 'footloose'. The successful introduction of trucks and vans advanced their flexibility. They no longer recruited their labour force exclusively on a local basis. Their staff commuted from suburbia to the new sites. Between the wars the exodus continued, despite the supply of building sites in a new and huge factory zone along the North Sea Canal, with optimal access for seagoing vessels, as well as modern docks and warehouses.

In the meantime, the expansion of the residential area went on as well. All industry was relocated. Yet in the older, pre-1900 parts of the city many industries maintained their presence. These medium-sized or small, often undercapitalized companies were not interested in expensive factory zones, which would inevitably increase the transport costs of their work-force. The successful introduction of electricity brought a clean source of power. However, at the same time the number of small firms multiplied. Their presence in what once were socially mixed pre-industrial neighbourhoods continued to depress these areas. By 1914 both the Jordaan and the Eastern and Western Islands were dominated by an all-pervasive poverty. Middle-class income earners had withdrawn *en masse* to new and better homes on the southern or western fringe (Wagenaar 1990, 310 ff.).

Epilogue

It would take well until the coming of the welfare state before local government disposed of the power to force out factories implanted in older, pre-1900 neighbourhoods. The most effective intervention in undesirable land use came with the wave of urban renewal in the 1960s and 1970s. The high rents of renovated buildings put a heavy strain on workshops and factories. Traffic regulations limited their accessibility. Ever-stricter rules on environmental protection further limited their profits. The end of the 1970s witnessed a dramatic closure of inner-city companies.

These changes helped to upgrade poverty-ridden inner-city areas into decent, sometimes even fashionable residential districts. At the same time they demonstrated the victory of interventionist policy over *laissez-faire* liberalism. In the nineteenth century such infringement upon private property rights was unthought of. All in all, the era of unrestricted free enterprise and the ideology of the hidden hand as a beneficial social mechanism did not last long. In the twentieth century Dutch cities reverted to planning practices more reminiscent of the seventeenth than of the nineteenth century.

Bibliography

Archives

Municipal Archives Amsterdam, Public Works Dept.
1875: file no. 5371.
1875: file no. 5433
1876: file no. 4483 (*Besier* v. *Meijlink*).
1876: file no. 5180 (*Terschotte* v. *Victor*).
1900: file no. 5180, no. 16.
1900: file no. 44 (*mr. Biederlaan* v. *Vereenigde Veehouders*).

Other References

Aalders, M.V.C. (1984), *Industrie, milieu en wetgeving. De hinderwet tussen synboliek en effectiviteit*, Amsterdam.

Delfgaauw, G.Th.J. (1934), *De grondpolitiek van de gemeente Amsterdam*, Amsterdam.

Gemeenteblad (1868), I.

Gemeenteblad (1905), II.

Gemeenteblad (1906), II.

Hohenberg, P. and L. Lees (1985), *The Making of Urban Europe, 1000–1950*, Cambridge, Mass.

Honderd jaar Zwavelzuur-fabricatie. Fa. G. T. Ketjen & Co., 1835–1935 (undated, anonymous).

Liafsen, J., Sr.,

De werking van de Hinderwet tÿdens de industrialisatie van Nederland. (1890–1910), *in*:

Jaarboek voor de geschiedenis van bedrÿf en techniek, H, 1986, 190–209.

Rapport van de Commissie voor het ontwerpen van een plan tot uitbreiding van de bebouwde kom der gemeente Amsterdam benoorden het IJ (1903) The Hague (further quoted as 'Industry Report').

Staatsblad van het Koninkrijk der Nederlanden (1875), no. 95.

Taverne, E. (1978), *In 't land van belofte: in de nieue stad. Ideaal en werkelijkheid van de stadsuitleg in de Republiek 1580–1680*, Maarssen.

Tijn, Th. van (1965), *Twintig jaren Amsterdam. De maatschappelijke ontwikkeling van de hoofdstad van de jaren '50 der vorige eeuw tot 1876*, Amsterdam.

Vries, Joh. de (1961), *Met Amsterdam als brandpunt. Honderdvijftig jaar Kamer van Koophandel en Fabrieken voor Amsterdam, 1811–1961*, Amsterdam.

Wagenaar, M. (1990), *Amsterdam 1876–1914. Economisch herstel, ruimtelijke expansie en de veranderende ordening van het ruimtelijk grondgebruik*, Amsterdam.

Wagenaar, M. (1984), 'Van "gemengde" naar "gelede" wijken. Amsterdamse stads-uitbreidingen in het laatste kwart van de negentiende eeuw', in M. Jonker and L. Noordegraaf (eds), *Van stadskern tot stadsgewest. Stedebouwkundige ontwikkeling van Amsterdam*, Amsterdam.

Zanden, J.L. van (1987), *De industrialisatie in Amsterdam, 1825–1914*, Bergen (NH).

13 The state, the élite and the market: the 'visible hand' in the British industrial city system

R.J. Morris

The basic outline of the urban history of industrializing Britain is well known. Economic growth, population growth, uneven but substantial changes in productivity and the organization of work were accompanied both by urban growth (towns became bigger) and by urbanization (more of the population lived in towns) (Morris 1986b, 164–79). In England and Wales, the proportion of the population living in settlements of more than 10,000 people rose from 21 per cent in 1801 to 62 per cent in 1911. In Scotland, the rise was on the same scale, from 17 per cent to 50 per cent (Robson 1973; Weber 1899, 59). C.M. Law's broader definition of 'urban' produced figures for England and Wales of 34 per cent to 79 per cent (Law 1967) This growth was marked by several features. The emergence of the 100,000-plus provincial city. Forty one British cities were in this category by 1911. There had been two possibly three, in 1801. The attention given to these cities should not hide the continued dominance of London. Its 'relative' decline involved a move from being eleven times the size of its nearest rival in 1801 to be just under six times in 1911. Despite this, London contained 11 per cent of Britain's population in 1801 and 16 per cent in 1911. These features were important for in so far as the interventions of the 'visible hand' were associated with specifically urban features of size, density and complexity, such interventions appeared first in London and the other great cities. Industrial change brought not only the industrial city, Salford, Preston, Paisley, Merthyr, Middlesbrough, but also an industrial city system. The older market and county towns, like Lincoln, York and Banbury were tied into the system through canals, railways and the growing demand of urban industrial populations (Hill 1974; Wright 1982; Armstrong 1974). Specialized towns like Oxford, leisure towns like Brighton, Harrogate and Blackpool, new towns like Swindon and Crewe were linked by the products of industrial change, railways, telephones and mass-produced goods (Walton 1983). An integrated urban system was created by the interaction of these specialized towns (Pred 1980; Morris, 1983a).

In the 1780s, most British towns could be described by Adam Smith's account of urbanism. They were market-places, encouraging the 'cultivation and improvement' of the countryside as a place of both agriculture and industry. They were sources of merchant capital and of 'order and good government' (Smith 1849, 181). In the next eighty years this situation was transformed. That section of industry concerned with mass production for 'distant markets' came in from the countryside. Industry came in from the countryside in response to a number of pressures created by the changing organization of production, by changing technologies and by the nature of the market for mass-produced goods. The town provided better supervision of high cost goods. The finishing end of many industries and the high quality end of several trades had always been urban. The size of the town made internal specialization possible. Urban locations provided services and skills which needed a substantial market to achieve economic viability. Lawyers, bankers, machine-makers, chemical producers and the makers of specialized glassware and packaging all sought urban locations. Technical change, such as chemical bleaching and taller factory buildings, reduced the demand for space, a high cost factor in towns. Water was the initial power source in towns but the steady growth of coal-based power was helped by the canal and railway, point delivery systems suited to coal. The railway, which had a more heavily capitalized point delivery system than the canal, encouraged the further concentration of production. As urban populations increased, many industries and services concentrated to serve the internal market thus created, notably breweries and leather. These developed to levels of efficiency which enabled them to seek external markets. The bulk of these processes were mediated through the market. The basic mechanisms of a cash economy, private property and the profit motive directed resource allocation and decisions of production and consumption.

At the same time, a variety of feudal and Early Modern economic relationships and rights were coming to a slow end. In 1837 the soke mill in Leeds was brought to an end by a private act of parliament. Under the soke mill, the owners of the manor of Leeds had a monopoly right to grind corn within the Manor or Borough of Leeds. This right was turned into a piece of property and purchased through a rate raised in the township (Leeds Soke Rate Assessment, DB 234 MH 1, Leeds City Archives). The 1832 Parliamentary Reform Act was celebrated for its political and constitutional effects. It also quietly set in motion a process by which certain ancient rights to vote based upon position like the potwallaper franchise in Preston or the widespread freeman franchises were transformed into a property-based franchise dependent upon marketable resources. Other forms of regulation like the Cloth Halls in Leeds were simply bypassed by market forms (Wilson 1971, 194–219). In many towns and cities guilds survived into the nineteenth century as part of the political process. After 1832 they either withered away or were transformed as the basis for charitable activity or inputs to the craft traditions of trades unions operating in the market economy (Gray 1976, 91–3).

The influence of the state seemed to be one of a benign neglect, providing the basic functions of law and order with occasional intervention to counter some of the more disruptive effects of urbanization. British urban growth took place in a capital-rich and population-rich economy. It took place in an organized capitalist economic space, a countryside with a highly developed property and market structure. These structures were related to the towns through a wide variety of agricultural and industrial products. There was little evidence of an 'urban policy' on the scale of the medieval *bastides*, North American boosterism or twentieth-century urban economic devel- opment and regeneration projects (Beresford 1967; Artibise 1982; Donnison and Middleton 1987). Was there any need for a 'visible hand' to intervene from the state or from any other structure of authority?

Adam Smith in his account of the virtues of the 'invisible hand' admitted a variety of situations which justified intervention.

The first duty of the sovereign, therefore, that of defending the society from the violence and injustice of other independent societies, grows gradually more and more expensive as the society advances in civilization. (*Wealth of Nations*, 5, 1, 319)

The rich, in particular, are necessarily interested to support that order of things, which can alone secure them in possesion of their own advantages. . . . Civil Government, so far as it is instituted for the security of property, is in reality instituted for the defence of the rich against the poor, or of those who have some property against those who have none at all. (*Wealth of Nations*, 5, 1, 321)

The third and last duty of the sovereign or commonwealth, is that of erecting and maintaining those public institutions and those public works, which, though they may be in the highest degree advantageous to a great society, are however of such a nature, that the profit could never repay the expense to any individual or small number of individuals. (*Wealth of Nations*, 5, 1, 325)

He gave an optimistic account of the manner in which the market and the profit motive would provide for most social and economic needs. Even when this failed he looked to specific taxes which would attribute costs to those who benefited most from the interventions offered. These were especially important for the location–specific services of local government and hence for urban places.

The outcome in the next century and a half was by no means so simple. The literature of British urban history not does deliver a clear and unified account of the relative part played by market and non–market forces in the allocation of resources to urban development. We have many important accounts of local party politics, constitutional structures and policy inno- vations (Fraser 1976; Garrard 1983; Hennock 1973). We have an excellent literature on the development of the built–up areas (Daunton 1983a; Olsen 1976; Parry Lewis 1965; Dyos 1966) and a substantial contribution to the understanding of issues of social structure and social control in an urban context (Morris 1986a; Smith 1982; Joyce 1980; Foster 1974). These supple- mented by information from contemporary parliamentary papers and sta- tistical studies make it possible to provide an outline of the 'visible hand'

and its part in urban economic development. This chapter will both provide this outline and indicate some of the ways in which non–market mechanisms for allocating resources may be related to the growing power of the market economy. Although local government must take a central place, closer inspection shows a variety of other forms for allocating space and resources, and taking decisions over their use. They could not work in isolation from market mechanisms but were never subordinate to them. The interaction of these two sets of processes produced the towns and cities of the British industrial system.

The visible hand or non–market mechanisms were used in quite distinct circumstances. They ensured that capitalist market relationships operated effectively. At its most basic this involved the provision of a legal system which enforced contracts, collected debts, validated property rights and ensured the smooth and certain transfer of property. One of the first institutions provided in the growing urban centres of Birmingham and Merthyr was a small debts court. Birmingham had its Court of Requests in 1752 well before the first Improvement Act began to attend to paving, lighting and cleansing in 1769 (Money 1977, 11–18). Merthyr acquired a Court of Requests in 1809 over a decade before the Select Vestry in 1822 (Williams 1978). There were many more aspects of the reproduction of capital and labour in a market economy which were essential to the working of that economy, yet because they did not attract immediate profit would be carried out only by non–market forces (Dunleavy 1980; Castells 1977, 246–75 and 393–420). The paving, lighting and policing of streets together with the care and control of the poor were early candidates. Water supply, sewage disposal and education were debated ground for the whole period. The provision of low–income housing was frequently fingered by the invisible hand but remained governed by the profit motive until the twentieth century.

In addition, British cities witnessed many localized interventions which eased the path of profit and development. The landscape of many British cities has been influenced by interventions which spread risk, assisted land assembly and allocated unprofitable or unpriceable aspects of property development to Corporations. Edinburgh's New Town remains an outstanding monument to this process. In the 1750s, a dirty patch of water called the North Loch provided a formidable barrier for development north from the crowded old town stretched along the medieval High Street. North Bridge was built across this water between 1765 and 1772. It was financed by a subscription fully backed by the credit and contributions of the Corporation. This was essential for sustaining work which cost £16,000 and lasted seven years. The economic return came not in the form of tolls after the manner of *Wealth of Nations* but from the opening up of the level open land to the north. On this land Edinburgh's New Town was built. The fluctuations of the capital market, the cost structures of builders and the demand schedules of potential owners and residents affected the timing and details of a process which took over eighty years, but interventions of Edinburgh Corporation in the form of land assembly, regulations and the provision of expensive infrastructure was an essential part of creating the

New Town in the controlled and classical form which emerged. Between 1767 and 1783, costs were £23,690, whilst the revenue from feus was only £15,957. Not until the late 1790s did a revenue of £35,664 exceed costs of £33,524 (Youngson 1966, 59–110). Edinburgh had a greater taste for this sort of operation than any other British town and spent its way to a protracted rescheduling of debts in the 1830s (Robertson and Wood 1928, 229–56).

Defence and public order have always been included even in the most minimal list of functions which the market cannot sustain. The years between 1790 and 1832 saw a number of disorders which were related by contemporaries to the lack of appropriate urban institutions. Although late eighteenth-century Birmingham was undoubtedly urban in terms of size, density and complexity, its citizens remained satisfied with a minimal level of urban institutions. The justices, the gaol, the election of Members of Parliament all took place in the nearby county town of Warwick. The local ratepayers refused to contemplate the cost of police and a stipendary magistrate. This was one of the reasons why the authorities lost control of a violent riot in 1793 in which tensions resulting from the French Revolution and divisions amongst the middle classes ended with the destruction of several bourgeois houses including that of Joseph Priestly, the experimental chemist (Money 1977, 15–18). Manchester survived into the 1830s with the same sort of rag-bag of institutions. When eleven people were killed in 1819 during the reform demonstration on St Peter's Fields (the 'Peterloo' massacre), it was as a result of action by the country yeomanry directed by county magistrates. Cobden in the 1830s was convinced that urban magistrates would have avoided this (Cobden 1907). In South Wales, Merthyr Tydfil grew from 8,000 residents in 1801 to 27,000 in 1831 as a result of the demand for labour from four giant iron works. Its density, death rates and poverty were urban and industrial but its leisure patterns and institutions were those of the village. The imperfections of this urban formation was one cause of the authorities' inability to control the main force of the takeover of the town in 1831. The short-term response was to bring troops to quell the rebellion. The longer-term strategy included making Merthyr a borough under the new parliamentary reform act with its own Member of Parliament (Williams 1978). Clearly, the nature of urban institutions was only one element in the course which these three riots took, but it is important to note that contemporaries in authority increasingly came to see urban institutions as the base upon which law and order could be maintained. When British policing was reformed in the 1830s, control and policy was demanded and placed firmly with urban authorities.

Recent geographical theory has given much attention to the management of externalities as an element in urban policy. This has received little coherent attention from historians although much evidence lies in studies of public health policy, local government development and planning history.

External effects may be said to arise when relevant effects on production and welfare go wholly or partially unpriced. Being outside the price system such external effects are sometimes looked upon as the by-products, wanted or unwanted, of other peoples' activities that immediately or indirectly affect the welfare of individuals. (Harvey 1973, 58)

Externalities consisted of the cost of access to work, housing, jobs or other amenities such as open space. Such access may be costed in terms of time, cash, noise or dirt. Pollution from industrial activity or decisions such as the placing of a fire station or library were important examples.

South Edinburgh expanded in a less orderly way than the north with its New Town. The Pleasance was the easternmost of the roads south. The building of substantial houses overlooking the royal park of Holyrood began in the late eighteenth century. They had a pleasant, prestigious and open environment until the arrival of the coal railway, the so-called 'Innocents Railway', from Dalkeith in 1825. The noise, dirt and dust of the coal yard destroyed the amenity of the houses at St Leonard's Bank and each new building boom saw a decrease in quality and increase in density (Robertson 1983, 63–5). Even more destructive were the negative externalities of the working-class and tradespeople's housing built in the Friar's district of St Ebbe's Parish in Oxford in the 1820s. The area was laid out and sold as small building plots suitable for between one and four houses, according to the resources of the builders. The tiny houses were tailored to the incomes of potential buyers. They were provided with privies and wells dug into the river gravel. This was fine until crowding and flooding mixed the contents of the privies with the water in the wells, causing all manner of water-borne diseases including the cholera epidemics of 1832, 1849 and 1854 (Morris 1971). In industrial towns like Leeds, smoke from the growing number of factories and dye-houses resulted in an unpriced reduction in the value of many properties (Beresford 1967). The inability of the market to control or allocate the costs of such externalities was one motivation for intervention.

Law and order, the sustaining of essential but unprofitable activities and the control of externalities were all partly or wholly supportive of a market economy which needed a minimal level of predictability and the conditions for the continued accumulation of capital to make profit-seeking decisions possible. Other motivations for intervention fit less easily into this subordinate role.

A wide range of urban-based activities were designed to sustain the authority and legitimacy of those with power. Certain aspects of policing and education, religious missionary work, cultural provision, buildings and monuments all played a long-standing role in this respect. From the start those who provided free or heavily subsidized education to children from low-income families were aware that they were creating both economic assets and a crucial set of attitudes to authority. In their first annual report, the committee of the Leeds Lancastrian Free School wrote: 'They hope that habits of decency, regularity, diligence and attention, and proper subordination may be formed and strengthened at the same time' (*First Annual Report of the Leeds Royal Lancastrian Free School*, Leeds 1814). In so far as this authority was the authority of the owners of capital, then such activity was subordinate to the smooth working of a market economy. In Britain, such authority contained two other elements. There was a respect for hierachy and continuity which irritated some intellectuals of the manufacturing class but formed an important element of élite ideology. There was also a debate between several major groups over the nature of the religious authority which could and should be contained in educational and cultural activities.

Most urban areas contained residues of older forms of property, especially in trusts and large estates which provided a distinct set of motivations. Such estates were bound by trust deeds or by family dynastic ambitions. They were concerned with status, continuity and survival, which gave them a much longer time horizon than most profit-seeking property and capital holders. Edinburgh's ability to control and shape urban development to the north of the city was assisted by the importance of a series of trusts as landholders. Educational and charitable trusts like Heriots and Trinity House as well as the Corporation itself eased planning and land assembly (Reed 1982; Robert Kirkwood, *A plan of the City of Edinburgh and its Environs containing all the recent and intended Improvements*, Edinburgh 1817). In Birmingham the part played by the Calthorpe estate in the creation of the high status suburb of Edgbaston has been well charted. The owners of the estate were willing to control externalities in the interests of the long-term value of properties on the estate and their own desire to be developers of high status properties (Cannadine 1980, 94–146).

Lastly, there was a series of motivations that can only be called 'localism'. Many urban leaders knew that they had a collective interest deriving from their common location in a town. Many were worried about the reputation of their town, which might be crucial when seeking powers from Parliament or attracting credit in business. They needed to act together when bargaining with a railway company in the private bill committees of Parliament. The elaborate symbolic system of town halls, statues, art galleries and other public buildings needed a coherence and dignity if it was to play its part in sustaining the authority of a local élite (Briggs 1963, 139–83; Meller 1976, 65–70; Kellett 1969, 100–5; Garrard 1983, 10–103).

The social and institutional structures which responded to these situations included much more than the structures of local government which have a major position in the literature. Local government was important in four major forms, the reconstructed corporations of the 1830s, the Poor Law authorities, the sanitary and urban district councils of the later half of the century and the school boards post 1870 (Hennock 1984). There were many other specialist and minor bodies which varied from improvement commissioners and docks and harbour boards to the Metropolitan Board of Works. In addition there was a growing and important group of voluntary societies which looked after the collective interests of the local bourgeoisie (Morris 1983b) These play an important part in the social control literature but have rarely been seen as deliberate and effective ways of overcoming the limitations of the market and the profit motive. The literature on urban development has also identified a series of legal structures which substantially modified the working of the market, notably covenants and the Scottish feu charter. Finally, participants in a range of prescriptive social structures developed strategies during the nineteenth century which modified major aspects of the market. The family often operated through age, gender and religion. In Britain, ethnic structures of religion, race and sometimes language were more rare (Anderson 1971; Roberts 1984; Smith 1986). The city, owing to its size, was able to sustain a variety of ethnic, language and religious communities. Such prescriptive structures operated generally throughout British society but their interaction with urban systems contributed to specific social and spatial effects like the middle-class suburbs which appeared in the later half of the century (Davidoff and Hall 1983).

Local government intervention can be divided into four major phases. An initial phase of fragmented government from the mid-eighteenth to about 1830 saw new agencies added to survivals from the seventeenth century and earlier. Local Acts of Parliament added Improvement and Highway Commissioners, Paving and Lighting Boards and Trustees of Toll Roads to existing Overseers of the Poor, Parish Vestries, Court Leets, Lordships of the Manor and Municipal Corporations. These corporations mostly derived from seventeenth century charters. They had various functions. Some were little more than agencies for electing a Member of Parliament. An important group provided Justices of the Peace for local Petty and Quarter Sessions and managed the local administration of justice. The coal-exporting city of Newcastle upon Tyne showed the nature of the activities of a wealthy and active municipal corporation in this period. There were two major items of income, tolls and dues on the trade of the city and rents and fines on property owned by the Corporation (Figure 13.1). The other major item was for conveying ballast from the ships which discharged ballast at special quays in the Tyne before taking on coal.

The 16 per cent devoted to the salaries and costs of the mayor and other officials was mostly a result of the administration of justice (Figure 13.2) although some was allocated ceremonial and regulatory activities. Such a corporation was a legal entity entrusted under charter with regulating local trade, administering justice and managing its own property in the interests of the local trading élite. Investments were of two kinds. Some consisted of property designed to add to the Corporation's own income. Others involved collective capital and formed part of a local economic development strategy which was not to be surpassed for over a century.

This was characteristic of ports and leisure towns. In such places the benefits of such investment were diffuse and long term, hence the collective agency of a corporation or trust was appropriate. Many of these corporations distorted the working of the market in different ways. They often attributed costs according to position rather than market or utilitarian considerations. In Newcastle the burgesses, like the freemen in other places, were free of many of the tolls. Such a position could be gained by inheritance, gift or purchase. The corporations were in no sense representative bodies of local ratepayers. That notion was contained in many of the local Improvement Acts (Keith Lucas 1980, 15–39; Select Committee on Municipal Corporations 1835; Mackenzie 1827, 601–53). The progress from small debt courts to improvement commissioners has already been outlined for Birmingham and Merthyr. Most areas had a various overlapping bodies. Growing towns without corporations showed little desire to acquire one. Birmingham's historian Hutton proudly declared that 'a town without

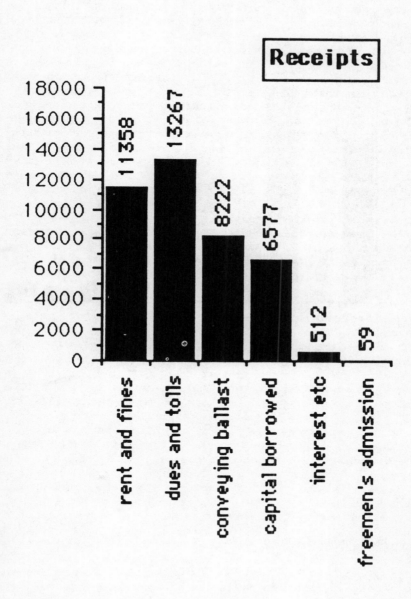

Figure 13.1   Income of the unreformed Corporation of Newcastle upon Tyne, 1832–3

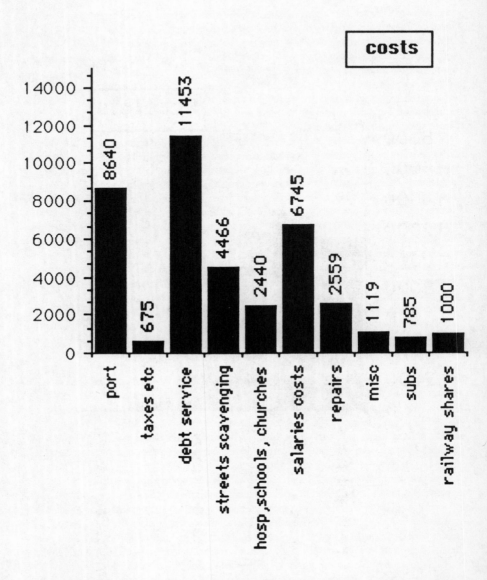

Figure 13.2   Spending pattern of the Corporation of Newcastle upon Tyne, 1832–3

a charter is a town without a shackle'. He meant that such a town had lower rates to pay and fewer political disputes.

This system was reconstructed from a series of reforms which began in 1835. The process involved a concern for urbanism both as a system of power and subordination which has dominated recent theory and for its spatial aspects more familiar to theorists of the 1930s and 1950s. Reconstruction centred upon 178 towns whose institutions were re-modelled by the Municipal Corporations Act, 5 & 6 Will. IV c.76. The concept of a town which the policy-makers had in mind was indicated by the instructions given to the Boundary Commission, which required that a clear line be drawn upon the map to include not just contiguity in terms of building but an integrated economic interest with enough voters to stand against other sources of power in an area, notably local landowners. The town was to be a spatially located power structure. More important for the future it was to be selected by local ratepayers and the local taxes on property (rates) were to be regarded as its principal source of income (*Instructions to the Parliamentary Boundary Commissioners* 1831–32; *Report of the Commissioners upon the Boundaries and Wards of Certain Boroughs and Corporate Towns* 1837).

In the next two decades, these bodies took on several aspects of local government. The Improvement Commissioners became committees of the corporation in legislation like the Leeds Improvement Act of 1842. They managed all aspects of the local state except the Poor Law which was located in Unions of Parishes which deliberately tried to ignore urban integrity and urban—rural divisions. Although historians have concentrated on the public health debates of those decades, the most successful inno-vations of the new local authorities concerned the regulation of the built-up areas to increase security, improve circulation, help policing and the provi-sion of services. The Leeds Act of 1842 was like many of the same period. It provided for the 'advantage and comfort of the inhabitants'. The corpor-ation took power through its inspectors to regulate building line, street width, thickness of walls, drainage and lighting. One result was the inven-tion of the street not just as a major thoroughfare but as the normal layout for all types of housing (Daunton 1983b). The acts extended older functions like regulating markets and scavenging. Newer provisions for ordering towns were provided. Streets were numbered and a public clock maintained (Leeds Improvement Act 1842). In the first decade very few places not included in the initial act applied for a charter. Most remained content with the older system. When the first Public Health Act was passed in 1848, the corporations were made the local health authorities, but the act left localities the option of becoming a local health authority without having a corpor-ation. Power was assigned to localities on the specific criteria of excess death rate. In the mid-nineteenth century such an excess was caused by water-borne diseases, notably infant diarrhoea. High death rates were a result of overcrowding. Thus locally specific authority was created on the basis of criteria related to the urban characteristic of density. Even in the 1870s, when the Public Health Acts were codified, the urban areas were given greater powers than rural ones (Public Health Act 1875, 38 & 39 Vic. c.55).

The debates were about public health, sewage systems and water supply, the effective innovations concerned the regulation of the built-up areas, but the spending patterns of the new corporations retained first place for the administration of justice and the management of local collective capital, both corporate and general. At the start of the 1840s only 20 per cent of income came from rates. For the four new boroughs, the figure was 80 per cent. On the expenditure side the greatest amount (27 per cent) was still allocated to the administration of justice. The other large sections went to debt service and the accumulation of local collective capital or public works and repairs (Fletcher 1842).

Around 1860 these corporations began to take a much broader and more active role in the accumulation and reconstruction of local capital. Large areas of several great cities were reconstructed to reduce density and ease the circulation of traffic. Although these actions were separate and uncoordinated, they all had much in common. They were unconnected but similar responses to the same economic and technological forces. Together they formed the first indication of a constructive and positive policy of economic development undertaken by the local state to counter the inability of market forces to provide for their own smooth and effective working. Sheffield gained its charter in 1843 and soon after acquired various regulatory powers under a new Improvement Act. By the early 1870s, the Corporation sought more positive powers of intervention. The city centre was congested and there was a shortage of suitable sites for retail and office accommodation in the growing central business district. Under a Provisional Order from the Local Government Board in 1875, Sheffield Corporation gained the authority to raise loans, purchase land and undertake the building of several new streets and widen others. The total cost was £575,055 of which £515,244 was for land purchase. Some £125,786 was regained from subsequent land sales (Furness 1893, 182–94). In Birmingham, this operation centred upon the building of Corporation Street. Joseph Chamberlain openly acknowledged the link between the spending and the development of Birmingham as a retail centre for the English Midlands. Corporation Street assisted the development of local capital, the prestige of the local élite and the success of Birmingham in inter-city competition. This sort of operation was the nearest the British industrial cities came to boosterism (Hennock 1973, 126–30). Many of these improvement schemes were linked to the rhetoric of the public health movement. In Edinburgh, Chambers Street was driven through crowded eighteenth-century squares and wynds under the 1867 City Improvement Act, a result of the constant nagging of the city's first medical officer of health. It did clear many unhealthy dwellings and replaced them with a new north–south link to bypass the congested High Street (Cousins and Lessels 1867; Morris 1986b, 177). A warren of courts and squares was changed into a major institutional street containing the University, the Watt Institution, the Church of Scotland Normal School (teacher-training) and the Museum of Science and Art. The scheme took over twenty years to complete. Several new streets were created and others widened. Death rates did fall and population densities were reduced, but the scheme was accompanied by complaints that it increased the working-class housing shortage. The Improvement Trust demolished 2,721 houses and built 340 (*Royal Commission on the Housing of the Working Classes*, 1884–5, 22; MacDonald, PhD 1968, 90–159). Low-income populations were decanted into nearby areas. In practice the scheme concentrated more on extending the central business district south than on health and welfare. The increasing size and specialization of the central business district was an important feature of the city in the second half of the nineteenth century (Whitehand 1987, 112–32). In Britain, this development was helped upon its way by the very visible hand of the municipal corporation improvement scheme.

By the 1880s an increasing number of urban authorities had begun to trade on a regular basis, providing a wide range of goods and services. The so-called 'reproductive undertakings' were dominated by three public utilities—water, gas and electricity—and by the tramways. Also included were markets, public baths and parks, with a number of innovations like Sheffield's pawnshop and Bradford's sterilized milk, which were small in economic importance but both promised and threatened ever-continuing expansion (Falkus 1977; Porter 1907, 108–9). Municipal trading originated with a group of characteristic activities. They were capital and land-intensive and spatially very specific. Services like water, gas and the trams tended to be monopolies which needed permission from the local authority for the use of roads or space under roads, initially financed by that authority. Many felt that the monopoly profits resulting from that permission should go to the 'ratepayers'. The output from much of this activity was often consumed collectively. Water and gas could be metered but the public health benefits of regular water supplies for all, or the public order benefits of well-lit streets and courts could not be allocated by conventional price mechanisms. Many of these activities were technically complex and required high technical standards if public safety and full collective benefits were to be ensured. In the last thirty years of the nineteenth century huge loans were raised on the security of the local rates. The position in 1898 showed the importance of the big four, water, gas, trams and electricity (Figure 13.3).

The water supply industry was the leading sector for municipal trading (Figure 13.4). The evidence available for about 80 per cent of the urban population showed that as technical demands, capital needs and the collective benefits of regular supplies became understood, so the supply of water moved from private and joint stock company provision to the municipal sector.

In contrast to many North American cities, British local authorities were in a strong bargaining position regarding private or joint stock local utilities. Despite this, little attempt was made to use this growing control of urban capital to mould the shape of the city or to compete with other cities to attract capital and labour after the manner of the 'boosters' (Artibise 1975; Linteau 1981). The Edinburgh tramways, joint stock and municipal followed the builders (Ochonja, PhD 1974; Ward 1964). A few street reconstructions in East Central London such as High Holborn and Queen Victoria Street which divided the central business district from the working-class east end contributed to some effective socio-spatial

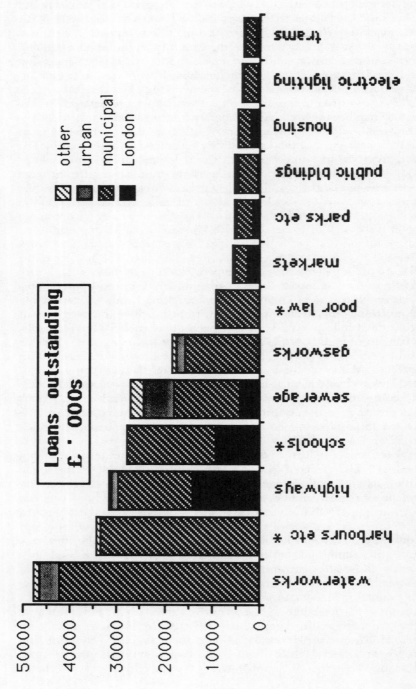

Figure 13.3 Outstanding loans on local authorities, 31 March 1898. (Fowler, 1900)

* These activities were carried on by authorities separately constituted from the Municipal Corporations and Urban District Councils.

engineering. Overt interurban competition was for prestige, first town halls and other public buildings, then parks, libraries and art galleries, designed to civilize the town and demonstrate the culture and liberality of urban élites (Briggs 1963, 139–83; Mellor 1976, 65–70; Kellett 1969, 100–5; Garrard 1983, 10–103).

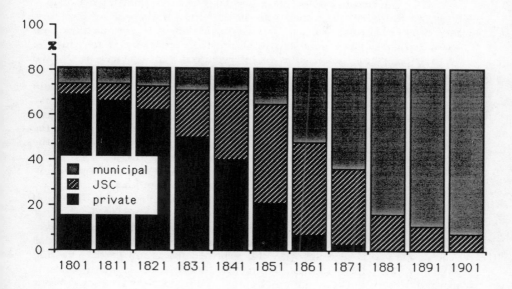

Figure 13.4 The organization of the water supply industry in 81 towns and cities in Britain expressed as a percentage of the urban population served. (Hassan 1985)

Evidence collected by Parliament gave some indication of the returns on capital valued at historic cost (Fowler 1900, 387–9). This varied between sectors.

	%		%
water	0.05	tramways	1.05
gas	1.8	electric light	0.14
markets	1.9	quays and harbours	1.3

These rates of return were well below anything expected for industrial capital or even in the securities market as a whole. The yield on consols in the 1890s fluctuated between 2.5 and 2.9 per cent. The ratepayer was held to benefit from the small net surplus made but then the credit of the rates was being used to mitigate the discipline of the market so that the point of supply in terms of quality, regularity and perhaps price could be shifted beyond anything which a market equilibrium might produce, especially under a monopoly.

These three phases of urban action, regulation, reconstruction and municipal trading, overlapped with one another, although the sequence was secure in each town and city. The timing, extent and impact of each phase was different according to the size, political traditions and economic and social needs of each place. So far non-market interventions have been accounted for in functional terms. It must be remembered that for the decision-takers the possibilities of intervention were opened up by two features of British élite ideology. At a local level, the religious traditions of nonconformity provided manufacturers and their professional and commercial allies with a motivation to seek legitimacy for their privilege and power through civic work. They inherited a concept of élite responsibility from the paternalistic traditions of the eighteenth century. From the 1830s onwards, this nonconformist Whig–Liberal tradition incited the creation of a Tory paternalist tradition located with the Tory–Anglican faction of local urban élites. This faction provided a powerful opposition to Liberal nonconformist dominance in most urban centres. Only in rare instances, as in Liverpool, did it achieve power (Hennock 1973, 61–79 and 154–69; Waller 1981). Central government was led by an aristocratic élite who had inherited the same paternalistic traditions. They saw themselves as the managers of social stability and the relationships of the lower social orders. They provided an open and general supervision of the enabling powers created for localities. In practice this involved a quasi-legalistic arbitration between local interests and between local and national needs with occasional inputs of policy from administrator 'statesmen in disguise'.

Restricting attention to the local state creates an impression that British urban élites played a minimal and reactive role between 1800 and 1860. Two other forms of intervention were especially important in that period.

Between 1780 and 1850 British urban élites created a wide range of voluntary societies which devoted substantial resources to the development of the urban economy and society by way of subscriptions, donations and legacies. Some societies like the Missionary Societies and the Literary and Philosophical Societies formed and asserted the identity of that élite and the middle classes they claimed to lead. Others like the Sunday Schools, school societies and Mechanics Institutions openly acknowledged a social control function. Together with Temperance Societies and Savings Banks they created a coherent ideology which sought to integrate the lower middle and working classes into a stable élite-led society. Many of these societies provided substantial amounts of collective capital in the form of hospitals, libraries, schools and meeting-halls (Morris 1983b). Although some, like the Edinburgh Society for the Suppression of Begging or the countless local Watch and Ward societies and Societies for the Apprehension of Felons, acted in support of existing local state agencies, the bulk of these societies deliberately avoided close association with the state. This enabled them to encompass the conflict between Tory–Anglican and Whig–nonconformist factions as competition between societies rather than as disruptive contests for the local state (Morris 1990a).

In the key period of minimal regulatory action by local government in the 1830s and 1840s, these societies commanded substantial local resources. It is very difficult to find comprehensive information on the overall quantity or nature of the resources controlled by these societies. Surviving figures are scattered in annual reports and local newspapers. Leeds was amongst the top half-dozen commercial and manufacturing centres of the first half of the century. Its experience must represent other major urban centres. A series of major voluntary funds were collected for the relief of the poor during trade depressions. These reached their peak in 1839 and 1842 when the sums collected equalled 30 per cent and 20 per cent of the sum collected for the same purpose through the local state. In those decades the Leeds General Infirmary received an income of between £4,000 and £6,000 from subscriptions, collections, donations and legacies. This was much on the same scale as the £7,427 collected in rates by the Improvement Commissioners in 1834 for lighting and street improvements. (*Leeds Mercury* 22 March 1834). Much of the collective and social capital created in this period was financed by quasi-commercial methods. The Philosophical Hall and the Leeds Public Baths were both financed by shares from which no one received or expected to receive an income. The Cemetery and the Zoological and Botanical Gardens were also joint stock companies from which in theory a dividend was expected, but statements made at the time indicate that income was not the main motive for subscribers, which was perhaps just as well for the Cemetery Company was limited to 5 per cent and the Gardens went bankrupt (Morris 1990b). The leading urban voluntary societies were concerned with the legitimacy and stability of dominant power structures, with expressing a collective local interest or some form of collective consumption and capital accumulation. These voluntary societies were an important episode in the development of urban resources. By the 1860s, urban leaders admitted that such societies could never amass sufficient resources for the tasks they set themselves and an increasing number of them worked in association with the state.

As the size of British towns and cities grew in the late eighteenth century, an increasing use was made of legal devices to control externalities in high status residential areas. In England, developers of large urban estates who looked for purchasers and future residents from the upper classes made use of the covenant. In Scotland the feu charter was used in the same way. Requirements about building line, drainage and minimum house size or value in Edinburgh's New Town ensured that any purchaser was guaranteed a neighbour of a minimum economic status (Youngson 1966, 81–3). A hundred years later in south Edinburgh, Sir George Warrender began to feu his estate in Marchmont. His feu charter determined the layout, the size and nature of the buildings and excluded all commercial and industrial activity and, above all, premises selling alcohol. The white-collar residents who moved in were assured of a neighbourhood of uniform and secure social status without the potential annoyance of back–court industry or street-level drinking-shops (Gray 1985). The Calthorpe estate in Birmingham was carefully disciplined through the estate office and the covenant. Even the resident who dared to let a chimney appear above his greenhouse had to remove it. The enforcement of the covenant was especially important for preventing workshops and retail premises entering the estate on the side closest to the city centre of Birmingham (Cannadine 1980).

There were many limitations to the effectiveness of these legal devices. The Wilson estate to the west of Leeds was laid out as a fashionable middle-class west end. The covenants successfully kept out public houses but could not keep out the smoke from Benjamin Gott's new factory to the west (Beresford 1967). Nor could such provisions succeed if they attempted to work against the market. The Duke of Norfolk attempted to create a 'west end' in Sheffield around Paradise Square. The Sheffield middle classes were not numerous enough and the Duke's agents had to reduce the quality of houses they envisaged (Cannadine 1980, 218). These legal devices assisted the creation of a series of middle-class social and culturally uniform residential areas, controlled in terms of retail and commercial development and free from the public sale of alcohol, the threat of industry and working-class housing. The 'west end' and nineteenth-century suburbs remain characteristic parts of many British cities as a result of this process.

This chapter has outlined some of the major features of interventions by the state and by urban élites in the economic and social development of British industrial cities. What were the directions, effects, limitations and general features of these interventions? Were they specific to industrial city systems or did they have specific British features? It is possible to make some preliminary suggestions.

Several features derive from the changing nature of cities in an industrial city system. As the size, density and complexity of these cities increased, so did the need for regulation to counter a wide range of destructive elements such as disease, fire and traffic congestion. These factors plus the nature of much industrial technology and the tensions and social attitudes of class consciousness meant that the potential gains from the control of externalities became greater. At the same time specialization meant that many unprofitable but essential items in the production process became separate and identifiable. The nature of the urban industrial system operating in a market economy in itself increased the need and the motivation for non-market interventions.

The actions of local government were limited by three disciplines. First, there was the attitude of local property-holders both as ratepayer voters and as representatives of local interests before the Private Bill Committees of the Houses of Parliament in London. The outcome was often structured by the result of a conflict between upper-class professional and commercial individuals who saw advantages in spending on local social capital and a *petite bourgeoisie* who found that the consequent increase in rates outweighed any advantage they might share. The politics of 'intervention', of 'collective capital accumulation' or 'collective consumption' took the form of a contest not so much between political parties as between status groups within the middle classes (Hennock 1973; Fraser 1976). The second major limitation was the influence of a powerful central state. The London Parliament was directly or indirectly the only source of authority available. The Private Bill Procedures of Westminster Parliament and after 1870 the Local Government Board regulated the ability of local authorities to raise finance and override individual property interests in pursuit of perceived collective aims. Local élites were linked to this central state by a series of political alliances which were structured by class, status and religion (Whig and Tory). This system was national, changed its form in 1830s, but because the national élite was divided, mitigated some of the constitutional weakness of localities in Britain. The third discipline, that of the market, was relatively weak. The Local Government Board had more effect on the ability to raise loan finance than the money market. The clearest market effect was that of the local rent geography. This pushed many institutional buildings away from potential clients towards the low-rent urban fringe, resulting in some bizarre conjunctions of poor houses and middle–class suburbs in the late nineteenth century (Whitehand 1987).

British cities lacked two features which appeared elsewhere in the economic development of cities in industrial systems. There was little need for intervention to aid reproduction of capital on a 'booster' basis. Instead, by the end of the century local government agencies had amassed a massive and specialized social capital. The town in Britain never became a unit of entrepreneurship as it did in other economies but it did react to the results and impact of entrepreneurship. Also missing from this history was the intense bargaining over locational decisions characteristic of nineteen-century North American and twentieth-century European cities. Locational decisions were taken in the context of the overall market and cost structures of a developed urban system. There were few financial, commercial or industrial units capable of bargaining over location with these established urban communities. The locational intertia of industrial capital was increased through its ownership by families embedded in local social and political networks. Even the railway companies were weak when bargaining with local authorities (Kellett 1969).

In the capital-rich and population-rich towns and cities of Britain, the interventions of the 'visible hand' were in the initial stages minimal. The logic of the developing industrial and market system created the need for more intervention, and more of that intervention became identified with a local state which saw itself as the creature of local property-holders and ratepayers. This brought an end-of-century crisis as the ability of the local tax base to expand failed to keep up with the demands for finance for intervention (Offer 1981, 283–315). There were two sorts of solution. Boundary extensions often led to bitter disputes, as low-taxed suburban municipalities sought to avoid association with larger high-taxed neighbours. The long-term solution was an increase in central government subsidies and grants in aid which began in the 1870s (Bellamy 1988). This led to the late twentieth-century situation in which the town was no longer able to contain urban social relationships and their associated needs for non-market controls and interventions (Dunleavy 1980; Castells 1977).

Bibliography

Anderson, Michael (1971), *Family Structure in Nineteenth Century Lancashire*, Cambridge, Cambridge University Press.

Armstrong, Alan (1974), *Stability and Change in an English County Town. A Social Study of York, 1801–51*, Cambridge, Cambridge University Press.

Artibise, Alan (1975), *Winnipeg. A Social History of Urban Growth, 1874–1913*, Montreal, McGill-Queens University Press.

Artibise, Alan (1982), 'In pursuit of growth: municipal boosterism and the urban development in the Canadian prairie West, 1871–1913', in G.A. Stelter and A.F.J. Artibise, *Shaping the Urban Landcape*. Ottawa, Carleton University Press.

Bellamy, Christine (1988), *Administering Central–Local Relations, 1871–1919. The Local Government Board in its Fiscal and Cultural Context*, Manchester, Manchester University Press.

Beresford, M.W. (1967), *New Towns of the Middle Ages. Town Plantation in England, Wales and Gascony*, London, Lutterworth.

Beresford, M.W. (1967), 'Prosperity Street and others: an essay in visible urban history', in M.W. Beresford and G.R.J. Jones (eds), *Leeds and Its Region*, Leeds, British Association for the Advancement of Science.

Briggs, Asa (1963), 'Leeds, a Study in Civic Pride', in A. Briggs, (ed.) *Victorian Cities*, London, Odhams.

Cannadine, David (1980), *Lords and Landlords. The Aristocracy and the Towns, 1774–1967*, Leicester, Leicester University Press.

Castells, Manuel (1977), *The Urban Question*, London, Edward Arnold.

Cobden, Richard (1907), 'Incorporate Your Borough', in William E.A.Axon, *Cobden as a Citizen*, London, T.F. Unwin.

Cousins, D. and J. Lessels (1867), *Plan of Sanitary Improvements in the City of Edinburgh*, Edinburgh, W. and A.K. Johnson.

Daunton, M.J. (1983a), *House and Home in the Victorian City. Working Class Housing, 1850–1914*, London, Edward Arnold.

Daunton, M.J. (1983b), 'Public place and private space: the Victorian city and the working class household', in Fraser and Sutcliffe, (1983): 212–32.

Davidoff, Leonore and Catherine Hall, (1983), 'The architecture of public and private life: English middle class society in a provincial town, 1780–1850', in Fraser and Sutcliffe, (1983): 326–45.

Donnison, David and Alan Middleton (eds) (1987), *Regenerating the Inner City. Glasgow's Experience*. London, Routledge and Kegan Paul.

Dunleavy, Patrick (1980), *Urban Political Analysis*, London, Macmillan.

Dyos, H.J. (1966), *Victorian Suburb. A Study of the Growth of Camberwell*. Leicester, Leicester University Press.

Falkus, Malcolm (1977), 'The development of municipal trading in the nineteenth century', *Business History*, 19 (2): 134–61.

Fletcher, Joseph (1942), Statistics of the municipal institutions of the English Towns, *Journal of the Statistical Society of London*, 5 (2): 97–168.

Foster, John (1974), *Class Struggle and the Industrial Revolution. Early Industrial Capitalism in Three English Towns*, London, Weidenfeld and Nicholson.

Fowler, Sir Henry (1900), Municipal finance and municipal trading, *Journal of the Royal Statistical Society*, 63 (3): 383–407.

Fraser, Derek (1976), *Urban Politics in Victorian England*, Leicester, Leicester University Press.

Fraser, Derek and Anthony Sutcliffe, (1983), *The Pursuit of Urban History*, London, Edward Arnold.

Furness, J.M. (1893), *Record of Municipal Affairs in Sheffield since the Incorporation of the Borough in 1843 to the Celebration of the Jubilee in 1893*, Sheffield, William Townsend.

Garrard, John (1983), *Leadership and Power in Victorian Industrial Towns, 1830–80*, Manchester, Manchester University Press.

Gray, T.M. and Associates (1985), *Marchmont, a Case for Conservation*, Edinburgh, Marchmont Community Council.

Gray, Robert Q. (1976), *The Labour Aristocracy in Victorian Edinburgh*, Oxford, Oxford University Press.

Hassan, J.A. (1985), 'The Growth and impact of the British water supply industry in the nineteenth century' *Economic History Review*. 2nd series, 38 (4): 531–47.

Hennock, E.P. (1973):, *Fit and Proper Persons. Ideal and Reality in Nineteenth Century Urban Government*, London, Edward Arnold.

Hennock, E.P. (1984), 'The creation of an urban local government system in England and Wales', in Helmut Naunin (ed.), *Städteordnungen des 19. Jahrhunderts*, Köln Böhlau Verlag.

Hill, Sir Francis (1974), *Victorian Lincoln*, Cambridge Cambridge University Press.

Joyce, Patrick (1980), *Work, Society and Politics. The Culture of the Factory in Later Victorian England*, Brighton, Harvester Press.

Keith-Lucas, Bryan (1980), *The Unreformed Local Government System*, London, Croom Helm.

Kellett, John R. (1969), *The Impact of Railways on Victorian Cities*, London Routledge and Kegan Paul.

Law, C.M. (1967), 'The growth of urban population in England and Wales, 1801–1911', *Transactions of the Institute of British Geographers*, 41 (2): 125–43.

Linteau, Paul-André (1981), *Maisonneuve. Comment des promoteurs fabriquent une ville, 1883–1918*, Montreal, Boréal Express.

Mackenzie, Enaes (1827), *A Descriptive and Historical Account of the Town and County of Newcastle upon Tyne*. Newcastle, Mackenzie and Dent.

Meller, H.E. 1976, *Leisure and the Changing City, 1870–1914*, London, Routledge and Kegan Paul.

Money, John (1977), *Experience and Identity. Birmingham and the West Midlands, 1760–1800*, Manchester, Manchester University Press.

Morris, R.J. (1971), 'The Friars and Paradise: an essay in the building history of Oxford, 1801–1861', *Oxoniensia*, 36: 72–98.

Morris, R.J. (1983a) 'The middle class and British towns and cities of the Industrial Revolution, 1780–1870', in Fraser and Sutcliffe, (1983): 286–304.

Morris, R.J. (1983b), 'Voluntary societies and British urban elites, 1780–1850', *Historical Journal*, 26 (1): 95–118.

Morris, R.J. (ed.) (1986a), *Class, power and social structure in British nineteenth century towns*, Leicester, Leicester University Press.

Morris, R.J. (1986b), 'Urbanization', in John Langton and R.J. Morris, *Atlas of Industrializing Britain, 1780–1914*, London, Methuen.

Morris, R.J. (1990a), 'Associations', in F.M.L.T. Thompson (ed.), *Cambridge Social History of Britain, 1750–1950 Volume 3: Social Agencies and Institutions*, Cambridge, Cambridge University Press.

Morris, R.J. (1990b), *Class, Sect and Party. The Making of the British Middle Class. Leeds, 1820–1850*, Manchester, Manchester University Press.

Offer, Avner (1981), *Property and Politics, 1870–1914. Landownership, Law, Ideology and Urban Development in England*, Cambridge, Cambridge University Press.

Olsen, Donald J. (1976), *The Growth of Victorian London*, London, Batsford.

Parry Lewis, J. (1965), *Building Cycles and Britain's Economic Growth*, London

Macmillan.

Porter, Robert R. (1907), *The Dangers of Municipal Trading*, London, Routledge.

Pred, Alan (1980), *Urban Growth and City Systems in the United States, 1840–1860*, Cambridge, Mass., Harvard University Press.

Reed, Peter (1982), 'Form and context: a study of Georgian Edinburgh', in Thomas A. Markus (ed.), *Order in Space and Society. Architectural Form and its Context in the Scottish Enlightenment*, Edinburgh, Mainstream.

Roberts, Elizabeth (1984), *A Woman's Place. An Oral History of Working Class Women, 1890–1940*, Oxford, Blackwell.

Robertson, C.J.A. (1983), *The origins of the Scottish Railway System, 1722–1844*, Edinburgh, John Donald.

Robertson, David and Marguerite Wood (1928), *Castle and Town, Chapters in the History of the Royal Burgh of Edinburgh*, Edinburgh, Oliver and Boyd.

Robson, Brian T. (1973), *Urban Growth*, London, Methuen.

Smith, Adam (1849), *Wealth of Nations*, 5th edn, Edinburgh, Adam and Charles Black.

Smith, Dennis (1982), *Conflict and Compromise. Class Formation in English Society, 1830–1914*, London, Routledge Kegan Paul.

Smith, Joan Class (1986), 'Skill and sectarianism in Glasgow and Liverpool, 1880–1914', in R.J. Morris (1986a).

Waller, P.J. (1981), *Democracy and Sectarianism. A Political and Social History of Liverpool, 1868–1939*, Liverpool, Liverpool University Press.

Walton, John K. (1983), *The English Seaside Resort. A Social History, 1750–1914*, Leicester, Leicester University Press.

Ward, David (1964), 'A comparative historical geography of the streetcar suburbs of Boston, Massachusetts and Leeds, England: 1850–1920', *Annals of the Association of American Geographers*, 54 (4): 477–89.

Weber, A.F. (1899), *The Growth of Cities in the Nineteenth Century*, reprint Ithaca, Cornell University Press, 1965.

Whitehand, J.W.R. (1987), *The Changing Face of Cities*, Oxford, Blackwell.

Williams, Gwyn (1978), *The Merthyr Rising*, London, Croom Helm.

Wilson, R.G. (1971), *Gentleman Merchants*, Manchester, Manchester University Press.

Wright, Neil R. (1982), *Lincolnshire Towns and Industry, 1700–1914*, Lincoln, Society for Lincolnshire History and Archeology.

Youngson, A.J. (1966), *The Making of Classical Edinburgh*, Edinburgh, Edinburgh University Press.

Unpublished Ph. D theses

Ochojna, A.D. (1974), 'Lines of class distinction: an economic and social history of the British tramcar with special reference to Edinburgh and Glasgow', Edinburgh.

MacDonald, Hector (1968), 'Public health legislation and problems in Victorian Edinburgh, with special reference to the work of Dr Littlejohn as medical officer of health', Edinburgh.

British Parliamentary Papers

Instructions to the Parliamentary Boundary Commissioners, 1831–2, vol. 36.

Report of the Commissioners upon the Boundaries and Wards of Certain Boroughs and Corporate Towns, 1837, vol.36.

Royal Commission on the Housing of the Working Classes, 1884–5, vol. 31 *Select Committee on Municipal Corporations in England and Wales*, 1835, vol. 35.

Select Committee on Smoke Prevention. British Parliamentary Papers, 1845, vol. 13.

14 Managing the market—regulating the city: urban control in the nineteenth-century United Kingdom

Richard Rodger

It has become a commonplace to regard the economic climate of nineteenth-century Britain as one of *laissez-faire*. Free trade, deregulation, and an increasingly unrestricted operation of the market—'the triumph of the entrepreneurial ideal' (Perkin 1969, 322)—are characteristically identified with the adoption of liberalism in the 1830s and extending to the international free flow of factors of production associated with the 'Atlantic Economy' in the half-century before the First World War (Kenwood and Lougheed 1971, 74–5; Thomas 1954; Cairncross 1953). The presumption remains that the emergence of a unified urban economic system associated with the growing sophistication of the British economy constrained the extent to which individual producers and customers could exert leverage on the system.

It would be a straightforward matter to consider the visible intervention of emergent town councils and regulatory bodies in the context of expanding municipal responsibilities for street lighting and cleansing, buildings, markets and fairs, parks and cemeteries, public health and hospital provision, poverty, police and public order, judicial functions, as well as those associated with a morally uplifting and purifying purpose—recreation, libraries, galleries and museums (Bellamy 1988; Keith–Lucas, 1977, 1980; Kellett 1978; Offer 1981; Fraser 1982; Hennock 1973). The catalogue could be extended. By means of local improvement acts, adoptive provisions and ultimately compulsory obligations associated with national minimum standards, these proliferating responsibilities came within the orbit of civic control, the finance, monitoring and enforcement of which themselves produced a spectacular growth in urban administration in the second half of the nineteenth century.

Such an approach takes legislative and administrative change and then traces the impact on an urban area. Public institutions—hospitals, asylums, workhouses, schools, slaughterhouses and cattle markets, police and fire departments, the town hall, water pumping, gasometers, electricity power generating and other aspects of municipal trading—each represented a sizeable, often impenetrable, zone of exclusive land use which determined urban spatial patterns into the twentieth century (Whitehand 1987). The monumentality associated with much of this building reflected an emergent civic consciousness and pride, intimidating citizens as it boasted self-importance (Lane 1979, 101). The image of the city was accordingly subverted by the acquisition of powers to direct the daily lives of the inhabitants; urban authority and the public building associated with it had a direct consequence for land use, price and availability in the city.

A different approach is adopted here. The central theme is that just like earlier bodies—medieval merchant and craft guilds, pre-industrial apprenticeship systems, London livery companies and chartered companies —the nineteenth century urban business élite were not predisposed to relinquish their power, privilege and prestige in the modern period. Examples drawn from the nineteenth-century housing market show that entrepreneurs frequently adapted the functioning of the market, directly and indirectly, so that their own power base, both economic and political, was not undermined. Or, at least, the urban élite attempted to regulate their own and the city's response to economic change since they perceived a close identity of interests. For example, in developing the urban infrastructure by means of the various responsibilities vested in civic authorities, businessmen simultaneously advanced their own interests as roads, drainage, public order, water supply and other amenities improved the efficiency with which day-to-day manufacturing and distribution was conducted. To the business community, the costs of such infrastructural investment were largely externalized, local taxes falling less on industrial premises and disproportionately on residential property, to the increasing anguish of both middle-class ratepayers and working-class tenants (Offer 1981; Englander 1983). The concept of external economies may not have been precisely formulated by eighteenth and nineteenth-century entrepreneurs, but they were acutely aware of the commercial advantage of forcing distributional and environmental costs upon the public purse rather than on the company balance sheet.

The presumption that the specialization of factor inputs and integration of regional markets associated both with industrialization and the emergence of a national distribution system weakened local entrepreneurial control in the cities needs to be tempered by the empirical evidence. First, numerous business histories such as those dealing with Jesse Boot, W.D. and H. O. Wills, the Vickers Brothers, and other major concerns—Cadbury, Lever, Singers and Beardmore—as well as many other studies of smaller though locally important family firms have shown how their influence over labour, housing and related markets remained secure (Alford 1973; Chapman 1974; Trebilcock 1977). Second, the continuing solidarity of business interests can be shown through the growth of imperfect competition, especially during periods of intense business integration, for example between 1880 and 1914; when controlling output, prices and production costs, and influencing market shares were precisely the objectives of entrepreneurs (Utton 1972). Attention to the growth of scale and the concentration of manufacturing and commercial power remains a central thrust of Marxist analyses, and one which, as formulated by Engels, had a specifically urban dimension.

Third, as reflected in the continued strong numerical representation of property interests, small proprietors and manufacturers generally in Victorian council chambers, from which stemmed civic influence and ceremonial appointments, as well as local patronage in parish councils, school and other boards, and the magistracy, the business community relinquished few of their policy-making opportunities. Despite the creeping encroachment of socialists, women, trade unionists and broader social groups in urban government at the close of the Victorian age, the ability of the business community to adapt and amend the urban scene, to use their wealth and economic power to endow schools, galleries and parks, to determine the fabric of the urban landscape through their industrial buildings and suburban residences, remained largely intact even in the late twentieth century. Whereas landed, aristocratic power was significantly eroded and increasingly assumed a decorative function as the nineteenth century progressed, so conversely business influence remained robust (Garrard 1983).

Managing the market is considered in the context of bankruptcy, employers' associations, company housing, suburban development, and town council appointees, and concludes that in many respects it was the market itself which prompted or forced legislative and institutional change to serve its own purposes, one of which was to regulate the city.

Factor and product markets: Features of the 'invisible hand'

Adam Smith's characterization of an 'invisible hand' to describe the workings of the market economy embody certain traits which are identified as central to the uncontaminated operation of the market. At the risk of an overdose of simple economic theory, certain features of the market model are worth attention simply to demonstrate how far Victorian business had departed from *laissez-faire*' principles.

In a general economic sense a market is a group of buyers and sellers. Close interaction between them affects the terms on which other buyers and sellers operate, and by extension, every transaction whether of commodities or services affects the activities of other participants in the market. The capital market, labour and land markets (factor markets) provide broad categories of buyers and sellers whose actions clarify the workings and functional relationships of constituent elements in the urban (and national) economy. Thus, in a product market such as housing, the prices and quantities of properties are determined by the responsiveness of demand to prices and incomes, and of supply to the costs of production. Costs of production depend on the quantities of factors used and their prices, which themselves are determined by supply and demand in the factor markets. These factor prices (wages, interest, rents, profits) together with the ownership of resources determine incomes. Unspent income is available for the capital market, and the terms on which these savings are made available influence the costs and thus the methods of production for other commodities and services. This, then, is the general sense in which the term 'market' is used, and is to be distinguished from the alternative and more specific spatial sense, the market-place for a commodity, which may take place in a single, usually urban location, and though transactions may be centralized —cattle, corn, flower, stock, gold, oil markets—members deal for buyers and sellers who are connected through their participation in the market even though physically scattered.

Market equilibrium implies a perfect match of trading options [either in all markets (general equilibrium) or a particular market (partial equilibrium)] so that at any given price demand and supply are equal. There is no incentive to change. Uniquely, there is one price at which producers wish to supply and the same price satisfies the amount consumers are freely prepared to buy. However, in most markets some buyers and some sellers are frustrated since the ruling price is below that at which some sellers are prepared to trade, and some buyers would trade at still higher prices. Whether a market is in equilibrium also depends on the period over which it is assessed. It could be

1. momentary—when market conditions relate to the disposal of a given stock of a commodity or service;
2. short-term—when the number of producers, stocks of equipment and consumers operating in the market are narrowly defined;
3. long-term—when the number of producers, consumers and scale of equipment are variable.

Market equilibrium may be stable—when shocks to price or output initiate adjustments which tend towards an new equilibrium—or unstable—when there is no such assurance that a new equilibrium will transpire.

Only in the purest theoretical terms did such markets exist; self-adjusting markets remain a textbook phenomenon. That factor allocation by means of a pricing mechanism, as formulated by Smith's 'invisible hand' and the non-interventionism advocated by the Manchester School and its *laissez-faire* disciples between 1820 and *c.*1860, rendered the business sector subservient to the dictates of the market was far removed from the particularities of modern British urban development. Imperfect information, inconsistencies between economic regions and within towns, and irregularities in the workings of markets counteracted such a unified market system. Indeed the durability of Norwich and Newcastle, Bristol and Exeter as regional centres, and, lower in the urban hierarchy, of county towns such as Chester, Cambridge and Carlisle is testimony to the continuation of their generalist economic functions, the absence of a genuinely integrated urban economy, the historically uneven nature of the market system and the stubborn resistance of traditional handicraft production (Corfield 1986; Samuel 1977; Sabel and Zeitlin 1985; Rodger 1988). The supremacy of the market implies the inability of producers (and possibly buyers) to influence the operation of the market itself. Both directly and more subtly the urban élite managed to do so.

Organising the market and defining the urban economic system

Markets exist to minimize uncertainty, unpredictability and risk. They represent an information system, networking details of prices, quantities and stocks, and transmitting perceptions of anticipated needs so as to iron out fluctuations. To produce in a vacuum of information increases risk and the possibilities of bankruptcy. Futures markets take the process a stage further in time. While individual operators might relish the opportunities afforded by inconsistencies in the market, and speculators depend on them, most manufacturers prefer assurances regarding the size of order books, timing of deliveries, maturity of loans, and customer preferences. Stock and credit control emphasize just that—control. Indiscipline amongst producers creates externalities for others—illiquidity in one producer contaminates the credit rating of business associates, cash reserves are increased or credit advances reined in, orders cancelled, production curtailed to avoid stockpiling. In reality, market intervention in the form of regulations introduces the concept of minimum standards of business behaviour, protecting the legitimate from the worst excesses of the unscrupulous, and thereby limiting the externalities. To avoid the commercial bruises of uncontrolled business operations is, therefore, a central justification for market management, and a vindication of departures from assumptions about profit maximization and optimal resource allocation. Judicious intervention promises limited damage.

Market volatility: bankruptcy and the dynamics of business

Bankruptcy, and the method of dealing with bankrupts, was subtly geared to regulating the market. Sanctions (imprisonment, disenfranchisement) and the social stigma of bankruptcy were buttressed by arguments of a moral nature (repayment of debts in full, personal responsibility for actions) so as to inhibit an element of entrepreneurial behaviour which in its irresponsibility might have adverse consequences for the product market as a whole, and for factor markets through its impact on creditor confidence. Debt recovery procedures together with a code of unwritten business ethics were part of an emerging market discipline geared to counteracting the activities of a few rogue producers so as not to impair the business operations of the majority. Instability at a given time resulting from the unacceptable excesses of a few operators was contained so as not to prejudice market disequilibrium in the longer term. Bankruptcy and related proceedings (announcement of insolvency, discharge, composition) were framed as a market control mechanism, developed by an urban élite for the maintenance of the *status quo*, accepted by producers and extended by them through the development, of their own regulatory standards and professional bodies. Streamlining and standardizing bankruptcy (and other regulatory) procedures were methods of advancing market unity. Expeditious bankruptcy proceedings produced a more efficient market, weeding out the inefficient producers before permanent damage to the market was experienced.

While the demise of the inefficient producer might seem an endorsement of the 'invisible hand' and of the supremacy of marginal analysis in microeconomics, refinements in debt recovery were prompted both by business considerations and administrative convenience. In eighteenth-century Scotland, bankruptcy proceedings encountered numerous difficulties: a means of distributing debtors' assets was lacking, decisions were not binding upon creditors not cited in proceedings, debtors remained undischarged and so subsequent accretions of wealth were liable to legal actions to recover earlier debts (Rodger 1985, 75–7, 89–91). The most inconvenient aspect, however, was the restrictive requirement that bankruptcy proceedings were confined to the Inner House of the Court of Session, centrally located in Edinburgh, and heard only on a limited number of days in the year. Quickening economic pace associated with industrialization in early nineteenth-century Scotland produced a mounting backlog of bankruptcy cases which impeded the recovery of debts. Archaic regulatory provisions inhibited market efficiency. Capital was tied up and confidence eroded.

In response to administrative and market needs, simplified procedures to manage indebtedness were developed gradually between 1772 and 1836. In 1839 expeditious discharge for bankrupts and payment of 'composition' to creditors was further streamlined when an act devolved responsibility to the county level and was supervised by the Sheriff Courts, and in 1856 the appointment of Accountants in Bankruptcy as a specialist wing of the courts took this a stage further. Indeed, when the inevitability of bankruptcy dawned, the debtor himself could initiate proceedings after 1836 by declaring his own insolvency. Early intimation of bankruptcy therefore limited the financial wreckage to the individual and his immediate business associates, and thereby minimized the damage to the market in general. With further refinements in 1856 and in 1881, when self-declared bankrupts could be discharged from further actions to recover funds, small firms whose net liabilities were no more than £100 continued to appreciate the merits of initiating their own bankruptcy proceedings, and from 1913 could also obtain summary sequestration.

Throughout the eighteenth and nineteenth century adverse publicity and moral opprobrium, the social stigma of bankruptcy, and other penalties, disciplined market behaviour. To supplement this indirect influence, the market, specifically the factor market for capital, amended the detailed workings of bankruptcy proceedings in 1772, 1814, 1836, 1839, 1856 and 1913, so that product markets generally functioned more efficiently, i.e. so that capital was not squandered on esoteric products or ill-conceived business ventures. Certainly there is sufficient Scottish evidence to argue that the sequence of procedural changes in bankruptcy arrangements contributed to a reduced dynamic in late Victorian business failures even when confronted with abrupt changes in market conditions. Prompted by the changing needs of Victorian business Scots law proved responsive (Campbell 1967).

The expeditious recovery of debts was one of several regulatory changes which the business community sought and obtained, the expense of which fell proportionately less on creditors as the legal procedures became standardized. Indeed more generally, as the registration of companies, limited liability, and related matters of industrial law became more fully regulated in the nineteenth century, expensive private legal actions were frequently superseded by standard forms for redress. Legal costs were to some extent externalized by the business community.

Market discipline and employers' associations

Central to the interests of the urban élite in nineteenth-century Britain was how far could markets be allowed to evolve independently, and how far was it necessary to manage the direction and pace of change. A *laissez-faire* approach with no barriers to new entrants in product markets undermined the interests of established, powerful firms and was contrary to the interests of the urban business élite, who sought by various means to ensure that the market worked to their advantage. To permit homogenization of product eliminated the leverage of the business élite, diminished their personal wealth and status, and standardized the participants in the market. New entrants threatened stability; market share was undermined. Tacit agreements over sales or factor inputs were vulnerable if newcomers represented a significant and uncontrolled element.

Associations of employers represented one response to changing market conditions. These were most conspicuous in wallpaper, tobacco, armaments, chemicals and soap, and railway engineering, where significant market shares were consolidated in the hands of merged firms or associations of producers, and by 1900 some formidable concentrations of economic power existed. For example, the Bleachers' Association controlled 50–60 per cent of their product market, Cotton and Wool Dyers controlled 85 per cent, the Salt Union had 90 per cent of the market by 1888, and in 1912 two groupings of cement producers shared 75 per cent of the market (Utton 1972, Table 1).

Builders, traditionally represented by a proliferation of very small firms, were not exempt from such trends after 1880 either, and embarked on several tactics aimed at self-regulation and tighter market control. For example, when paralysed by the collapse of the building boom in the west of Scotland after the failure of the City of Glasgow Bank in 1878, the remnants of the building industry willingly acquiesced to tighter money-lending practices from banks and informal financial sources because they recognized that though this constrained their operations in the short term, their own long-term continuation in the industry was more assured if excessive overproduction and the domino effect of building bankruptcies did not recur. Managing the market for building finance gave a measure of self-preservation to existing firms, and one indication of their success in this respect was that after 1880 the proportion of larger Scottish building firms declared bankrupt declined (Rodger 1985). By contrast, in Bristol the rates of attrition amongst new building firms rose in the 1860s and 1870s compared with bankruptcy levels earlier in the nineteenth century (Powell 1986, 66).

Employers' associations can be viewed as conceding a limited amount of entrepreneurial autonomy in return for tighter market control. Such motives may be seen across a spectrum of urban industries, but are particularly illuminating in the case of the building industry in England and Wales. Two major influences combined to encourage employer collusion: first, deteriorating control over a major factor cost, labour, between 1850 and 1914; and second, an amplitude of annual building fluctuations more than twice that of average industrial production (Maiwald 1954, 193; Feinstein 1972, Tables 111–12). The dynamics of Victorian building production were inherently unstable and control over factor and product markets was not improving.

At least four factors redefined building employers attitudes towards collusion from *c.* 1890 (McKenna and Rodger 1985). First, the London building industry experienced an abrupt recession in the late 1880s. Second, builders were faced with the growing power and financial strength of building trade unions, and this threatened to circumscribe their independence of entrepreneurial action. The financial position of London building labour and their masters diverged significantly in the 1890s: membership of London building unions had risen by 43 per cent and subscriptions by 56 per cent between 1892 and 1898 compared with a reduction of 40 per cent in the London Master Builders Association membership and a 29 per cent fall in subscriptions. This disparity between their respective financial resources 'makes one blush' commented the chairman of the MBA, though the Carpenters' and Joiners' president feared that 'the knowledge of our increasing strength' would induce alternative employers' strategies to manage the labour market (McKenna and Rodger 1985).

Third, there was the pressing political need to embrace arbitration machinery, since a Royal Commission on Labour acknowledged:

The most quarrelsome period of a trade's existence is when it is just emerging from the patriarchal condition in which each employer governs his establishment and deals with his own men with no outside interference but has not fully entered into that other condition in which transactions take place between strong associations fully recognising each other. (Royal Commission on Labour, Final Report, *PP 1894 XXXV*, para. 93)

It was judged preferable to intervene in the workings of the market so as not to relinquish power in an arbitrary manner. The concern was that negotiating and conciliation procedures would be compulsorily imposed, as indeed they eventually were in 1896, resulting in an industrial relations framework which placed the labour market outside the exclusive influence of building employers. Fourth, there was a more favourable disposition towards mergers and employers' organisations not just in neo-classical economics but more importantly as recorded by a series of court decisions which ruled against the restrictive practices of unions in the building industry.

Two further internal rule changes redefined market opportunities for building employers. First, in recognition of a plateau of membership reached in the 1890s, eligibility was broadened so as to embrace almost any employer concerned with building or the supply of building materials. Amended rules for entry were not easily or evenly adopted, but by 1901 the change was formally acknowledged in the change of name, the National Association of Master Builders being superseded by the National Federation of Building Trades Employers (NFBTE). The second decision was the application of a sanction, 'the inter-trading rule' (ITR), which moulded employers into a cohesive and effective force. The principal intention of the inter-trading rule was to offer a premium for membership of the employers' federation, and to impose penalties on those intent on remaining free agents outside the employers' ring. Members agreed only to deal with fellow members—the inter-trading aspect of the rule. In Lancashire, Cheshire and North Wales membership more than doubled within the first year of the introduction of the ITR and virtually tripled within two years (McKenna and Rodger 1985). By 1909 the Sheffield building employers' association had doubled the membership level of 1906, and in Birmingham an NFBTE membership of 84 in 1908 had risen to 179 in 1910. Collusion, sanction, and co-operation combined to produce tighter market control.

The formation of the NFBTE and the implementation of the ITR were intended to control competitive tendering, to distribute building work in an orderly manner amongst members, to enhance employer solidarity so that strikes were not aimed at one firm alone, to negotiate wage settlements for a prescribed period, to offer preferential discounts on materials to members, and, perhaps most importantly in the longer term, to develop a coherent builders' view which could be presented to local councils and parliamentary inquiries.

For the urban environment, the gluts of overproduction were to a degree avoided, the intensity of the cyclical upturn modified, and there existed some prospect of a more orderly housing supply. (In practice other factors intervened: rising interest rates, decline in house values, threats of capital gains taxes on houses and land, and uncertainty in the housing market caused by the spectre of council building.) The principal point to be made is that the building industry attempted to gain a measure of control over participants' activities by collusive arrangements aimed to secure stability for producers. Builders as producers were not simply passive. Their organizations, which took several decades to mobilize but moved relatively swiftly in the later stages, were geared towards amending the operation of the housing and factor markets so as to provide a more informed and thus secure basis on which to form commercial decisions. So, as a corrective to the 'invisible hand' and the inability of the housing market to develop and sustain long-term partial equilibrium, interventionism was acceptable, though the visibility of the market management strategy varied locally, depending upon particular circumstances of producers.

Company housing and market leverage

In 1833 the Royal Commission on Factories (*PP 1833 XX*) reported that 168 out of 881 large firms (19 per cent) provided some housing for their workers as part of their need to attract labour to remote locations. Like the eighteenth-century factory villages at New Lanark, Styal and Hyde, the mid-Victorian model housing schemes of Titus Salt (Saltaire, Bradford 1853), Edward Ackroyd (Ackroydon, Halifax 1861), Crossley (West Hill Park, Halifax 1863), Richardson (Bessbrook, N. Ireland 1846), Pim (Harold's Cross, Dublin), and Wilson (Bromborough, Cheshire 1853) provided some benefits to workers, but were conceived by employers as an integral part of factory discipline and labour supply (Ashworth 1954, 126). Management motives also embraced a Christian desire to improve workers' living conditions, an influence more pronounced in the later company housing of Cadbury's Bournville (begun 1879), Lever's Port Sunlight (begun 1888) and Rowntree's New Earswick (begun 1902), though the emphases on profitable housing investment and management, and sound if conventional housing design indicates that only rarely was company housing overtly philanthropic (Gaskell 1986, 131). Some employers like the jute firm of Baxters in Dundee were compelled, though unwilling, to house their work-force, while geographical isolation continued to oblige others to do so, for example, steel and shipbuilding firms in Barrow, railway companies at Crewe, Swindon and Wolverton in the 1840s, and collieries which commonly housed 3–11 per cent of their work-force in England and Wales, more locally in Durham and Scotland (Roberts 1977, 109; Ball 1971; Daunton 1980, 145).

In some northern mill and mining towns company housing continued to be used to secure a regular labour force, and in Clydeside burghs from 1880 company housing formed part of a management strategy to obtain the compliance of supervisory grades, introduce new work practices, or dismiss inefficient workers, using the pretext of delayed rental payments (Melling 1981, 258, 280; Bedale 1980, 50). In this sense company housing extended capital–labour relations from the arena of production to that of consumption; it was already well established as a means of influencing political allegiance in mill towns. Clearly the number and extent of company towns in Britain should not be overstated, but locally, employers' housing was significant, and lower down the urban scale, in mining communities, colliery companies were often the sole provider of housing. Implicitly and explicitly, leverage over the work-force was exerted in a very direct manner.

At the very least company housing represented an attempt to exert a degree of control over the local factor market in labour. Simultaneously, however, it extended regulation and control of other aspects of urban life. Where they were provided, churches and meeting-houses tended to reflect the religious affiliation of the 'benefactor' only. The durability of the housing stock ensured that street lay-outs, land uses and spatial patterns, together with building materials, colours and the aesthetic of the built environment generally bequeathed a legacy of urban land use for several generations. In addition, the domination of a single major employer skewed the social structure of the town, its housing and related infrastructural investment, and produced conditions unlikely to be attractive to other manufacturers. The urban physical and social structure of company-dominated towns effectively placed a ring fence around them, though some, like Crewe and Darlington, did manage a degree of economic diversification.

Developing suburbs: perpetuating market control

British cities typically developed discrete suburbs between 1815 and 1850. Architectural trends, domestic ideology, separation of work and home, and advancing urban scale each contributed to this process (Davidoff and Hall 1987; Thompson 1982; Olsen 1976). So, too, did the workings of the housing market in the city centre which itself produced externalities—contagion, overcrowding and a hostile environment generally—sufficiently repellent to encourage relocation. Yet behind these influences were the new market opportunities provided by this shift in housing preferences. Suburbs provided an integrated, self-sustaining capitalist mechanism in pre-1850 years, and indeed beyond, by generating custom for suppliers of building materials and furnishings, for transport operators and property developers, retailing and entertainment interests, and by providing opportunities for water and gas companies, not to mention new outlets for lenders and landlords, and the professional activities of solicitors, bankers, savings institutions and others associated with property transactions. An 'ecological marvel', the suburb was a spatial device for generating income and employment opportunities and which inoculated the middle class against the hazards of the city without requiring them to relinquish their political control over it (Dyos and Reeder 1973).

Two principal mechanisms can be identified by which suburbanization contributed to the management of the market and the regulation of the city:

1. as a means of developing social networks through which urban management was retained by means of personal contacts, church and other associational institutions; and
2. by the perpetuation of slums and the indirect management of factor inputs for labour through the mechanism of low wages.

Suburbs assisted the process by which the middle classes developed institutions to control power and influence in the face of significant changes caused by industrialization and urbanization. Peterloo (1819), the Merthyr Rising (1831), emergent trade unionism and other expressions of class tension prompted several responses:
- the defensive posture of cultural and residential unity in the suburbs;
- the manipulation of urban institutions such as the town council and law enforcement through the instruments of legitimate power, the ballot box and the judiciary; and

- the management of informal networks through professional bodies and employers' associations, or by a combination of these methods. (Morris 1983)

Suburbs and the suburbans were, therefore, a consciously developed cog in the mechanism for maintaining, consolidating and defending urban political power and the Great Reform Bill (1832) and municipal reform (1834/5) only recognized a process already under way by 1830 and which continued thereafter.

The switch of capital to the suburbs and the deterioration of the urban fabric in the city centre were systematically linked, and the tension between slum and suburb can been viewed as a deliberate perpetuation of the *status quo* in social relations through the mechanism of low wages (Castells 1977, 263). Profits were reinvested with a view to deriving productivity gains and further profits, a process dependent upon low-priced labour abundantly replenished by natural increase and urban immigration (Dyos 1968). Capital accumulation and reinvestment therefore neglected environmental improvement unless it directly impaired workers' health and efficiency and landlords' rental incomes (Foster 1979). The work-force were too poor and employers were unwilling to consider substantive improvements. Viewed thus, capitalist accumulation generated two crises in the urban scene. One was the deterioration of significant portions of the capital stock, to which suburbs contributed and from which cities never fully recovered; the second was the creation of increasingly homogeneous inner-city neighbourhoods in which working-class consciousness ultimately ran counter to capitalist interests. In these senses suburbs created inherent, though not fatal, weaknesses in the control of cities which they were designed to perpetuate (Rose 1981).

Yet in the not so short term—indeed over many generations—suburbanization offered varied opportunities to control the urban economy, either directly through product markets and prominent business interests, or indirectly by means of the retention of urban political power through the perpetuation of middle-class ideology by means of church, magistracy and municipal appointees. In this sense the revolution in nineteenth-century government was more an evolution of the existing oligarchic control of the city—a perpetuation of the caste system.

Fixing the market: appointees and urban influence

The nature and timing of urban development and the outcome in the housing market was to some extent fixed before the market deployed its 'invisible hand' to achieve factor allocations. Decisions taken in the chambers of the town council and its committees shaped the outcome. For example, in mid-Victorian Lancashire boroughs mayors and committee chairmen were almost exclusively drawn from a conjunction of large-scale business and property concerns and the identity of municipal–property–business interests was clearly expressed when in 1847 a candidate for the mayoral chain in Salford was described as: 'the proprietor of a considerable manufactory . . . the employer of a great number of hands. His sympathies were consequently connected with the prosperity of the borough. One of the largest ratepayers . . . his son was also a large ratepayer' (Garrard 1983, 24).

In Edinburgh, 80 per cent of burgh councillors in 1875 were landlords, and in 1905 the figure stood at 72 per cent (McCrone and Elliott 1989). Councillors had also extended their numerical interest in Edinburgh properties, owning 1,000 properties in 1875 and over 1,300 in 1905. Was it conceivable that urban policy and administration was undertaken independently of such vested interests? Even more emphatically, the composition of crucial council committees further demonstrated this partiality of interests. Most powerful of these sub-committees was the Lord Provost's Committee, which drew 95 per cent of its composition in 1875 from landlords, and the Treasurer's Committee, another critical instrument of council administration because it set the level of local taxation, 87 per cent of whom were landlords. Over 80 per cent of City Improvement Commissioners were Edinburgh landlords, and their slum clearance responsibilities clearly produced externalities for landlords generally in terms of compensation payments for compulsory purchase, environmental amenities, and consequently for the enhanced capital values of property. The scrutiny of building applications, permission to build, and authorization of housing for human habitation fell within the jurisdiction of the Dean of Guild Court—a medieval legacy overseeing plans and works in Scottish burghs. Edinburgh landlords represented 86 per cent of the committee membership in 1875, and perhaps more significantly, the constitutional composition of the Court provided for the permanent representation of builders (Miller 1896). The solid phalanx of property interests was therefore complete.

It was councillors, Merchant Company representatives on the Town Council, and influential individuals such as the chairman of the plans committee, Sir James Gowans, who campaigned for tramway extension lines into areas of Edinburgh which they owned and whose value was subsequently inflated by improved transport access. As expressed by the manager of the Edinburgh Street Tramway Company, commercial policy emphasized the need to 'feu' or develop housing prior to transport services: 'If tramways were to succeed feuing must precede, and (he hoped) that tramways would not precede that feuing might succeed' (Edinburgh Town Council Minutes, 20 December 1881). The Town Council put pressure on the company to advance routes beyond the built-up area into sections of North Merchiston with a view to enhancing the capital value of land owned by prominent individuals and wealthy trusts such as the Merchant Company (Ochojna 1974, 171–2).

It would be naïve to claim that town councillors served only their own class interests. Many contributions in urban social welfare were generally beneficial, though it is easy, and convenient, to overlook the disruptive impact of slum clearances, land use changes, regulations, and the construction of infrastructural investment on certain elements of the community.

Long and short-term horizons to such urban initiatives provide divergent conceptions of private and public costs and benefits. The 'visible hand' of regulation, though it existed to protect tenants' interests when, for example, their accommodation was demolished to make way for railway terminals or civic projects, in practice was mostly disregarded and rehousing rarely undertaken. Particular town 'improvement' schemes, therefore, frequently depended upon enhanced site value, the gains of which normally went to businesses in the form of improved turnover, and to landlords in the form of compensation for demolition of their property (Yelling 1986). Only in a minor way did councils gain since their revenue base might be affected only marginally. This was the case when Glasgow Town Council cleared sites in the 1860s and 1870s under their ambitious improvement schemes, but then failed to sell or develop those sites, the demolition costs of the work being borne by ratepayers, with no offsetting gain to the public purse from land sales, or house rents (Allan 1965). Public benefits and the common good were frequently jettisoned in favour of private gains.

Conclusion

What entrepreneurs were increasingly successful in achieving after *c*.1850 was both the adoption of social costs by the public purse with tangible private benefits, and the adaptation of regulations governing their sphere of operations. The transfer of private companies into public, i.e. municipal, ownership in the major utilities—water, gas, tramway operation—and the adoption of environmental services such as park maintenance, along with responsibilities for public order, street regulation and upkeep of roads meant that both the capital and recurrent costs of these amenities were shared amongst the wider community while bestowing commercial advantages on private firms. Had not the municipality accepted these functions, additional costs of production and distribution would inevitably have fallen more heavily on the business community. It was no accident that, for example, in Leeds and Birmingham business interests were most strongly represented in the council chambers during the years before 1890 when the assumption of civic responsibilities was in its infancy, and manufacturing and small proprietors overwhelmingly formed the majority occupational group in Rochdale (70–80 per cent during 1856–80), Bolton (67–81 per cent during 1843–75, 59 per cent during 1876–80) and Salford (55–65 per cent during 1845–80) (Garrard 1983, Tables 3–5; Hennock 1973).

Only from about 1880 was there a suggestion that businesses should pay higher local taxes, given the narrow and regressive nature of local taxation based on the rating of domestic property, a suggestion which was successfully resisted. Taxation of commercial property, betterment and land value taxation, and ideas regarding a 'single tax' associated with Henry George made only a modest impact between 1880 and 1914 (Offer 1981). In Glasgow and the burghs of the west of Scotland it was the political pressure exerted by house factors and landlords in the quarter-century before the

First World War which stalled the introduction of short leases, contained the extent of direct council intervention in the local housing market, and secured more aggressive conditions for eviction of tenants, all in return for a greater responsibility on the part of landlords for the collection of local property taxes (Morgan and Daunton 1983). Chambers of commerce, professional bodies such as Factors' Associations and Federations of Building Trades Employers each contributed to pressure group politics locally, influencing the nature and pace of change in their sphere of operations and for the broader evolution of spatial and functional change within the city.

Resistance, subverting the original intent, obstruction and non-compliance, and ultimately amendments to the implementation of the 'visible hand' of regulation provided a spectrum of entrepreneurial options which shaped the operation of the market. For example, building by-laws were vociferously condemned by contemporary builders who claimed that fixed minimum standards would raise costs of building, diminish affordable space, and exacerbate the overcrowding problem in Victorian cities (Beresford 1971). Yet simultaneously, building regulations discriminated against the jerry-builder, increased public confidence in the standards of construction, and generated other externalities beneficial to the builder with a long-term commitment to the market. In a related manner, the transference of property in Scotland was widely castigated for the legal costs associated with searching a central register of property—the Register of Sasines. Yet this public document safeguarded property rights, established ground burdens, recorded financial obligations, cited the superior and vassal, and thus represented an unchallengeable record of title. Public opinion was antagonistic to the costly procedures, but confidence in the land market was firm. So capital supplies were forthcoming on the basis of guaranteed collateral— unequivocal land titles. The original intent, to establish title to land, was successfully adapted by those in the capital market so as to deepen the reservoir of finance for building. Indeed, land assumed a character not unlike gold which, if not invariably redeemable, was unlikely to be devalued. Similarly, the contemplation of council housing was initially unpalatable to the building industry when first seriously proposed in the 1890s and early 1900s. Yet, by the 1920s the squeals of anguish were almost imperceptible.

Why was there a turnaround? First, because the least profitable sector of house-building and the most problematical element of housing management had been taken into the arena of public responsibility; second, because there was a considerable amount of contract building for private firms, with financial assurances from the Treasury; and third, to improve the housing supply the public sector sponsored the necessary research and development to test alternative materials and construction systems (Morgan 1987). Again developmental costs assumed by the public sector produced external economies for the private firm, which gained substantial market experience with very limited financial risks in poured 'no-fines concrete', slag and clinker blocks, steel and timber-framed houses, and prefabrication.

Builders rarely proposed regulations. They opposed, as did business generally, interventionist attempts to curtail their entrepreneurial autonomy. Once change was acknowledged as inevitable, however, and further resistance judged futile, they redirected the impact of the 'visible hand' so as to procure some commercial advantage from it. The same might be said of land developers. It has been claimed that land tenure affected urban form; that legal instruments influenced the density of building. In short, that legal provisions predetermined the functioning of the land market and that the 'visible hand' had tangible, visible repercussions. This type of argument assumed that builders required more capital to purchase freehold land compared to leasehold sites, and that they were therefore obliged to build intensively upon freehold land so as to recoup their capital outlay (Mortimore 1969). Accordingly, back-to-back housing in northern England and local variants such as Tyneside flats have been offered as geographical exemplars of the impact of tenurial characteristics. However, the reversionary value and rack-renting possibilities of leasehold tenure also offered landlords attractive options at the end of a lease, and so few lessees troubled to maintain or repair property which was shortly to revert to their landlord (Dyos 1966, 87–9).

Recently the assumptions about the need for intensive building on freehold land have been questioned (Daunton 1983, 66), while other studies of leaseholding, for example of the Calthorpes in Birmingham, Devonshire family in Eastbourne, and 'feuing' by the Heriot Trust in Edinburgh, have demonstrated the landowner's ability to monitor and enforce the quality of housebuilding on his land (Cannadine 1980). In 1914 about 60 per cent of urban tenures in the United Kingdom were freehold and the remainder were various types of leasehold (Offer 1981). Although some geographical concentrations did exist, for example, Leeds, Bradford and West Riding towns were dominated by freehold and Lancashire boroughs by long leases, a blend of tenures existed in most boroughs and serious housing deficiencies were not confined to one type of tenure or location. No longer is the simple equation between type of tenure and quality of housing sustainable because, though legal restrictions imposed different conditions in the factor market (land), the product market (housing) responded to local demand conditions to produce similar accommodation irrespective of the tenure. To assume, as studies of municipal intervention almost invariably have done, that supply-side regulations have been a major influence on urban development is to underestimate seriously the effect of demand factors, specifically the composition and local variations in incomes.

By focusing on builders and the housing market certain points have been highlighted which illustrate the specific ways in which cities adapted to changing economic circumstances. The mechanisms presented in this nineteenth-century context can partially explain the urban morphogenesis in the city—the adaptation of the city and its reconstructed urban form from one temporal span to another (Vance 1977; Lynch 1960, 1981; Whitehand 1977, 1981; Konvitz 1985). From archaeological sources, maps, and documentary evidence the mutating pattern of urban form has been revealed; the spatial dimensions of temporal change in the city have been admirably presented. Against such physical changes social scientists have provided detailed analyses of the changing social, political and economic structures associated with urbanization. Against static or snapshot views of urban structure at a given time must be placed the dynamic of urban change, the processes or linkages by which cities were recast. Establishing the morphological change in cities and its origin now requires a further dimension: how the process was carried out. By concentrating on part of the urban élite, and illustrating certain of the principles which underlay business methods, more is to be learned than merely concentrating on the regulations themselves. This is principally because the interventionism associated with the 'visible hand' of regulation was usually *ex post*—it formalized incremental changes already undertaken informally by builders and developers. The spatial adaptation of the city thus emerged as a by-product of business, financial and other economic pressures rather than as a conscious initiative. Put more crudely, and to return to the initial proposition, if there were power blocs in the city, then there was little need to be demonstrative in the use of power; behind the scenes pressure could be applied to great effect and urban control exerted without the ostentatious introduction of regulations.

In only a limited sense did the urban economy approximate textbook assumptions for resource allocation through the price mechanism. Nor were rationality or optimizing strategies or profit maximization invariable. Irregularities in the operation of the market abounded. To some extent this was inevitable, since private and social costs and benefits conflicted, and the market—buyers and sellers—sought to combat the marginal advantage secured by one or other grouping. So to view interventionism as a corrective to the distributional consequences of the 'invisible hand' and the inability of factor and product markets to develop and sustain long-term general equilibrium is to sidestep an important issue, namely, that interventionism involved daily market management and was normally undertaken behind the scenes in an effort to control and dampen the dynamic of directional change. Managing the housing market was simply a less overt method of regulating the city than with by-laws and civic interventionism; it was an important cog in the mechanism of urban economic and social control.

Acknowledgement

Part of the research on which this paper is based has been financed by the Research Board of the University of Leicester.

Bibliography

Alford, B.W.E. (1973), *W.D. & H.O. Wills and the Development of the UK Tobacco Industry 1786–1965*, London.

Allan, C. M. (1965), 'The genesis of British urban redevelopment with special reference to Glasgow', *Economic History Review*, 17: 598–613.

Ashworth, W. (1954), *The Genesis of British Town Planning*, London.

Ball, F.J. (1971), 'Housing in an industrial colony: Ebbw Vale 1778–1914' in S.D. Chapman (ed.) *The History of Working Housing: A Symposium*, Newton Abbot:, 277–300.

Bedale, C. (1980), 'Property relations and housing policy: Oldham in the late nineteenth and early twentieth centuries', in J. Melling (ed.) *Housing, Social Policy and the State*, London.

Bellamy, C. (1988), *Administering Central–Local Relations, 1871–1919: The Local Government Board in its Fiscal and Cultural Context* Manchester.

Beresford, M.W., 'The back-to-back house in Leeds 1787–1937', in S.D. Chapman, *Working Class Housing, A Symposium*, Newton Abott

Cairncross, A.K. (1953), *Home and Foreign Investment 1870–1913*, Cambridge.

Campbell, R.H. (1967), 'The law and the joint stock company in Scotland', in P.L. Payne (ed.) *Studies in Scottish Business History*, London: 136–51.

Cannadine, D. (1980), *Lords and Landlords: The Aristocracy and the Towns 1774–1967*, Leicester.

Castells, M. (1977), *The Urban Question*, London.

Chapman, S.D. 1974, *Jesse Boot of Boots the Chemists: a Study in Business History*, London.

Corfield, P.J. (1986), 'Slopmen and specialists: urban occupations in the early industrial revolution', unpublished paper to Urban History Group Seminar, Cheltenham.

Daunton, M.J. (1980), 'Miners' houses: South Wales and the Great Northern Coalfield', *International Review of Social History*, 25: 145.

Daunton, M.J. (1983), *House and Home in the Victorian City: Working Class Housing 1850–1914*, London.

Davidoff, L. and C. Hall (1987), *Family Fortunes: Men and Women of the English Middle Class 1780–1850* London.

Dyos, H.J. (1966), *Victorian Suburb: A Study of the Growth of Camberwell*, Leicester.

Dyos, H.J. (1968), 'The speculative builders and developers of Victorian London', *Victorian Studies*, 11: 641–90.

Dyos, H.J. and D. Reeder (1973), 'Slums and suburbs', in H.J. Dyos and M. Wolff (eds) *The Victorian City: Images and Reality*, London: 359–86.

Englander, D. (1983), *Landlord and Tenant in Urban Britain 1838–1918*, Oxford.

Feinstein, C.H. (1972), *Statistical Tables of National Income, Expenditure and Output of the U.K. 1855–1965*, Cambridge: T.111–2.

Foster, J. (1979), 'How imperial London preserved its slums', *International Journal of Urban and Regional Research*, 3: 93–114.

Fraser, D. (1982), 'Introduction' to his *Municipal Reform and the Industrial City*, Leicester.

Garrard, J. (1983), *Leadership and Power in Victorian Industrial Towns 1830–80*, Manchester.

Gaskell, S.M. (1986), *Model housing: from the Great Exhibition to the Festival of Britain*, London.

Hennock, E.P. (1973), *Fit and Proper Persons: Ideal and Reality in Nineteenth Century Urban Government*, London.

Hume, J.R. and M.S. Moss (1979), *Beardmores: the History of a Scottish Industrial Giant*, Heineman, London.

Keith–Lucas, B. (1977), *English Local Government in the Nineteenth and Twentieth Century*, London.

Keith–Lucas, B. (1980), *The Unreformed Local Government System*, London.

Kellett, J.R. (1978), 'Municipal socialism, enterprise and trading in the Victorian city', *Urban History Yearbook*, 36–45.

Kenwood, A.G. and A.L. Lougheed (1971), *The Growth of the International Economy 1820–1960*, London.

Konvitz, J. W. (1985), *The Urban Millennium: the City Building Process from the Early Middle Ages to the Present*, Carbondale.

Lambert, R.J. (1964), *Sir John Simon and English Social Administration*, London.

Lane, B.M. (1979), 'Changing attitudes to monumentality: an interpretation of European architecture and urban form 1880–1914', in l. Hammarström and T. Hall (eds) *Growth and Transformation of the City*, Stockholm.

Lynch, K. (1960), *The Image of the City*, Cambridge, Mass.

Lynch, K. (1981), *A Theory of Good City Form*, Cambridge, Mass.

Maiwald, K. (1954), 'An index of building costs in the U.K. 1845–1938', *Economic History Review*, 7: 193, Index B, Table 2.

McCrone, D. and B. Elliott (1978), 'Property and political power: Edinburgh 1875–1975', in J. Garrard et al., *The Middle Class in Politics*, Macmillans, London.

McCrone, D. and B. Elliott (1989), *Property and Power in the City: the Sociological Significance of Landlordism*, London.

McKenna, J. A. and R.G. Rodger (1985), 'Control by coercion: employers' associations and the establishment of industrial order in the building industry of England and Wales 1860–1914', *Business History Review*, 59: 203–31.

Melling, J. (1981), 'Employers, industrial housing and the evolution of company welfare policies in Britain's heavy industry: west Scotland 1870–1920', *International Review of Social History*, 26: 258, 280.

Miller, R. (1896), *The Edinburgh Dean of Guild Court: A Manual of History and Procedure*, Edinburgh.

Morgan, N. J. (1987), '£8 cottages for Glasgow citizens: innovations in municipal house-building in Glasgow in the inter-war years', unpublished paper to Strathclyde University conference 'Glasgow—From No Mean City to Miles Better', Glasgow, December.

Morgan, N.J. and M.J. Daunton (1983), 'Landlords in Glasgow: a study of 1901', *Business History*, 25: 264–81.

Morris, R.J. (1983), 'The middle class and British towns and cities of the industrial revolution 1780–1870', in D. Fraser and A. Sutcliffe (eds) *The Pursuit of Urban History*, London: 286–306.

Mortimore, M.J. (1969), 'Landownership and urban growth in Bradford and its environs in the West Riding conurbation 1850–1950', *Transactions of the Institute of British Geographers*, 46: 105–18.

Ochojna, A.D. (1974), 'Lines of class distinction: an economic and social history of the British tramcar with special reference to Edinburgh and Glasgow', unpublished PhD thesis, Edinburgh: 171–2.

Offer, A. (1981), *Property and Politics 1870–1914: Landownership, Law, Ideology and Urban Development in England*, Cambridge.

Olsen, D.J. (1976), *The Growth of Victorian London*, London.

Perkin, H.J. (1969), *The Origins of Modern English Society 1780–1880*, London.

Powell, C.G. (1986), 'He that runs against time: life expectancy of building firms in nineteenth century Bristol', *Construction History*, 2: 66.

Roberts, E. (1977), 'Working class housing in Barrow and Lancaster 1880–1930', *Transactions of the Historic Society of Lancashire and Cheshire*, 127: 109.

Rodger, R. G. (1988), 'Concentration and fragmentation: capital, labor and the structure of mid-Victorian Scottish industry', *Journal of Urban History*, 14: 178–213.

Rodger, R.G. (1985), 'Business failure in Scotland 1839–1913', *Business History*, 27: 75–91.

Rose, D. (1981), 'Accumulation versus reproduction in the inner city: the recurrent crisis of London revisited', M. Dear and A.J. Scott (eds) *Urbanization and Urban Planning in Capitalistic Society*, London: 339–81.

Sabel, C. and J. Zeitlin (1985), 'Historical alternatives to mass production: politics, markets and technology in nineteenth century industrialization', *Past and Present*, 108: 133–76.

Samuel, R. (1977), 'The workshop of the world: steam power and hand technology in mid-Victorian Britain', *History Workshop Journal*, 3: 1–72.

Thomas, B. (1954), *Migration and Economic Growth*, Cambridge.

Thompson, F.M. (1982), 'Introduction: the rise of suburbia', in Thompson (ed.) *The Rise of Suburbia*, Leicester.

Trebilcock, C. (1977), *The Vickers Brothers: Armaments and Enterprise 1854–1914*,

Utton, M.A. (1972), 'Some features of the early merger movements in British manufacturing industry', *Business History*, 14: 51–60.

Vance, J.E. (1977), *This Scene of Man: the Role and Structure of the City in the Geography of Western Civilization*, New York.

Whitehand, J.W.R. (1977), 'The basis for an historico-geographical theory of urban form', *Trans. Institute of British Geographers*, 2: 400–16.

Whitehand, J.W.R. (1981), 'Background to the urban morphogenetic tradition', in Whitehand (ed) *The Urban Landscape: Historical Development and Management*, Institute of British Geographers Special Publication, no.13, London: 1–24.

Whitehand, J.W.R. (1987), *The Changing Face of Cities: A Study of Development Cycles and Urban Form*, Oxford.

Yelling, J.A. (1986), *Slums and Slum Clearance in Victorian London*, London.

Index of names & places